# SORTING OUT THE SUPERNATURAL

# SORTING OUT

# THE

# SUPERNATURAL

K. NEILL FOSTER

**Christian Publications**
CAMP HILL, PENNSYLVANIA

# ⁽ᵈⁱ⁾ Christian Publications

3825 Hartzdale Drive
Camp Hill, PA 17011
www.cpi-horizon.com
www.christianpublications.com

*Faithful, biblical publishing since 1883*

*Sorting Out the Supernatural*
paperback edition
ISBN: 0-87509-867-3

LOC Control Number: 2001-130453

© 2001 by Christian Publications

To

*Paul G. Hiebert*

Professor, Mentor, Friend

# Contents

## Part II: Prophecy—A Major Understanding

# Part III: Nine Other Polarities

# The Wheat and the Tares

J esus told them another parable: "The kingdom of heaven is like a man who sowed good seed in his field. But while everyone was sleeping, his enemy came and sowed weeds among the wheat, and went away. When the wheat sprouted and formed heads, then the weeds also appeared.

"The owner's servants came to him and said, 'Sir, didn't you sow good seed in your field? Where then did the weeds come from?'

" 'An enemy did this,' he replied.

"The servants asked him, 'Do you want us to go and pull them up?'

" 'No,' he answered, 'because while you are pulling the weeds, you may root up the wheat with them. Let both grow together until the harvest. At that time I will tell the harvesters: First collect the weeds and tie them in bundles to be burned; then gather the wheat and bring it into my barn.' " (Matthew 13:24-30)

# Foreword

True Christianity is by its very nature supernatural. But in this fallen world, the supernatural is often imitated by the kingdom of darkness. Not everything that looks supernatural comes from God. Sometimes the line between true spiritual manifestations and the counterfeit which comes from the demonic is difficult to detect. Satan is a master at deception. He is especially expert in the field of religion. As a fallen angel, religion is his stock and trade. Satanic manifestations often look like the real thing. He is very good at imitating an angel of light.

It is when God's people meet that the enemy most often displays his religious wares. His intention is to deceive the saints and make them captive to his lies. The first century Church faced this reality as has every generation of the Church since then.

This truth has never been more relevant than it is today. The present generation of evangelicals is exposed to a wide spectrum of supernatural manifestations. Technology makes it possible for almost everyone to view all kinds of religious services in his or her own home. Many of the television ministries specialize in manifestations, not all of which are valid.

God's people are warned against being gullible. A bottom-line principle was laid down by the Apostle John in his first letter. "Believe not every spirit, but try the spirits whether they are of God" (1 John 4:1, KJV). We dare not believe the lie that testing manifes grieves the Holy Spirit. Just the opposite is true. The Holy Spirit is grieved when Christians fail to try the spirits.

This book begins with the premise that the Church of Jesus Christ in modern times can experience the supernatural. It is folly to renounce all manifestations because imitations exist. The instruction to try the spirits is clear evidence that John anticipated the supernatural as a norm in the Church. The basic question is the origin of the manifestations. The Bible equips the believer to make that judgment.

Neill Foster brings into focus the major spiritual manifestations likely to occur today. He shows how each can be imitated by the devil. Speaking from his rich personal background as an international evangelist and as a scholar, in a sane and irenic manner he states his case. Supernatural manifestations are addressed from the historical, biblical and theological points of view, followed by a listing of biblical tools for sorting. This study will be helpful for the growing group of evangelicals who believe that all of the gifts of the Holy Spirit can be manifest in our day.

The author calls believers to learn discernment from revealed truth. Anything less will compromise the gospel and grieve the Holy Spirit. Sorting out the supernatural is not an impossible task.

Keith M. Bailey, L.L.D.
Minister at Large
March 2001

*Preface*

# One Clear Worldview

Soccer referees are often in physical peril after a match and sometimes they may seem to be an endangered species. The very act of placing oneself in the position of an umpire in the kingdom of God involves a mind-set that embraces the idea of absolutes—true and false, right and wrong.

Interestingly enough, the Scriptures have something to say about umpires. "Let the peace of God rule like an umpire in your heart" (Colossians 3:15, author's paraphrase). In Christian decision-making, there is no more sage advice than to urge the peace of God as the umpire or arbiter of the soul. With such peace, we are free to decide, to proceed, to be finally at rest.

The absolutes of true and false, right and wrong, are of the essence in this book. I am not talking here about the carnal nature or the pseudo-supernatural. Rather, the worldview embraced within these pages focuses on the distinct and stark polarities—good and evil, false and true—of the supernatural world within the Judeo-Christian context and beyond.

The choices are not easy. The magicians of Egypt initially seemed quite adept at facing the clumsiness of Moses and Aaron. And, for a while at least, the miracles matched. In the end, the question becomes, "What is of God, and what is of the devil?" When it comes to the supernatural, the prevailing human passion is to declare the field as either wheat or tares. However, the Scripture declares that the wheat and the tares grow together.

Surely a referee is needed to define such monumental issues. That referee is the Word of God. Just as a referee introduces both tension and order into an athletic event, so God's Word brings both tension and order to bear upon spiritual chaos. It is, thank God, a divine tension which produces holy order. The proper outcome of the swirling game of life is dependent upon its illuminating role.

The singular purpose of this book, then, is to point out the biblical reality of the true and false—the polarities within the realm of the supernatural—and thereby raise the level of discernment. This thesis will be illustrated with biblical, historical and contemporary incidents which emphasize the constant need to "prove all things; hold fast that which is good" (1 Thessalonians 5:21, KJV).

Please join me in the journey.

# Introduction

WHAT ON EARTH does a title such as *Sorting Out the Super-natural* mean? Those words in and of themselves are not difficult to understand, but the process that has led to combining them in this title has, to say the least, been a journey. It began when I was about seventeen years old.

While attending the Christian high school which was part of the Prairie Bible Institute campus at Three Hills, Alberta, Canada, I found myself checking out the Prairie Book Room. In the literature offered there was a small booklet written by an obscure (at least to me) author named Archie Ruark. Those musty pages introduced me to the focus of this book—the possibility of true and false spiritual phenomena.

I was intrigued.

Through the intervening years, I have come to see and experience firsthand many of the things about which Ruark wrote. More than thirty-five years later, when the time came to write my Ph.D. dissertation, Ruark's little booklet framed the research which by that time had been buttressed by the words and works of many others who had written on similar themes.

Also during those years, I experienced a lot of things, engaged in far too much travel and voraciously consumed thousands of pages written by others. Even as I organize the thoughts and themes of this manuscript, I am again fascinated by the plurality of supernaturals (plural intended) in Christine Trevett's *Montanism, Gender, Authority and the New Prophecy*. The book describes the supernaturals in the primitive Church of the second century.

All these—the scriptural declarations, the writings of others and my own experiences—have led to what you now hold in your hand. The competing phenomena on all sides only affirm the need for it. We will begin by building a foundation upon which the main structure will be erected.

## Naturalism vs. Supernaturalism

Naturalism as a philosophy was first advanced by Benedict Spinosa in 1670 and later affirmed by David Hume in 1730. These men were primarily responsible for the philosophical unbelief which has greatly troubled the Church. Naturalism is the stark opposite of supernaturalism. It sees no supernatural in the Scriptures nor in the spiritual life of the Christian.[1] Sorting out the supernatural is incomprehensible and nonsensical if philosophical naturalism rules. For me, belief in the supernatural is not a problem.

While attending Fuller Theological Seminary, I was required to take a Signs and Wonders course called MC510 which was taught at that time by John Wimber. Since I was an older student who had seen a lot of supernatural events, I had no problem understanding or accepting the basic premise of the course. There were no doubt illustrations of the miraculous presented during the classes, though I do not particularly remember any. What I do recall is processing the events connected with the class in view of what I had already seen and experienced. Some of the results of that processing form the thesis of this book.

## Biblical Vandalism

Christians today are as supernaturalistic as their belief in Scripture allows. A certain segment of Christendom seems content to relegate such events to New Testament times. That view is safe and honor-able, but restrictive. Positive supernatural events such as answers to prayer, healings, deliverances and even angelic visitations, are not so likely to take place in those circles.

R.C. Sproul notes that

> Christianity is based upon and rooted in miracles. Take away the miracles, and you take away the Christian faith. Church history, of course, is replete with attempts to do this. From the efforts of the Enlightenment thinkers to re-duce Christianity to a form of naturalism, to the biblical vandalism of nineteenth-century Liberalism to explain away biblical miracles with fancifully contrived ethical parables, to Bultmann's systematic program of "de-mythologizing," the attacks have been relentless.[2]

Such a belief system also tries to rule out the supernatural today. I have neither the will nor the space to engage such a belief here. It is, however, a position held by many and, given the title of this book, is probably relevant to this readership. It is also a position which obviously fails to engage the increasing occultism of our times. While in process on this book, I have watched several spiri-tualistic mediums openly plying their trade on television. I have yet to see anyone quoting the biblical prohibitions of communication with the dead (Leviticus 19:31; 20:6-7, 27; Deuteronomy 18:10-12). Naturalism and secularism have no way of dealing with such powers except to discount them.

One Sunday school teacher affirmed the dual nature of the super-natural, but interestingly illustrated that it occasionally impinges upon the natural mind as reflected in Figure 1. The protruding ar-rows from above and below reflect that reality. Such an event as the angelic manifestation when Christ was born would be one of the down arrows. Likewise, the behavior of the Gadarene demoniacs would be an up arrow intruding into the human realm from Satan's domain.

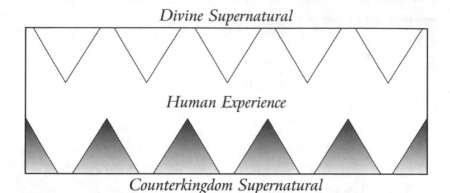

*Divine Supernatural*

*Human Experience*

*Counterkingdom Supernatural*

**Figure 1**[3]

Whatever the source, the supernatural is disconcerting. On the subterranean side, cultists pursue it relentlessly. Observe the arrows directed downward and reaching upward. Some believers today, particularly those with Montanistic/charismatic tendencies, pursue the miraculous as the downward arrows indicate. I do not place myself among them. Rather, I view myself as a believer in miracles who welcomes the supernatural, and who at the same time reminds himself that those who have never seen the supernatural and yet have believed are held up in Scripture as the receptors of special blessing from God (John 20:29).

If one does not believe in the supernatural in the present day, there is not much possibility that a book like this which compares the assumed polarities of true and false supernaturalism will be of significant benefit. However, if you do believe in the supernatural and recognize its presence, welcome. If you find these pages as exciting and illuminating as the lifetime of study and experience which has made them possible, I will be grateful.

## The Supernatural

To insure that we are all on the same page, let's define "supernatural." According to *Merriam-Webster's Collegiate Dictionary,* it means "1: of or relating to an order of existence beyond the visible observable universe; esp: of or relating to God or a god, demigod, spirit, or devil 2 a: departing from what is usual or normal esp. so as to appear to transcend the laws of nature b: attributed to an invisible agent (as a ghost or spirit)."[4]

Since I am obviously writing from a Christian perspective, you may properly expect me to be a believer in the resurrection of Jesus Christ which was the ultimate supernatural event of history. My faith is vain if I cannot embrace the resurrection of Christ (1 Corinthians 15:14). And, of course, the Scriptures affirm numerous other supernatural events: creation in Genesis—the first book of the Old Testament; the Virgin birth in Matthew—the first book of the New Testament; and, of course, the plagues that Moses and Aaron orchestrated were as supernatural as the healings and deliverances of Jesus Christ. Those too I happily embrace.

## Lori's Deliverance

The most supernatural event in my experience, at least in terms of variety, took place at Camp Nakamun in Alberta, Canada, in 1963. There, a girl just seventeen years old asked for spiritual help. In a matter of minutes, as the authority of the believer and the force of Scripture were applied, she was groveling on the ground in front of a wood-frame, sawdust-strewn camp-meeting tabernacle.

Over the next six weeks many other Christian workers joined us, and every supernatural event in the New Testament related to deliverances seemed to replay itself before our eyes. As there was a Legion in Jesus' day, so there was in ours—the name, the voices, the violence. We saw physical strength that required five men to subdue, demons that claimed to be from the Hungarian war, the exotic and exquisite dances of Thailand performed by evil spirits through this Canadian teenager who had never been in the Orient, and much, much more.

The awesome power of the Name of Jesus Christ was daily exhibited in expulsion of those evil powers in and through the authority of the believers in whom Christ lived. Prayer and fasting were the weapons of power. The instruction manual was the New Testament. I had been a supernaturalist before the struggle began, but after six weeks in that war, I had participated in an intensive course in the supernatural available in no seminary. Others carried the battle through to victory. From the perspective of forty years later, I must admit that my ministry has been and continues to be profoundly influenced by the relentless supernaturalism of those days.

## Sorting It Out

The verb "sorting" infers the necessity of ranking, classifying or defining events by characteristics, of examining them and hopefully, in the process, clarifying fact from fiction and eliminating confusion. "Sorting" also suggests a plurality of supernaturals. The Bible not only describes the supernatural power of God, but it also affirms the reality of supernatural evil. In Moses' contest with Pharaoh, the magicians of Egypt were initially able to wield supernatural evil which had nearly the same effect as the supernatural power of Almighty God (Exodus 8:16-32).

There is one important caveat in this discussion. There are phenomena in human experience which may seem to be supernatural, but are not. They are, rather, psychological in nature. An immense literature focuses on these phenomena. This book, however, does not include them.

# A Warning

Another significant observation must be made here. Dr. Arnold L. Cook has said that there are two bookends[5] from Scripture which supply the parameters in evaluating religious phenomena: 1) the possibility that all spirits do not proceed from God and therefore need to be "tried," i.e., tested (1 John 4:1-6), and 2) the possibility that in the testing of them one may commit the unpardonable sin by attributing the work of God to Satan (Matthew 12:22-37).

The admonition of John is clear: ". . . do not believe every spirit, but test the spirits to see whether they are from God, because many false prophets have gone out into the world" (1 John 4:1). In Matthew 12:22-37, Christ spoke of the unpardonable sin in the context of His healing a demon-possessed man who was blind and mute (12:22). The Pharisees were accusing Him of casting out demons through Beelzebub, the prince of demons (12:24). Immediately following this interaction, Jesus intentionally addresses the issue of "blasphemy against the Spirit" (12:30-32).

For centuries, theologians have vigorously debated the definition of and potential for committing such a "final" sin. This link between their accusation and Christ's declaration that blasphemy against the Spirit is unforgivable has always served as a strong check in my own spirit. The point is well taken and tremendously important. In sorting out the supernatural, as we hope to do, we need these two bookends to enclose our thinking. We must at all cost avoid the blasphemy of the Holy Spirit by attributing the work of the Holy Spirit to Satan, and, with only slightly less ardor, we must try the spirits—every single one—since many antichrists have gone out into the world. *Holding biblical balance while sorting out the supernatural is of the most profound importance.*

Christian supernaturalism, finally, is biblically deduced, and it flows from the authority of the Scriptures themselves. The supernatural that emerges from the counterkingdom, while acknowledged in the Scriptures, emerges from another source. J. Hudson Taylo known for his missionary exploits with the China Inland Mission, laid out the supernatural element of the Christian faith as follows: "We are a supernatural people born again by a supernatural birth, kept by a supernatural Teacher from a supernatural Book. We are led by a supernatural Captain in right paths to assured victories."[6]

Nothing more need be said.

*"Test everything. Hold on to the good.*
*Avoid every kind of evil." (1 Thessalonians 5:21-22)*

## Endnotes

1. Norman Geisler, "Beware of Philosophy: A Caution to Biblical Exegetes" (Orlando, FL: Evangelical Theological Society, 1998), tape recording.

2. R.C. Sproul, *The Invisible Hand* (Dallas: Word Publishing, 1997), 181.

3. Janet Paull, a diagram used in a Sunday school class, 2000.

4. Frederick C. Mish, ed., *Merriam-Webster's Collegiate Dictionary,* 10th ed. (Springfield, MA: Merriam-Webster, 1999).

5. Arnold L. Cook, *Historical Drift: Must My Church Die?* (Camp Hill, PA: Christian Publications, 2000), 260-261. "I find two bookends from Scripture [Matthew 12:22-37] helpful in evaluating religious phenomena. . . . Christ spoke to this issue in the context of His healing a demon-possessed man who was blind and mute (v. 22). The Pharisees accused Him of casting out demons through Beelzebub, the prince of demons (v. 24). . . . Immediately following this interaction, He intentionally addresses the issue of 'blasphemy against the Spirit' (12:30-32). Theologians have debated this question vigorously. This close link between their accusation that He had acted through the power of Satan, and then Christ's declaring that blasphemy against the Spirit is unforgivable, has served as a strong check in my spirit."

6. Leona Choy, "Conversations with Andrew Murray," *Classic-Christianity* e-zine, April 1, 1999.

# PART I

# THREE VITAL

# CONTROLS

IN THIS SCIENTIFIC AGE, all valid experiments must have standards of comparison or procedure—commonly called controls—to be valid. Controls have two functions: 1) they inject consistency, order and discipline into the gathering and collation of information, and 2) they frame the results of the investigation. As one authority noted, "Careful, controlled and scientifically designed experiments are not only morally justified but morally required. . . . When the controls can also be standards, additional advantages are gained."[1] Controls may also be defined as rules of engagement, restrictions which are predetermined before the sorting process begins.

*Sorting Out the Supernatural* is an exploratory, deliberately nonexhaustive look at common phenomena in the Judeo-Christian spiritual realm. While this volume is far from a scientifically designed experiment complete with blinds and double blinds, etc., it is, nevertheless, an investigation of another sort—a theological one.

Controls in the spiritual and doctrinal realms are both necessary and evident. I have chosen three biblical ones with which to frame the discussion. At the heart of these ideas is the full and uncompromised authority of Scripture: The holy texts of the Old and New Testaments are inerrant and the only rule for faith and practice. Without them, there is no viable way to make any sense at all of dissonant voices and competing phenomena.

In Part I, we will begin an enumeration and consideration of the various controls and standards which will mark this journey.

## Control 1: Nonverbal Communication

This research comes out of both the Scriptures and sociology. It shows nonverbal communication to be of the essence in the Bible.

## Control 2: Truth and Heresy

Heresies must come, the Scriptures say. This section deals with the marks of heresy, the willingness to call error heresy and the point at which error clarifies and becomes heresy.

## Control 3: The Scriptures

The rule of Scripture is probably the most critical control, impinging upon and coloring all other controls. It is without question the main control.

### Endnote

1. Bright Wilson, Jr. *An Introduction to Scientific Research* (New York: Dover Publications, 1990), 40-41.

# 1

# Nonverbal

# Communication

# The Clintons and Nonverbals

*(The inclusion of this vignette is not intended to be political.)*

AMERICAN HISTORY IN THE LATE 1990s and early years of the twenty-first century was dominated by presidential politics. Bill Clinton, the then occupant of the White House (1993-2001), was at one point under fire for alleged improprieties with women other than his wife. The nonverbal response by the Clintons was masterful. In response to accusations in the media, the President and his wife were photographed holding hands. When the fires of accusation were most intense, Mrs. Clinton was seen leaning tightly against her husband's chest. The message was obvious: "Forget all these allegations. There is nothing wrong here."

When President Clinton was preparing to testify before a grand jury, his chief lawyer made a trip to Arkansas to view a deposition video the President had made earlier. The lawyer already had received written transcripts, but he felt compelled to check the nonverbals of the video.

After the President was impeached by the House of Representatives, his trial moved to the Senate. His persistence in nonverbal behaviors was duly observed by a columnist of the *New York Times* who noted in Clinton's defense against conviction in the Senate an ever-increasing power . . . to set the agenda of even his fiercest adversaries.

The President who promised a cabinet that looked like America had, in typically shameless fashion, done the same with his defense team: one disabled lawyer, one black woman lawyer, one white woman lawyer, one Brooks Brothers lawyer and, to wrap it up, one Good Ole Boy. The 13 managers [prosecutors from the House of Representatives] clearly, if belatedly, took this stage-managed diversity to heart. Given the choice between calling a black woman [Betty Currie] who might actually help their case . . . they blinked. The politics of P.C. [political correctness] trumped the legal imperatives and inviolate principles that supposedly governed their prosecution.[1]

## *Endnote*

1. Frank Rich, "Betty Currie's P.C. Pass," *New York Times*, January 30, 1999, B1.

# Nonverbal Communication

———————◆————————

BASEBALL IS THE AMERICAN PASTIME. The game is known for its deliberately created tensions and its dramatic home runs. It is also known for its incessant and sometimes humorous use of nonverbals by the managers and coaches. Any good coach knows that the careful communication of nonverbal instructions to his players can make the difference between victory and defeat.

Animals, too, are experts at nonverbals. Take, for instance, our little white bichon. When he wants to go for an evening walk, he stands and begs, ready at the least movement on his master's part to head to the door. His black eyes gleam, and the curled tail is waving hopefully, faster or slower according to the signal he's reading. It is clear what he wants. No words are needed. (Could it be that I am the one who is trained?)

I have read somewhere that in the time of the British Empire when a colony became disorderly, the Royal Navy would sail a ship into its port city and drop anchor in the bay in plain view of the citizenry. Predictably, the disorder would subside. At one point in my pastoral career, when the "troops" were getting a little restless, I invited the district superintendent to drop by for a visit. (Thank God for district superintendents!) He sailed into our town, dropped anchor at the Wednesday night prayer meeting and gave a brief message to the assembled saints—appropriately entitled "Trouble in the Church." At the end of the service, he sailed out. The rumblings subsided.

So, what do nonverbals have to do with sorting out the supernatural? In this chapter I propose to show that many of the clues to determining true and false, right and wrong, divine and devilish, are often nonverbal. This control has wide impact as the book unfolds. It is especially significant in addressing prophecy, music and an extensive list of competing polarities.

## A Definition

In the midst of an abundance of definitions for nonverbal communication, one of the briefest is as follows: "Nonverbal communication means all the messages other than words that people exchange."[1] Apparently the term was first coined by Ruesch and Kees in 1956.[2] Other writers further observe that

> nonverbal communication *differs* from verbal in that it concerns itself with the entire range and scope of communication over and above the use of words. In our view, whatever the message, whatever the channel, whatever the nature of the intensity, of intentionality—where *words* are not involved, the communication is nonverbal. The vast majority of the message content in virtually all messages we send and receive is encoded and decoded in nonverbal channels.[3]

Paul Kruger, a South African theologian, insightfully insists that "a distinction has to be made between 'information' and 'communication.' Many forms of behavior are informative, but only some of them can qualify as communicative."[4]

The definition of nonverbal communication which I happen to prefer (since it is my own!) is the following, which allows for behavioral, cultural and spiritual realities in the communicational realm:

Nonverbal communication is the conveyance of information from one entity to another without the use of verbal expression, resulting in understanding being exchanged without the exactness of speech in any form.

## An Ever-present Danger

Nonverbal communication has at least one significant peril attached to it: There is always the danger of misunderstanding what has been "said." For example, in Anglo culture, to stretch one's hand forward and flat to indicate the height of a child is correct nonverbal communication. That same gesture is insulting in at least some Spanish cultures where the hand flatly extended indicates the height of an animal. In Colombia and elsewhere, the hand must be extended and held vertically, thumb on top.

In high school, my wife served as an accompanist for an orchestra. One evening, as they were rehearsing a certain Gilbert and Sullivan operetta, she muffed her part of the introduction and grimaced disgustedly at her error. The conductor, however, took the nonverbal as an assault against his direction and the abilities of the other members of the orchestra. She became the recipient of an undeserved public reprimand.

In a 1999 incident in New York City, four white officers fired forty-one bullets at an unarmed Nigerian immigrant. According to news reports, miscommunicated nonverbals exacerbated the situation. The man had apparently made movements which were thought to be the drawing of a gun. It was later determined that he had been unarmed. As a foreigner, he may have had no concept of what such movements might mean in big-city television culture where "freeze" has nothing to do with temperature. One policeman fell in the midst of the fusillade, possibly giving further impression that the Nigerian was returning fire. Misunderstanding of the nonverbals was, according to testimony, part of that tragic event.

## Up to Sixty Percent

It is commonly stated that sixty percent of all communication is nonverbal, and in some cases, as high as ninety percent. "Simultaneous verbal, vocal and facial attitude communications account for seven percent, thirty-eight percent and fifty-five percent respectively of the total communication."[5]

Among the social sciences, studies on the nonverbal are exceptionally interesting. The homosexual community, for example, has sometimes been called the "silent community" which penetrates a culture almost wholly by nonverbal means.[6] In law enforcement, contradictions between verbal and nonverbal communication is commonly discussed.[7] (I must add parenthetically that evangelicals, properly enamored as they are with words such as "inerrant" and "infallible," sometimes are so word-oriented that they fail to read even the most obvious nonverbals, particularly the contradictions and dissonance between verbals and nonverbals. More about this later.)

One academic volume contains a chapter written by DePaulo and Rosenthal entitled, "Ambivalence, Discrepancy, and Deception in Nonverbal Communication."[8] Further, Druckman, Rozelle and Baxter devote an entire chapter of their work to "Decoding Nonverbal Clues to Deception."[9] Both of these chapters describe at length the dissonance that may be observed between various physical responses and the human voice when lying.

## "Dr. Fox"

A celebrated case in point involved the presentation of a fabricated academician, a certain "Dr. Fox," to a group of educators. The perpetrators of the hoax hired a professional actor who "looked distinguished and sounded authoritative." He was coached to present his lecture with "excessive use of double-talk, neologisms, non sequiturs, and contradictory statements."

The unsuspecting teachers gathered for the occasion and listened to Dr. Fox with all due respect and attention. Not surprisingly, "the professional educators rated [him] favorably on eight general items including organization of material, use of examples, arousal of interest, and stimulation of thinking."[10] Nonverbal communication by a phony speaker had carried the day.

## The Medium/the Message

A key theorist in this whole area of the nonverbal has been Marshall McLuhan. Among his premises is one which has become rather famous: "The medium is the message."[11] "The 'content' of a medium is like the juicy piece of meat carried by a burglar to distract the watchdog of the mind," he said.[12]

Applying his principle to music, McLuhan adds: "Since the advent of pictures, the job of the . . . copy is as incidental and latent as the 'meaning' of a poem is to a poem, or the words of a song to a song. Highly literate people [or highly verbalized people] cannot cope with the nonverbal . . . so they dance impatiently up and down to express a pointless disapproval."[13]

McLuhan was an ardent Roman Catholic whose views had theological color.

> [He] applied his pronouncement of "the medium is the message" to Christ. It is not only the sayings of Christ that are important but His very person . . . "the incarnation was the ultimate extension of man, the ultimate technology." For him all human technologies were negligible compared to the coming of the Christ. In fact, McLuhan . . . was fond of pointing out, especially in his later years when the television generation seemed intent on abandoning traditional morality, that "Satan is a great electrical engineer."[14]

The main point in this chapter, not divorced from McLuhan, does not necessarily have to do with the findings of science, so-called, but rather with the use of nonverbals in the Scriptures. If nonverbals really are as pervasive in communication as the evidence indicates, then the presence and power of nonverbals in the Scriptures should be briefly explored and examined.

## The Early Church

One of the fascinating documents coming down to us from the early Church was written by Appolonius. In writing about false prophets and against Montanists in particular, he complained that "the receiving of gifts and the multiplication of wealth is [sic] . . . a sign of false prophecy."[15]

Curiously, or perhaps obviously, Appolonius goes on to cite several nonverbal complaints against the false prophets: "Tell me, does a prophet dye his hair? [Nonverbal] Does a prophet use stibium on his eyes? [Nonverbal] Is a prophet fond of dress? [Nonverbal] Does a prophet play at gaming tables and dice? [Nonverbal]."[16]

The Didache, an earlier and more reliable document than the Appolonius material, contains similar warnings about nonverbals.[17] Here is a list of six statements from the Didache, all but two of which deal with the nonverbal:

> If the teacher himself turns away and teaches another doctrine, so that he destroys [the correct teaching], do not listen to him. (Didache 11:2) [Verbal]
>
> If he stays three days he is a false prophet. (Didache 11:5) [Nonverbal]
>
> If he asks for money he is a false prophet. (Didache 11:6) [Verbal]
>
> So the false prophet and the prophet will be recognized by their behavior. (Didache 11:8) [Nonverbal]

> The prophet who orders a meal in the Spirit and eats of it himself; if he does so, he is a false prophet. (Didache 11:9) [Nonverbal]
>
> If any prophet does not do what he teaches he is a false prophet. (Didache 11:10) [Nonverbal][18]

Small wonder then that by the time the Church reached the fourth century, Augustine was already quite observant in this area. In the view of one writer, he "saw more clearly than anyone before him [or for a long time after him] that issues of supreme importance are raised by the problem of the relation of words to the reality they attempt to describe. He was a pioneer in the critical study of nonverbal communication."[19]

I believe it is fair to say that historically the Church has been at least somewhat and sometimes observant of nonverbal communication.

## American Politics

In his long career, President Richard Nixon was dogged by bad nonverbals. When he was required in 1974 to surrender tapes of conversations in the White House, he offered transcripts. Congress refused them. Evidently, they wanted to—and ultimately got to—hear the nonverbals, "the voice inflection, stress, and other such nuances."[20]

Earlier in Nixon's 1960 debate with John F. Kennedy, many who heard it on radio or read the text felt that Nixon had won. However, the television audience pronounced Kennedy the winner. Consequently, the Kennedy handlers, observing that their man was getting slightly more exposure than his opponent, issued the following directive: "Keep the camera on Nixon. Every time his face appears, he loses votes."[21] Could it be that sometimes the children of this world are wiser than the children of light?

## A Scriptural Survey

Without probing the entire Bible for every instance of the nonverbal, let's look at some of the more memorable and obvious. The rainbow of Genesis quickly comes to mind. God chose to make a beautiful nonverbal promise very early in the history of mankind. The pillar of cloud by day and the pillar of fire by night likewise dramatically and supernaturally directed Israel's focus toward God in a show-stopping, nonverbal way. And what about the second commandment? "You shall not make for yourself an idol in the form of anything in heaven above or on the earth beneath or in the waters below" (Exodus 20:4). How significant is it?

Art, too, is nonverbal communication. Sculptures have messages; however, the making of a form to attract worship is clearly prohibited. A more lengthy survey might include the tree of the knowledge of good and evil and the tree of life in Genesis 2-3 and Revelation 22; the dove and the olive branch in Genesis 8:11; circumcision as initiated in Genesis 17; the tabernacle in Exodus 25-40, and the bronze snake in Numbers 21:8-9.[22] The Levitical sacrifices, too, were rich in nonverbals. The smells, the blood, the incense, the sounds, the music—all combined to make such scenes forever memorable.

## True and False Prophets

The twin admonitions against false prophets in Deuteronomy 13 and 18 are curious in that the first false prophet is false not in his initial statements *which all come true*, but in his later influence and advice. Curiously, this first warning to Israel against false prophets directs the nation away from the verbals:

> If a prophet, or one who foretells by dreams, appears among you and announces to you a miraculous sign or wonder, and if the sign or wonder of which he has spoken takes place, and he says, "Let us follow other gods" (gods you have not known) "and let us worship them," you

must not listen to the words of that prophet or dreamer. The LORD your God is testing you to find out whether you love him with all your heart and with all your soul. (Deuteronomy 13:1-3)

The second warning against false prophets focuses on the content, the verbalizations of the seer. Five chapters later, Moses explains to the nation that words which do not come true also mark false prophets. *If the actual words were the main thing, one would expect the order of the Deuteronomy 13 and Deuteronomy 18 warnings to be reversed.*

You may be asking, "How [then] can we know when a message has been spoken by the Lord?" The answer is a biblical one: "If what a prophet proclaims in the name of the LORD does not take place or come true, that is a message the LORD has not spoken. That prophet has spoken presumptuously. Do not be afraid of him" (Deuteronomy 18:21-22).

## The Hebrews

I have not found a great deal of writing on the subject of nonverbal communication and the Bible, but what there is seems to focus on the Old Testament accounts of Hebrew history. Paul Kruger makes some fascinating observations about "leaving the garment in one's hand" as with Joseph when he fled the sexual advances of Potiphar's wife.[23] And, in the case of Boaz and Ruth, Kruger sees the romantic nonverbals flowing from "when they first see each other," to "social distance" when they begin talking, to "personal distance" when they eat together and finally to "intimate distance" when Boaz covers Ruth with his cloak on the threshing floor.[24]

## Three to One, Four to One

Farther on in the Old Testament, the writer of Proverbs sees "[a] scoundrel and villain, who goes about with a corrupt mouth [one channel of verbal communication], who winks with his eye, signals with his feet and motions with his fingers [three channels of non-verbal communication]" (Proverbs 6:12-13).

In the list of the seven things that God hates, the catalog alternates between the nonverbal and the verbal. Indeed, to think both verbally and nonverbally and then to read this passage provides remarkable insight: "There are six things the LORD hates, seven that are detestable to him: haughty eyes [nonverbal], a lying tongue [verbal], hands that shed innocent blood [nonverbal], a heart that devises wicked schemes [nonverbal], feet that are quick to rush into evil [nonverbal], a false witness who pours out lies [verbal] and a man who stirs up dissension among brothers [verbal]" (6:16-19).

In the New Testament, too, examples abound. John tells us that the purpose of baptism (a nonverbal) is "to fulfill all righteousness" (Matthew 3:15). John the Baptist's dress and manner were nonverbal reinforcements of his message of repentance. The bread and the cup of the Lord's Supper were (and are) nonverbal representations of the body and blood of the Lord Jesus Christ.

Then there was Jesus Himself. He denounced humanity's foolish tendency to depend on the verbals: "Not everyone who says to me, 'Lord, Lord,' will enter the kingdom of heaven, but only he who does the will of my Father who is in heaven" (7:21). Many of those who profess to have prophesied in His name are going to be rejected. Notice that Jesus does not warn against false prophecies, but against false prophets—against the prophets, yes; against the prophecies, no. Perhaps Jesus was concerned that the Church miss the nonverbals by paying too much attention to the verbals, that they would be awed by the vocabulary and miss the spirit behind the message. "For false Christs and false prophets will appear and perform great signs and miracles to deceive even the elect—if that were possible" (24:24).

## The Nonverbals in Postresurrection Events

The 24th chapter of Luke is particularly striking in that it illustrates the ascendency and significance of nonverbal communication in the postresurrection appearances of Jesus.

> *Verse 2:* The stone rolls away and hints at the drama inside the sepulcher of Jesus. Has Roman authority been breached? The nonverbal says "yes."
>
> *Verse 12:* Peter runs to the tomb, suggesting profound interest and perhaps expectancy. A trudging trip to the tomb would have communicated a very different message. The strips of linen lying by themselves say even more. They hint at a resurrection or removal of Jesus' human body.
>
> *Verse 17:* The downcast faces of the disciples nonverbally demonstrate that the Emmaus road was a heavy-hearted trail of shattered hopes.
>
> *Verse 28:* Jesus acts as if He is going farther. He really isn't.
>
> *Verse 30:* Jesus takes the bread and breaks it. The nonverbal act of breaking the bread, particularly how He did it, suddenly reveals who He is. What had been hidden from the disciples for a time was now nonverbally revealed.

There are as many as twenty incidents of nonverbal communication in this death and resurrection chapter. The point I am making is that nonverbals in the Bible are not only numerous but they are also crucial to the full meaning and intent of Scripture. Even in the Apocalypse of John, there are angels, beasts, trumpets, seals and sounds—all part of the final thunder of nonverbal end-time statements.

In summary, nonverbal communication is part of divine revelation and divine communication to mankind. It is at the very heart of Christian discernment and sorting out the supernatural. It is an essential part of the mosaic of the understanding we are seeking to accumulate here, and it is wholly futile and counterproductive to discuss later the polarities in this book if the reader has not grasped the reality and significance of nonverbal communication.

## *Endnotes*

1. Joseph A. DeVito and Michael L. Hecht, *The Nonverbal Communication Reader* (Prospect Heights, IL: Waveland Press, 1990), 4.

2. Paul A. Kruger, " 'Nonverbal Communication' in the Hebrew Bible: A Few Comments," *Journal of Northwest Semitic Languages,* vol. 24:1, no. 144.

3. Albert M. Katz and Virginia T. Katz, *Foundations of Nonverbal Communication* (Carbondale, IL: Southern Illinois University Press, 1983), xv.

4. Kruger, 144.

5. Bert E. Bradley, *Fundamentals of Speech Communication: The Credibility of Ideas* (Dubuque, IA: Wm. C. Brown Publishing, 1991), 224.

6. Edward William Delph, *The Silent Community* (Beverly Hills, CA: Sage Publications, 1978).

7. Loretta A. Malandro, Larry L. Barker and Debrah G. Barker, *Nonverbal Communication* (New York: Random House, 1983), 14.

8. Robert Rosenthal, *Skill in Nonverbal Communication* (Cambridge, MA: Oelgeschlager, Grum and Hein, 1979), 204.

9. Daniel Druckman, Richard M. Rozelle and James C. Baxter, *Nonverbal Communication: Survey, Theory, Research* (Beverly Hills, CA: Sage Publications, 1982), 6.

10. Sid Hecker and David W. Stewart, *Nonverbal Communication in Advertising* (Lexington, MA: Lexington Books, 1988), 190.

11. Marshall McLuhan, *Understanding Media: The Extension of Man* (New York: McGraw Hill, 1964), 7, 13-19.

12. Ibid., 18.

13. Ibid., 231.

14. Philip Marchand, "Marshall McLuhan," *Canada Portraits of Faith* (Chilliwack, BC: Reel to Real, 1998), 109.

15. Alexander Roberts and James Donaldson, *Anti-Nicene Christian Library* (Edinburgh: T & T Clark, 1916), volume 5, 114.

16. Ibid.

17. Elio Cuccaro, personal correspondence, April 6, 1999.

18. Kurt Niederwimmer, *The Didache* (Minneapolis, MN: Fortress Press, 1998), 171-183.

19. Henry Chadwick, *Augustine* (Oxford: Oxford University Press, 1986), 3.

20. Nancy M. Henley, *Body Politics, Power, Sex, and Nonverbal Communication* (New York: Simon and Schuster, 1977), 7.

21. Ken Cooper, *Nonverbal Communication for Business Success* (New York: AMACOM, a division of American Management Association, 1979), 184.

22. Elio Cuccaro, April 6, 1999.

23. Paul Kruger, 147-148.

24. Ibid., 158-159.

# 2

Truth
and Heresy

# The Bathhouse Encounter

CHURCH HISTORY HAS SOME interesting things to tell us, not the least of which is how the Christian Church dealt with heresy.

The Apostle John, as was the custom in that time, habitually visited a public bath. However, on a certain day, Cerinthus, a widely known heretic, happened to visit the same bath. Cerinthus was known for "severing" Christ, i.e., "loosening Jesus" from Christ.[1]

The apostle's response to the arrival of Cerinthus (questioned by some)[2] was immediate and dramatic: he fled from the bathhouse lest the judgment of God be immediately unleashed upon the heretic.[3] John did not want to be caught in a calamity. Such a reaction may help us to understand John. ("Under assault from the Gnostics, and Cerinthus [first, we note], John . . . demands that every spirit be tried and that every spirit confess the Lordship and incarnation of a very specific Jesus."[4])

Such was John's godly fear that he trembled even to be near a heretic. The bathhouse story gives us a glimpse into the heart of the apostle when faced with an antichrist in the flesh.

### Endnotes

1. K. Neill Foster, "Discernment, the Powers and Spirit-Speaking," unpublished dissertation (Pasadena, CA: Fuller Theological Seminary, 1988), 171.

2. David J. Wright, "The Gnostics," *Eerdmans Handbook to the History of Christianity* (Grand Rapids, MI: Eerdmans, 1977), 100. Wright doubts the bathhouse story.

3. Frederick W. Farrar, *The Early Days of Christianity* (New York: Cassell, Petter, Galpin, & Co., 1882), vol. 2, 163.

4. Foster, 221.

# Truth and Heresy

---

"**H**ERESIES MUST COME" (1 Corinthians 11:19, author's paraphrase). This statement is one of the most unusual in the New Testament, but there are those who are willing to argue with Paul for the necessity, even usefulness, of heresy in guiding the Church to orthodoxy.[1]

In the context of this book, some discussion of heresy is essential since by definition it is the opposite of orthodoxy. One might even call this chapter "Doctrines and Doctrines," with the basic understanding being that one set of doctrines is orthodox, the other heretical, or heterodox. (Please be reminded that the supernatural is found both in orthodoxy and heterodoxy.)

One author, H.O.J. Brown, has suggested that heresy seems to come first, though in reality orthodoxy has come first, but has often failed to enunciate and express itself. Practically speaking, it is only when heresy emerges that latent orthodoxy expresses itself.[2]

The list of heresies that have harassed the Church is long: Galatianism, the Colossian heresy, Montanism, Marcionism, Pelagianism, Arianism, Antinomianism and Universalism to name just a few. A little insight into the characteristics of those named reveals that basic errors tend to repeat themselves. Pelagianism, for instance, was the natural heir of Galatianism, because salvation by works was at the heart of both errors. Another example demon-

strates that the universalism which tainted Origen keeps resurfac-
ing, as in the nineteenth century and now in the twenty-first, as
inclusivism, a miniaturized form of universalism. Further, the contemporary isms of Modernism and Liberalism were anticipated by
Marcionism. (Marcion had a habit of eliminating parts of the Scriptures he didn't like!) In both cases, the Scriptures were/are eroded
or discounted.

Montanus was the other first-century heretic who anticipated (as
did Marcion) the struggles the Church has had through the centuries
with prophecy and tongues movements. Indeed, the first time any
such movements since the Corinthian excesses ever achieved formal
orthodoxy was in twentieth-century America.

## *"Other Jesus" Trouble*

Along with the heresies, or even because of them, we now have
sharper and more refined expressions of orthodoxy. The creeds,
while not Scripture, are nevertheless scriptural expressions of the
Church under fire. The Apostles' Creed, for example, identifies
which Jesus the Church is talking about. Perhaps the beginning of
the necessity for the Apostles' Creed can be traced back to the Corinthians. They certainly had "other Jesus" trouble (2 Corinthians
11:4).

The Montanists, as inheritors of the Corinthian error, also had
"other Jesus" trouble. And, of course, John wrestled with the "antichrists" who had emerged (1 John 2:18; 4:1). The modern Church
also has many antichrists and alternate Jesus teachings too—contemporary "Jesus trouble."

One should never assume that heresy is all error. Since the purpose of heresy is to win over sections of the Church to its adherence, in reality, heresy is mixed with large doses of truth. Such a
"conversion" would neither be possible nor likely unless the heresy
were made up in large part of commonly held truths.

## Everyone Has Some Error

It should be admitted that all Christian teachers have error at some points in their systems. For instance, dichotomists (man is body and soul/spirit) and trichotomists (man is body, soul and spirit) cannot both be right, but both can be orthodox in that doctrinal statements and expressions of truth rarely get so specific as to pronounce on the finer points of theology. Jesus understood this beforehand and gave us a helpful encouragement to careful study. "Anyone who breaks one of the least of these commandments and *teaches others to do the same* will be called least in the kingdom of heaven" (Matthew 5:19, emphasis added). Note that the Lord Jesus recognized that getting one's theology wholly correct was a very difficult job and that error on some points would not keep one out of the kingdom. That ought to serve as an encouragement—but not an excuse—to us all.

Will Calvinists and Arminians ever totally agree? Can both be rightly dividing the Word of Truth? And what will they ever do with me, an "occasional" Calvinist? If we proceed with Calvin's definition of a true Church which must include the Word of God, the sacraments and church discipline, most of Protestantism would not qualify as the true Church. Certainly on the point of discipline, Calvin would dismiss us for the most part as nonchurchly, sectarian or worse.

I believe it must be said that errors (plural intended) are held by all Christians, if for no other reason than the depravity of the human heart. Some, even most, errors relate to obscure points of theology. Other errors are more significant. Some become heresy in the biblical sense, and some finally become doctrines of demons. One of the best ways to understand this is as a continuum. See Figure 2.

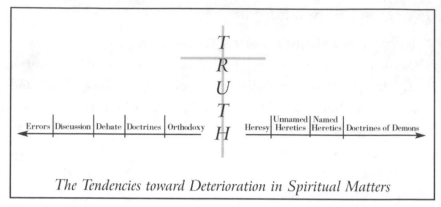

*The Tendencies toward Deterioration in Spiritual Matters*

**Figure 2**

One of the most famous statements about heresy comes from Irenaeus in *Against Heresies*: "Error indeed is never set forth in its naked deformity, lest, being thus exposed, it should at once be detected. But it is craftily decked out in an attractive dress, so as, by its outward form, to make it appear to the inexperienced (ridiculous as the expression may seem) more true than truth itself."[3]

Once identified, however, heresy must be counteracted and expunged from the body of the Church. Otherwise, the little leaven will finally permeate the whole loaf (1 Corinthians 5:6; Galatians 5:9).

## Exposing Error

Exposing error can be a dangerous business. Some theological whistle-blowers have even lost their heads. The tendency, whether in the corporate world or in the corporate church, is to blame the messenger. Heretics often exhibit a charisma and "anointing" that makes them very difficult to connect fully to obvious error. Bowman's advice on ecclesiastical or theological whistle-blowers is exceptionally apt: "Who is it, according to Paul, that causes dissensions? Is it those who teach different, false doctrines, or those who point out those who teach false doctrines? Obviously, it is those who teach the false doctrine. Those who 'blow the whistle' on false teachers in the church are *not* causing the division."[4]

Bowman, of course, was resonating the words of Paul: "Now I urge you, brethren, keep your eye on those who cause dissensions and hindrances *contrary to the teaching which you learned,* and turn away from them" (Romans 16:17, NASB, emphasis added). Sometimes names must be named. Paul's pattern, it seems, was to attack error, sometimes frontally, sometimes obliquely. The Colossian error, for instance, is not identified with an individual, though there undoubtedly were leaders who could have been identified. But in writing to Timothy about problem people, Paul names Hymenaeus (twice), Alexander and Philetus (1 Timothy 1:20; 2 Timothy 2:17) as being heretical.

Should names be named? It all depends. Once again, Bowman responds, giving two reasons why false teachers should be named:

> One reason why giving names can be important is that if false doctrines are spoken of in generalities, people will often deny that their teachers are responsible for those doctrines. In many cases people will not believe that their favorite teachers are espousing false doctrines unless exact quotes are produced from their writings or sermons documenting the errors. . . .
>
> If someone is an unrepentant false teacher, we need to do more than reject that person's specific false doctrines. We need to have nothing to do with that person. "Reject a factious man after a first and second warning, knowing that such a man is perverted and is sinning, being self-condemned" (Titus 3:10-11, NASB). These are strong words, even harsh, but they are also inspired words from God. The person who creates factions by teaching different, false doctrines is to be rejected. For that rejection to

be consistent throughout the church, the false teacher needs to be publicly named.[5]

So long as there is the possibility of reconciliation, for the repudiation of evil by the holders of error and heresy, while there are signs of hesitancy in the proclamation of that error, then names should not be named. The first two stages of Matthew 18 procedure (go to the person, go with a witness to the person) come before the announcement to the Church and perhaps even public rejection (18:15-17).

## The Protestant Smile

Tom Oden talks about the "Protestant smile," meaning that in the presence of error "the tendency of the Protestant church [is] to be unwilling to exert discipline in its midst."[6] Again, tongue in cheek, Oden continues on about heresy in the seminary context:

> It seems worth noting that the liberated seminary at its zenith has finally achieved a condition that has never before prevailed in Christian history: Heresy simply does not exist. Christian doctrine and catechesis, after long centuries of struggle against heresy, have finally found a way of overcoming heterodoxy altogether, by banishing it as a concept legitimately teachable within the hallowed walls of the inclusive multicultural, doctrinally experimental institution. . . . No heresy of any kind any longer exists. You cannot find one anywhere in the liberated seminary—unless perhaps you might consider offenses against inclusivism.[7]

How right he is! The denouncing of error is sadly lacking today. The naming of heresy is sometimes facetiously called the identification of the losing side.[8] That is not correct. Richard Hooker properly observed, "Heresy is more plain than true, whereas right belief is more true than plain."[9] Sound doctrine has to be "endured" (2 Timothy 4:3, NASB). False doctrine is smooth and goes down rather well (2 Corinthians 11:4). Preachers who have "bite" in their message are likely to be preaching the straight gospel. (Too much bite, of course, could also indicate plenty of error!)

Paul's admonition to prove all things (1 Thessalonians 5:21) and his further exhortation to Timothy to pay attention to doctrine (1 Timothy 4:16) must not be ignored. Some doctrine is true, and some doctrine is false. Truth sets some folks free and leads to eternal life. Heresy plunges others into hell and eternal punishment (Matthew 25:46). Surely distinguishing between orthodoxy and heresy is not the place to make a wrong call: "Therefore, brethren, be even more diligent to make your call and election sure, for if you do these things you will never stumble; for so an entrance will be supplied to you abundantly into the everlasting kingdom of our Lord and Savior Jesus Christ" (2 Peter 1:10-11, NKJV).

In summary, orthodoxy and heresies must be identified if we are to sort out supernatural manifestations accurately.

## Endnotes

1. Harold O.J. Brown, *Heresies* (Garden City, NY: Doubleday, 1984), 4-5.

2. Ibid.

3. Ibid., 6.

4. Robert M. Bowman, *Orthodoxy and Heresy* (Grand Rapids, MI: Baker Book House, 1992), 34.

5. Ibid., 37-40.

6. Thomas C. Oden, *Requiem* (Nashville, TN: Abingdon, 1995), 46-47.

7. Ibid., 29.

8. Wayne House, "With an Apology to Arius: When and How Should We Deal with Heretics and Heresy?" *Journal of Christian Apologetics* (Plymouth, MI: Michigan Theological Seminary, 1997), 31.

9. Ibid., 29.

# 3

The

Scriptures

# Under the Book

I HAD RETURNED TO SEMINARY at age forty-five and was attending a Sunday night service at the Alliance Church in Pasadena, California. The preacher was a student at Fuller Theological Seminary as was I, but he was in the School of Psychology, whereas I was in the School of World Mission. Our contacts had been fleeting. That night there was a defining moment in my life as I listened to this graduate student, a mature man himself.

The theme of the message I have forgotten. I recall no text. But at one dramatic moment the preacher lifted up his Bible and placed it over his head. Then he said, and I am paraphrasing, "I am under this book, and I am controlled by Scripture." It was a personal statement about the biblical rule of his life.

In that moment, I recognized that I too believed that. His way of expressing it has become mine as well. I am nothing if I am not a man under authority—the rule of Scripture.

# The Scriptures

T HE REALITY OF TRUTH AND FALSEHOOD and the absoluteness of truth in a world of confusion is uncompromisingly set forth in both testaments of the Bible. My attempted sorting of the supernaturals (plural intended) has no hope of success apart from the rule of Scripture. I happily embrace the Bible as inerrant. My affirmation of inerrancy is without qualifications or equivocating disclaimers. I seek to live and expect to die (apart from our Lord's return) by its precepts. Its authority and demand for absolutes come early and often in the biblical text. If you do not fully trust the Scriptures, you will never be able to sort out the supernatural accurately or adequately.

## True and False in the Old Testament

It does not take long for error and deception to arrive on the scene in the book of Genesis. Creation has hardly cooled and man has hardly gotten over the discovery of a lovely creature called woman when Satan is introduced. He is a talking serpent—he is able to communicate verbally. His first attack on God is directed in the form of a question to the woman. "Did God really say, 'You must not eat from any tree in the garden?' " (Genesis 3:1). Eve had only one commandment to obey. The single prohibition was not to eat the fruit of one of the trees. Her temptation and fall are history. The results are no less than incomprehensibly catastrophic.

Satan apparently already knew about God, as did Eve. The theological expertise of the counterkingdom is evident elsewhere in the Scripture. The devils believe and tremble (James 2:19). So Satan has his information. In fact, he betrays his communicational traits when he says to Eve, "Did God really say . . . ?" Tim Warner suggests that the Prince of Darkness works in two powerful ways: 1) to intimidate and cause fear, and 2) to entice humans into taking power or knowledge from him instead of God.[1] The obvious intent of his engagement of Eve was to kill her, even though the serpent assured her, "You will not surely die" (Genesis 3:4). In building his temptation of Eve, Satan questioned the integrity of God, challenged the honesty of God and argued persuasively about the desirability and attractiveness of the fruit, actually speaking the truth to move the temptation on to sin and death.

## Touch Not, Taste Not

We all know that the final result was that Adam as well as Eve partook of the forbidden fruit. We also know that even as Eve was deceived, Adam was held responsible in that sin, and death passed upon all men through his actions. "Therefore, just as sin entered the world through one man, and death through sin, and in this way death came to all men, because all sinned. . . . So . . . just as sin reigned in death, so also grace might reign through righteousness to bring eternal life through Jesus Christ our Lord" (Romans 5:12, 21).

The unpleasant reality is that creation has been spoiled by sin and the devil. Although it has been redeemed by Jesus Christ, the passage through this "vale of tears" is continually buffeted by the reality of evil—with its malevolence and deception—through the person and work of Satan and his legions. Eve was simply the first person to engage. Her surrender to deception and Adam's willful capitulation irrevocably marred and damned us all. But Christ has come. His kingdom has been launched (Luke 4:18-19). It will be further enlarged (Matthew 13:31-32), and it will finally and fully arrive (6:10).

It falls to man in this "now" of time to struggle against temptation, to be sober, to be vigilant, to recognize that Satan goes about as a roaring lion seeking to devour (1 Peter 5:8), to not be ignorant of his devices (2 Corinthians 2:11) and to resist steadfastly his schemes (Ephesians 6:11). And, as well as we may do and as faithfully as we may follow hard after God, there is still the possibility of being deceived as were Eve and Adam.

That possibility we *must* accept and admit.

## Joshua and All Israel

Just as Israel was entering into the land of promise, while they were still flushed with the victories of Jericho and Ai, they encountered the wily Gibeonites. Most of Israel's enemies had come together in vain to make war against Joshua and the people of God (Joshua 9:2). The Gibeonites had already observed which way the wind was blowing. It was obvious that they too were doomed to destruction, so they "resorted to a ruse" (9:4). Accordingly, they sent a delegation to Joshua and the elders. Notice the dominance of the nonverbals in this story. The Gibeonites' sacks are worn out, their wineskins old and mended, their clothes tattered, their sandals patched. And so they lie. They had come, they said, from a far country wanting to make a treaty with Israel (9:3-6).

The tale they spun was eloquent—and (mostly) false. They had heard, they said, of the exploits of Jehovah (undoubtedly true). Their elders had sent them from a very far country to make a treaty with Israel. Their bread, now moldy, had been fresh and warm when they had left, and their wineskins had been new. Their sandals and clothes, likewise, had obviously been in mint condition (all lies).

The Scriptures then tell us: "The men of Israel sampled their provisions *but did not inquire of the LORD.* Then Joshua made a treaty of

peace with them to let them live, and the leaders of the assembly rat-
ified it by oath" (Joshua 9:14-15, emphasis added). Just three days
after the accord, Israel found out that the Gibeonites were their
neighbors. Embarrassed at having been deceived, the men of Israel
marched on their cities. However, according to the instructions of
Moses, they did not wipe them out. Instead, the Gibeonites were
made hewers of wood and haulers of water, but they were not destroyed. Israel had sworn to its own hurt, and the oath they had
made saved the lives of the Gibeonites.

But the story was not over. In the ensuing years, the Gibeonites
came back to haunt and trouble Israel. Gibeon became a place of
war, treachery and murder (2 Samuel 3:30). The murder of Amasa by
Joab took place in Gibeon (20:8-10), and Solomon's sin of sacrificing
in the high places was indulged in Gibeon (1 Kings 3:4).

Nevertheless, it was in Gibeon that Solomon made his famous request for wisdom, and it was there that God said to him, "Since you
have asked for this and not for long life or wealth for yourself, nor
have you asked for the death of your enemies but for discernment in
administering justice, I will do what you have asked. I will give you a
wise and discerning heart, so that there will never have been anyone
like you, nor will there ever be" (3:11-12).

Moreover, what God did in appearing to Solomon was so
impactful that at the dedication of the temple the author of First
Kings harked back to the Gibeon encounter (9:2). That remem-
brance in itself shows that the errors of Joshua and all Israel were
swept up into the redemptive purposes of God. That is encouragement to believe that, when grievous errors are made today, God will
still work out His redemptive purposes and that He abides faithful
and cannot deny Himself (2 Timothy 2:13).

He proved that later in the Bible. When Nehemiah enumerated
those who had been taken in captivity, there were ninety-five from
Gibeon. And Jeremiah identifies a prophet's father named Azzur
from Gibeon (Jeremiah 28:1), a prophetic voice for God's people

from among the families of "woodcutters and water carriers" (Joshua 9:21). Also, when the sun stood still over Gibeon (10:12), there could be no doubt that this site of deception and shame had become the showcase of one of Israel's saving miracles. Even deception, as disastrous as it may be at the outset, is frustrated and overturned by the persistent grace of God. The works of God at Gibeon should encourage every once-deluded soul.

## True and False in the New Testament

The New Testament begins with a powerful gospel of true and false—Matthew. Though I will make a number of observations on Matthew, my purpose again is not to collate all the "true-and-false" passages exhaustively; rather, I simply want to demonstrate that true and false now, as then, have to do with reality.

Just as the Old Testament opens with Satan in the garden, so Matthew moves directly to the temptation of Jesus in the wilderness (Matthew 4:1-11). The Son of God faces a sophisticated enemy who uses the very thing in which Jesus has utmost confidence—the Word of God—to tempt Him. In the first two incidents, Satan twists the intent of Scripture to match the temptation. Indeed, God could make stones into bread. So the tempter says, "If you are the Son of God, tell these stones to become bread" (4:3).

Jesus, in His after-fast hunger, nevertheless realized that the issue before Him was not bread, but one of trust and faith. Satan had slyly suggested that He might not be the Son of God if He did not do this. He had reinforced the temptation with an awareness of divine power, a realization that God by words alone had power to create. Christ's response was biblical: "Man does not live on bread alone, but on every word that comes from the mouth of God" (Matthew 4:4; Deuteronomy 8:3). In the core of the temptation there was a devilish invitation to distrust. Jesus met it head on.

The second temptation was similar. After taking Jesus to the pinnacle of the temple, Satan again prefaced his temptation with, "If you are the Son of God . . ." (Matthew 4:6). Along with the question of Jesus' divinity, there was the temptation to the spectacular. "Throw yourself down, and the angels will intervene" (author's paraphrase). Moreover, Satan quoted Scripture to support his case. (So often we evangelicals fall prey to those who eloquently quote Scripture to substantiate their causes.) Jesus' veneration of the very words of God could surely be used against Him here. But not so; Satan found himself stymied once again by a scriptural reply, "Do not put the Lord your God to the test" (Matthew 4:7; Deuteronomy 6:16).

## A Passion to Be Worshiped

In the final temptation of Jesus, Satan puts aside the niceties. He sets aside the twice-used "if you are the Son of God" theme because Jesus was not biting. Instead, Satan is raw and frontal. With the world in full view, he says, "All this I will give you . . . if you will bow down and worship me" (Matthew 4:9). There, he had said it. Now the truth was out. Worship was what he was after. Jesus' response, again citing Scripture, was swift and sure: "Worship the Lord your God, and serve him only" (4:10; Deuteronomy 6:13). It is also noteworthy that Satan was willing to sacrifice all the kingdoms of this world if Jesus would bow down and worship him. We can almost hear him singing, "Take the world, but give me Jesus." Satan had enough sense to value Jesus more than the whole world. Would that more Christians had that same desire.[2] For Jesus to have yielded would have been false worship.

Satan is a fallen though created being who desperately wants worship. His address of human passion (hunger) was repudiated by Jesus. His lust for spectacle was likewise rejected by our Lord. The final desperate quest for worship was also rejected—all by Jesus' use of Scripture. Woven through this fascinating account of temptation and victory is the importance of scriptural knowledge. What if Jesus had not known the Scriptures? Surely that is why God's people today are so often overcome: "My people are destroyed from lack of knowledge" (Hosea 4:6).

## False Religion

In Matthew's 6th chapter, Jesus plunges forward in His exposure of false religion. He is not at this point speaking about the pagan worship of false gods; instead, He is addressing the attempts of the doctrinally orthodox to worship aright. That they fail miserably is all too obvious. In 6:1-18, "Jesus highlighted six areas in which wrong motives and distorted ideals tainted religious life. Specifically, Jesus put his finger on false giving, false praying, false fasting, false security, false counseling and false prophets."[3]

One of the questions we should be continually asking about our worship is this: Is the worship in which we are now engaged true worship of Almighty God? If the list given us by our Lord in Matthew 6 is significant at all, it ought to drive us continually to the most devastating question of all: Is this worship in which we are now engaging the true worship of the Sovereign Lord God?

John Wesley's view of false worship was clear—even if it lacks a biblical base, "all emotional religion is false."[4] The reality undoubtedly is that "emotion in worship is quite appropriate and likely necessary."[5] Still, Wesley had a point.

Similarly, Tozer had his own pithy views about false religion: ". . . the way of the cross is never easy. The shine and glamour accompanying popular religious movements is as false as the sheen on the wings of the angel of darkness. . . ."[6] Even concerning his own books, Tozer gave himself no mercy: "All I can hope is that this book may be a right emphasis coming at a right time. If the reader should discover here anything really new he is in conscience bound to reject it, for whatever in religion is new is by the same token false."[7]

He warned as well that there was in his day confusion about the old cross and the new:

The new cross does not slay the sinner, it redirects him. It gears him into a cleaner and jollier way of living and saves his self-respect. To the self-assertive it says, "Come and assert yourself for Christ." To the egotist it says, "Come and do your boasting in the Lord." To the thrill seeker it says, "Come and enjoy the thrill of Christian fellowship." The Christian message is slanted in the direction of the current vogue in order to make it acceptable to the public.

The philosophy back of this kind of thing may be sincere, but its sincerity does not save it from being false. It is false because it is blind. It misses completely the whole meaning of the cross.[8]

Jesus was compellingly clear:

If those days had not been cut short, no one would survive, but for the sake of the elect those days will be shortened. At that time if anyone says to you, "Look, here is the Christ!" or, "There he is!" do not believe it. For false Christs and false prophets will appear and perform great signs and miracles to deceive even the elect—if that were possible. See, I have told you ahead of time. (Matthew 24:22-25)

Similarly, the Apostle Paul warned the Thessalonian church about the perils attendant to the end. "The coming of the lawless one will be in accordance with the work of Satan displayed in all kinds of counterfeit miracles, signs and wonders, and in every sort of evil that deceives those who are perishing" (2 Thessalonians 2:9-10).

D. Martyn Lloyd-Jones sums it up rather well.

Do you agree with those who say that a spirit of love is incompatible with the negative and critical denunciation of blatant error, and that we must always be positive? The simple answer to such an attitude is that the Lord Jesus Christ denounced evil and false teachers. I repeat that he denounced them as "ravening wolves" and "whited sepulchres," and as "blind guides." The Apostle Paul spoke of those "whose God is their belly and whose glory is in their shame." That is the language of the Scriptures. There can be little doubt but that the Church is as she is today because we do not follow New Testament teaching and its exhortations, and confine ourselves to the positive and so-called "simple Gospel," and fail to stress the negativeness and the criticism. The result is that people do not recognize error when they meet it.

It is not pleasant to be negative; it is not enjoyable to have to denounce and expose error. But any pastor who feels in a little measure, and with humility, the responsibility . . . is compelled to utter these warnings. It is not liked and appreciated in this modern flabby generation.[9]

Peter likewise reminds his hearers, "But there were also false prophets among the people [Israel], just as there will be false teachers among you" (2 Peter 2:1). And John was just as clear, "Dear friends, do not believe every spirit, but test the spirits to see whether they are from God, because many false prophets have gone out into the world" (1 John 4:1).

In summary, the point I am making is that the New Testament, as the Old does, clearly exhibits strong affirmations about both true and false. All too often today's Christians are like the woman one man encountered in a Florida church. Noting his concern about whether the Holy Spirit was the author of the events he was witnessing, she brightly assured him that it had to be the Holy Spirit.

"What else would it be? We're in church, aren't we?"[10]

Jesus first met a demonized man in the synagogue—in church if you will (Luke 4:33). One of the largest battlefields in spiritual warfare is the actual worship service of faithful, authentic Christian churches. The gospel is always being preached to a trifold audience—the human congregation, the heavenly host and the observing powers (Ephesians 3:10; Hebrews 12:1). Those dark powers are there to seek to pervert, deceive and delude. At the same time, the all-powerful Holy Spirit of Almighty God is there as well. The immediate potential for true and false is continually before us all.

## *Endnotes*

1. Timothy Warner, "The Power of Truth to Dispel Deception," unpublished lecture notes (Gettysburg, PA: Susek Evangelistic Association, 1997), 10.

2. David E. Schroeder, *Matthew* (Camp Hill, PA: Christian Publications, 1995), 31.

3. Ibid., 49.

4. John Wesley, *The Journal of John Wesley* (Chicago: Moody Press, 1980), 24.

5. W. Robert Willoughby, personal correspondence, 1998, 1.

6. A.W. Tozer, *The Pursuit of Man* (Camp Hill, PA: Christian Publications, 1997), 132.

7. Ibid., xiii.

8. A.W. Tozer, *The Best of A.W. Tozer* (Camp Hill, PA: Christian Publications, 1978), 176.

9. D. Martyn Lloyd-Jones, "Biblical Intolerance," *Banner of Truth*, August-September 1994, 371-372.

10. Hank Hanegraaff, "Pensacola Outpouring," *Christian Research Journal*, November-December 1997, 17-18.

# PART II

# PROPHECY—

# A MAJOR

# UNDERSTANDING

TAKING TIME TO UNDERSTAND why prophecy is a key issue when it comes to sorting out the supernatural will pay dividends later. For that reason, a major section of this book is developed here. All that has preceded and will follow rests on this fulcrum.

Our goal in this second section of *Sorting Out the Supernatural* is to define and describe prophecy from the Scriptures. We will do that by comparing and contrasting the biblical, traditional and historical meanings of prophecy with the current definition of prophecy which has emerged and gained credence in the years surrounding the turn of the twenty-first century.

> *"Prove all things; hold fast that which is good."*
> *(1 Thessalonians 5:21, KJV)*

# 4

# Prophecy
# and Prophecy

# "False" True Prophecy?

*Excerpted from* Thus Saith the Lord? *by John Brevere*[1]

IT WAS MY FIRST TIME to this city. I'd only spoken briefly with the pastor twice, once by phone and later when he picked me up at the airport. I've made it a policy not to discuss church matters before ministering. I do this to keep from being influenced one way or another incorrectly. This makes it easier to remain sensitive to the Spirit of God. I had done this with this pastor and his associates also.

As I prepared for the first service I planned to speak along the lines of what I normally do on Sunday mornings. I'm usually drawn to the lost in the church—those who confess to be believers but still live for themselves. Yet that morning during worship I felt an uneasiness in my spirit. I sensed something amiss in this church's spiritual climate. I recognized it as what I come up against when divination or the counterfeit prophetic ministry has influence over a church. I sensed something had been released against this church.

Repeatedly I heard God say, "Deal with the error."

I asked for direction. "Where do I begin?"

I heard the Lord say, "Begin by reading Ezekiel 13."

After being introduced, I immediately instructed the congregation to turn to Ezekiel 13 and began to preach from that chapter. I confronted the counterfeit prophetic ministry that is sweeping through the Church unchecked today. I shared how these prophets are speaking under inspiration, yet it is not the inspiration of the Holy Spirit. As I preached I was aware that a stronghold in their thinking was being confronted. I also noticed the leadership was listening intently.

After the service, I went to lunch with the pastor and his wife. As soon as we were alone, the pastor shared. "We needed this so much. You don't realize how on target you were this morning."

I responded, "Tell me. I am not used to preaching along this line at a Sunday morning service." He went into great detail. "We had a prophet come into our church to minister, and the fruit was devastating. Let me tell you of a situation that occurred with a couple in our church."

He went on to share a tragic story of a couple in his church whose greatest desire was to work for an internationally known evangelist on the East Coast. The desire was strongest with his wife. Anytime the evangelist was anywhere near, they both attended every meeting they could, hoping to hook up with him.

Their pastor had invited a prophet to minister to the congregation. This man had never been to this church before and was unaware of any personal situations or desires within its body.

During the course of the service, he picked out this couple and asked them to stand up while he gave them a "word from God." His message went something like this, "Thus saith the Lord, 'I've called you to the ministry of healing. I am going to remove you from this fellowship and send you to the East Coast. There you will serve and be mentored by (at this point he named the evangelist they had desired to be with by name). He will pour himself into you, and it is there I will equip you for the healing ministry and bring his mantle upon you. Then after a season he will launch you, and I will bring you back to this part of the country where you will establish a powerful healing ministry.'"

The pastor said, "John, the couple was weeping with joy and amazement. Those in our congregation who knew they desired to work for this evangelist either wept along with them or stared in amazement at the accuracy of this word. Almost everyone in our fellowship was excited except my wife and me. We knew something was wrong."

Why? Because the pastor and his wife knew this couple well. They had sat with them through several sessions for marriage counseling. They were also concerned that this couple was overly enamored with ministry. They were not drawn to minister to people as much as they were drawn to the spotlight they saw coming with it.

The pastor shared how this couple began to pursue actively a position with this ministry. The husband finally quit his job, and they left for the East Coast. They met with one of the evangelist's right-hand men and shared what God had put on their hearts and their desire to serve the ministry in any capacity necessary.

The assistant thanked them but no position was offered. So they waited for a door to open. After a period of time and after great disappointment, the couple returned home. Nothing at all had happened. . . .

Recently the pastor informed me that this couple is now divorced.

> *"You say, 'The LORD declares,' though I have not spoken."*
> *(Ezekiel 13:7)*

### Endnote

1. John Brevere, *Thus Saith the Lord?* (Lake Mary, FL: Creation House, 1999), 44-46. Used by permission.

# Section A

# Prophecy Defined

B URKINA FASO IS A FAR-OFF LAND which will never be visited by large numbers of people. But in 1972, in a spin-off of the Western Canadian Revival which had begun a year earlier, revival came to one of Burkina's major cities, Bobo Dioulasso.

The revival featured agonizing confessions of sin, restitution, great joy, powerful music, a contagion which spread to other cities, an evangelistic harvest and more. There was no falling, no barking and no disorder.

It also, I am told, featured a prophecy—one that, as the evangelist, I apparently gave. Returning in later years, I was told about the prophecy.

"I don't think I said that. I don't talk that way," I responded in unbelief. I now surmise that my interpreter cast my words with a prophetic nuance. Nevertheless, I was assured by friends at Bobo that I had indeed prophesied that there would be twelve churches in the city. That was in a day when Bobo had only one evangelical congregation—the church where the revival was taking place.

Some years later, I paid another visit to the city. By that time, our own Mission had eleven churches with the expectation of more. Other Missions and groups now have churches in Bobo, the second largest city of this sub-Sahara African nation. The number has certainly exceeded twelve churches and, according to missionary Jim

Albright, there is a campaign in process even as I write to found a dozen more churches there.

Apparently I was not a false prophet—if the criteria of the Old Testament is applied to New Testament experience, i.e., prophecy in the predictive mode being either true or false.

Traditionally, prophecy has long been associated with inspired preaching, speaking forth and forthtelling, as the etymology of the word suggests.[1] It is biblically described as for "edification, and exhortation, and comfort" (1 Corinthians 14:3, KJV), and sometimes it dips into the predictive mode, as in the case of Agabus in Acts 11:28 who foretold a famine that would spread over the entire Roman Empire. Almost invariably, when prophecy is referenced the clear implication is that what was prophesied predictively came to pass as prophesied (Acts 2:17-21; 11:28; 21:10, etc.).

Commonly, in its narrowest expression, prophecy appears in utterance form within and as an inspired part of prayers and preaching—a manifestation of the Holy Spirit (1 Corinthians 12:7-11). It is also a gift whose pursuit is advocated (14:1), and it connects viscerally with several other expressions such as music, tongues and perhaps even revelation.

## A Current Definition

Today, an alternate definition of prophecy is being promoted. The following quotes from its proponents clarify their position. Briefly stated, prophecy is being defined as 1) "telling something that God has spontaneously brought to mind";[2] and 2) "an unreliable human speech act in response to a revelation from the Holy Spirit."[3]

The current definition is enunciated as follows: "Prophecy in ordinary New Testament churches . . . was simply a very human—sometimes partially mistaken—report of something the Holy Spirit brought to mind."[4] Thus it appears that *prophecy becomes the ability to interpret and tell accurately and appropriately what God has brought to mind.* Inaccuracies in prophecy in this line of thinking may no longer indicate false prophecy.

For example, Agabus, who is sometimes accused of the false prophecy that Paul would be bound by the Jews but instead was imprisoned by the Romans (Acts 21:10-11; 28:17), is portrayed by the present definition as having failed to convey accurately what God was showing him. (In defense of Agabus, there are situations in Scripture where responsibility for an act is considered the same as actually doing it. Did Pilate actually scourge Jesus? No. Did the Jews actually physically crucify Jesus? No. Yet, Peter directly lays the blame on the Jews and specifically says, "God has made this Jesus, whom you crucified, both Lord and Christ" [Acts 2:36].) Indeed, "It was the violent hostility of the Jews that prompted the Roman soldiers to take Paul into protective custody."[5]

An important caveat needs to be inserted here before we begin to compare and contrast the biblical/traditional/historical definition with this one. Let it be clear that no one who is defining prophecy on either side of this conversation is suggesting that any utterance can conflict with the biblical canon and still be a true manifestation of the Holy Spirit. With that understanding in place, we proceed.

The emerging definition of prophecy is as follows:

> Why did Jesus choose the term *apostle* to designate those who had the authority to write Scripture? It was probably because the Greek word *prophetes* ("prophet") at the time of the New Testament had a very broad range of meanings. It generally did not have the sense "one who speaks God's very words" but rather "one who speaks on the basis of some external influence" (often a spiritual influence of some kind). Titus 1:12 uses the word in this sense, where Paul quotes the pagan Greek poet Epimenides: "One of themselves, a *prophet* of their own. . . ." [NASB]

Many writings outside the Bible use the word *prophet*
. . . in this way, without signifying divine authority in the
words of one called "prophet." In fact, by the time of the
New Testament the term *prophet* in everyday use often
simply meant "one who had supernatural knowledge" or
"one who predicts the future"—or even just "spokes-
man" (without any connotation of divine authority).[6]

In working through Professor Wayne Grudem's explanation
above, I exposed the material to two friends who are also published
authors. Their reactions caught me by surprise. Robert Willoughby,
a professor and scholar, observes that Grudem's definition is derived "from extra-biblical sources . . . [where] the term 'prophet'
does not mean 'one who speaks God's very words,' but rather 'one
who speaks on the basis of some external influence.' "[7]

Albert Runge, a Jewish believer and long-time pastor and writer to
whom I also sent the material, reacted similarly to Willoughby and
expressed a heightened alarm about the definition:

Grudem redefines the word "prophecy" in order to conform it to the [current] belief, claims and exercise of the
gift of prophecy. . . . Redefining words is dangerous and
can be misleading. . . . In order to prove his premise about
the vagueness of the [New Testament] gift of prophecy he
uses . . . [a] pagan prophet as supporting evidence for his
view of the fallibility of the gift of prophecy.[8]

Runge's observation is exceptionally serious. Certainly, the citing
of a pagan prophet to redefine prophecy for the Christian Church is
one of the weakest links in this view of prophecy. We know, of
course, that the gods prophesy (Deuteronomy 18:20). It is for that
reason that the Scriptures include means of testing the source of
prophecies. If pagan prophets such as Epimenides were anointed

from subterranean sources—and by definition they were—then Christian prophecy, intended to be from the Holy Spirit, is in one bold stroke being redefined in subterranean terms. I find this emerging tendency to attribute error and inaccuracy to the Spirit of Truth greatly disturbing (John 14:17).

## Fallible Prophecy?

This is a profoundly troubling definition in that by going "outside the Bible" and by citing a "pagan" prophet in the context of "everyday use" rather than biblical texts, the author introduces into the modern era a cultural and theological affirmation that ultimately permits inaccuracy and fallibility and indeed makes truth optional in manifestations attributed to the Holy Spirit, the Spirit of Truth (John 14:17).

The fallible view of prophecy just set forth is clearly presented in Professor Grudem's paraphrase of First Corinthians 13:9: "This is because we know imperfectly and we prophesy imperfectly"[9] in place of the NIV's statement, "For we know in part and we prophesy in part." The use of "imperfectly" as derived from the Greek *merous* seems accommodational and slanted, possibly not warranted.

Vine sees the words "in part" as meaning "in some measure" or "partly," but does not suggest imperfection.[10] If one is advocating the imperfection and even fallibility of New Testament prophecy, then the choice of "imperfect" is apt, though probably not the best.

The use of "imperfect" in this text, however, does have support in *A Greek English Lexicon of the New Testament and other Early Christian Literature*,[11] but the passage concludes that "[t]he bulk of its usage indicates [its use of the meaning] a part."[12]

C. Samuel Storms explains that the present definition of prophecy does say that "though rooted in revelation, prophecy is occasionally fallible."[13] Like others, he argues against the "strict standards applied under the Old Testament" and wonders, "Might it not rather be that

New Testament prophecy is occasionally fallible and therefore has to be carefully judged (1 Corinthians 14:29; 1 Thessalonians 5:19-22)?"[14]

One way of allowing for fallibility in prophecy is to suggest that there are layers of prophecy. Robert Saucy, for example, does not agree with such an idea. "The attempt to see prophecy as having different levels, ranging from that which is totally God's Word and therefore inerrant to that which is mixed with varying degrees of human error, is difficult to support biblically."[15]

His protest is correct but inadequate in that the problems with prophecy are seen as only "human error." While not discounting human depravity, the possibility of demonic error should not be overlooked in the matter of prophecy. Both the Old and New Testaments are brimming with references to false prophets, especially in the Apostle John's vocabulary in which he barely distinguishes between spirits and prophets (1 John 4:1-3).

Furthermore, Paul's equation of tongues and interpretation with prophecy connects glossolalia to this discussion (1 Corinthians 14:5), though that connection cannot be pursued in view of the immensity of such an investigation.

## Allowable Error?

The very idea of allowable error in prophecy should be pushing us toward several other biblical ideas. My major concerns are as follows.

### 1. Prophecy and Biblical Polarities

The current definition of prophecy backs away from the polarities of both Testaments. In the Old Testament false prophets were a plague. Similarly, in the New Testament false prophets are furiously denounced. Even in John's day he noted that "many false prophets have gone out into the world" (1 John 4:1). Today's definition of prophecy potentially legitimizes a host of false prophets. If "false" no longer means "false," then we are in a quagmire of semantics. If something is to be advocated in our era as being biblical, it should be prefigured or at least intimated in the Old Testament. One of the key verses of the New Testament still is this one: "For everything that was written in the past was written to teach us, so that through endurance and the encouragement of the Scriptures we might have hope" (Romans 15:4; c.f. 2 Corinthians 10:11). When I see no Old Testament erosion of the stark opposites in prophecy, I remain doubtful about the meanings of prophecy now being advanced.

The present stance on predictive prophecy exhibits a reluctance to label prophecy false. The utterance movements of today in which prophecies abound have an immense stake in this definition. They also have an immense problem if even a small percentage of the existing prophecies are fallible—hence they cannot help but have an increasing openness to an accommodated definition.

The next and most uncomfortable question must then be: Why the passion to allow for prophecies that are fallible? Does it mean that a large percentage of the current prophecies are not turning out to be true? Or is it that there is broad unwillingness to admit such a possibility?

## 2. Prophecy and the Old Testament

The Old Testament is intended to prefigure the New. It is evident and accepted that Old Testament prophecy is false when one of two criteria are not found—when the hearts of the people are led astray (Deuteronomy 13:1-4), or what the prophet pronounces fails to come to pass (18:20-22). And we must be further reminded that Old Testament prophets had life-and-death responsibility to line up with Moses. Any prophet who counseled rebellion against the Law (thus turning away the hearts of the people) was to be put to death (Deuteronomy 13). And in the case of predictive prophecy, it had to stand the test of fulfillment. If what a prophet prophesied did not come to pass, that prophet was to be ignored ("not to be feared") (Deuteronomy 18).[16]

If Old Testament prophets had to line up with an established authority (Moses), how is it that New Testament era prophets may, under the present definition, have no obligation to line up with the Old and New Testaments on the matter of accuracy? (I am not referring to the biblical canon at this point but to the necessity of integrity and truth. This necessity and passion for truth, along with a corresponding abhorrence for falsehood, is contextually pervasive in both testaments. Willoughby is correct when he says, "[A] good hermeneutic [not derived from culture] demands that the meaning of a New Testament word is based primarily upon its usage in the Old Testament Scripture."[17])

The current definition of prophecy rejects the hermeneutical principle which has been called "the analogy of antecedent Scripture." It is significant because it focuses

> on the milieu in which the discourse was first delivered. Our eyes and ears are not attuned to catching the obvious signals that meant so much to the original speakers and listeners who heard old themes and phrases ringing through the new revelations from God. *It is at this point that most people make their biggest mistake in the interpreting process* (emphasis added).[18]

One of the early rules of interpretation of the Bible is to allow the definitions established in the Old Testament to follow through into the New Testament. "God," as understood in Genesis chapter 1, is elaborated upon and reinforced in John chapter 1. Similarly, concepts such as the glory of God, the trinity and redemption are launched in the Old Testament and carried into the New. Also, the numerous Old Testament references to anointing, for example, find further expression in the Messiah, the Anointed One of the New Testament.

Where there are changes as the result of New Testament revelation, such as in Paul's discussion of the Old Adam and the New Adam (1 Corinthians 15:45-49), the explanations are clearly laid out in the New Testament. Likewise, the shift from law in the Old Testament to grace in the New is fully explained and underscored. Even names announced and used in the Old Testament are carried forward into the New.

If solid biblical interpretation depends upon a flow of meanings from the Old Testament into the New, by what measure is anyone authorized to explain prophecy differently in the New Testament than it has already been explained in the Old? Jesus explained that the law and the prophets were until John (the Baptist), but there was no announcement of a change that had been effected in prophecy. In fact, the direction is the other way in that John the Baptist, the evangelists, Peter and later the Apostle John in Revelation act and write as if the Old Testament definition of predictive prophecy continues to prevail in the New. Those who advocate fallible prophecy must overcome one of the most basic rules of hermeneutics: unless otherwise informed, interpret the meanings in the New Testament as you have interpreted those same meanings in the Old Testament; ". . . we must take into consideration the usage of the word in the Old Testament when attempting to arrive at its New Testament meaning. . . . Of course the New Testament may add to its meaning, or colour it with exclusively Christian overtones."[19]

Similarly, the early church saw New Testament prophecy as an extension of Old Testament experience.

Justin Martyr (A.D. 110-165), the eminent Greek apologist of the second century, also advocated a direct continuity between Old Testament and New Testament prophets. In *Dialogue with Trypho 82*, he wrote that the prophetic gift of the Old Testament had been transferred to the church. ("For the prophetic gift remains with us, even to the present time. And hence you have to understand that [the gifts] formerly among your nation have been transferred to us [the church].") By this statement we may infer that Justin Martyr viewed the New Testament prophetic gift as a direct continuation of the gift as it was practiced in the Old Testament.[20]

I will later argue that repeatedly in the New Testament references to prophecy continue to be set with undiminished force in the format and context established in the Old Testament.

Wayne Grudem is not alone in his advocacy of fallible prophecy, but his prominence as a writer makes him a focal point. I find it remarkable that from the outset of his published dissertation (1982) he embraces this definition.[21] As already observed, he derives his definition from potentially pagan sources "outside the Bible," and then moves into the discussion without key controls in place.

To venture without controls into the study of prophecy is a perilous excursion. It would have been a great place to install a resolute adherence to the established Old Testament definition of prophecy from Moses and the hermeneutical principle of antecedent Scripture. Biblical controls such as those would never have allowed him to say early in his writing, "But if he [the prophet] only claims a divine authority of general content, then his audience will not brand him as 'false' simply because occasional details of his prophecies turn out to be wrong."[22] Such a definition affords ample wiggle room for the flesh and the devil. That they (the flesh and the devil) readily seize the opportunities is not in doubt.

Nostradamus (1503-1566) was a famous French seer. Some of his prophecies apparently came true. Louis XVI and his queen, Marie Antoinette, were captured at Varennes and later beheaded on the guillotine. Nostradamus' phrases written 200 years earlier were "Varennes" and "bloody slicing."[23]

But many of Nostradamus' prophecies did not come true. According to Francis King, "It is prophesied that in the seventh month (July) of 1999, or perhaps in early August, just after the end of the seventh month, the 'King of Terror' will descend upon the earth."[24] This date is already past, and the King of Terror seems to delay. The astrological (and therefore occult) nature of his almanacs is beyond dispute. Nostradamus was not an authentic Christian prophet—unless of course the modern definition of prophecy prevailed then as apparently now. By the measures of the Old Testament, he would have been buried in a hail of stones. By the newer definitions of prophecy, however, the occultist Nostradamus might have approached orthodox sainthood.

### 3. Prophecy and Accommodation

Briefly stated, the current definition of prophecy is accommodational. In departing from definitions of long standing, it fits only what has been going on for the last 200 years or so, particularly in America. It must also be linked to the Azusa Street events in Los Angeles at the turn of the last century, along with the emergence of the Pentecostal, Charismatic and Vineyard movements. Broad sectors of Christendom continue to have an unwillingness to admit that Azusa Street may have been a mixture of false and true, the demonic and the divine. Many are still willing to categorize those events wholly divine or wholly diabolical. Not so many, however, are willing to see both wheat and tares.

Charles Parham, one of the fathers of the Pentecostal movement and the originator of the tongues evidence doctrine (which emerged in 1901 in connection with his Bible school in Topeka, Kansas), became unsure about the authenticity of the movement he helped found. Ten years after the Azusa events, he was denouncing demonic penetration of the movement that later exploded into worldwide prominence.

Hear this: Three-fourths of the so-called Pentecosts [sic] in the world are counterfeits, the devil's imitation to deceive the poor earnest souls. . . . Many hundreds, in seeking Pentecost, were taught to yield to any force, as God would not permit them to be misled; under those conditions they were ripe for hypnotic influence. . . . Two-thirds of the people professing Pentecost are either hypnotized or spook-driven, being seized in the first place with a false spirit or coming under control of one afterward. We cannot be too careful to try or test the spirits, and any person unwilling to have their [sic] experience tested by going to God for themselves or with the brethren, reveal [sic] the fact that they are demon-controlled. . . . They plead the blood and claim to be Jesus, giving messages, and imitate every gift of the Holy Spirit and Pentecostal tongues. . . .[25]

In the current era it must be admitted that the suggestion that New Testament prophecy may be fallible and mistaken in its predictive mode has emerged almost exclusively from the movements that broke into public view after Parham's doctrine had been popularized at Azusa Street. Defenders of the fallible view of prophecy frequently use charismatic and Pentecostal writers for validation.

In rigorously arguing contra Wayne Grudem, I should add that I affirm the book he coauthored with John Piper[26] and his academic credentials. On hundreds of theological points, I warmly concur with his views. However, the definition of prophecy is a point of departure. The reason is clear: The fallible view of Christian prophecy is not biblical but cultural. It seeks to interpret from the Greek milieu of the day. The result is a definition that is linguistically and culturally, but not biblically, defined. Any definition which is derived from non-biblical sources is potentially accommodational. The biblical definitions of prophecy simply do not fit or match the current phenomena. Could that be why the following definition, cited more extensively earlier, is offered?

> [The word *prophet*] at the time of the New Testament had
> a very broad range of meanings. It generally did not have
> the sense "one who speaks God's very words" but rather
> "one who speaks on the basis of some external influence"
> (often a spiritual influence of some kind). Titus 1:12 uses
> the word in this sense, where Paul quotes the pagan Greek
> poet Epimenides. . . "a prophet of their own."[27]

From this it appears that a definition must be chosen which fits the current phenomena—or, unthinkably, so it seems—the phenomena should be rejected.

Richard Gaffin's views are explicitly opposite. "[T]he material in Acts and Paul provides a picture of a single unified prophetic activity present in the various church centers . . . mentioned in the New Testament, and that picture is one of marked continuity with both the apostles and the Old Testament prophets."[28]

David Farnell concludes his third article in the series on the fallible prophecy view by likewise arguing vigorously against such an accommodated view: "Close examination of [the] hypothesis reveals critical weaknesses and also outright contradictions of the biblical data."[29]

If the present definition is indeed accommodational to the events within Christendom in this century, if it is indeed only a twenty-first-century definition, then it is undoubtedly a wrong definition.

One's definition of prophecy may not be a test of orthodoxy, but the definition one holds has the potential either to resist or to accommodate the destructive currents abroad today in evangelicalism. Do the habits and traits of the movements which emerged after 1900 *require* this definition for legitimization? The importance of definition on this issue is immense.

## 4. Prophecy and Hermeneutics

The definition of prophecy now in vogue switches from the meanings of the biblical texts to hermeneutics, i.e., from the actual meaning of "prophecy" to the interpretation of the same. It is basically a switch from "saying God's words" to "resaying what God told me."

One of the slippery slopes in the kingdom of God is hermeneutics. By this time there are probably a hundred brands of supposedly biblical interpretation. Moving the definition of prophecy away from the traditional grammatical/historical plain-sense hermeneutic into the interpretive minefield is fraught with explosive and deceptive dangers.

Hermeneutics itself is a vital and honorable theological trade which is essential to understanding what the Scriptures say. To even discuss biblical texts means interpretation. The key, finally, is distinguishing between an authentic hermeneutic and various agenda hermeneutics which champion unusual and novel positions.

Two generations ago, the battle for the Bible focused on inerrancy. That battle has been fought and apparently won—but lost. Lately, the hermeneutical adventurers have done an end run around inerrancy. It is now possible to gather evangelicals under the name of inerrancy (which the Evangelical Theological Society does on an annual basis), but that banner, thanks to a plethora of hermeneutics, no longer means what it once did. Theologians may now blithely embrace inerrancy and in the same breath proceed to deny whatever they wish with hermeneutics.

The classic illustration in the Bible is "corban" (Mark 7:8-13). The Pharisees would never willingly break the law which required fidelity to parents. But of certain gifts they would say, "This is corban"—that is, a gift devoted to God. They then had no obligation to care for their parents with that gift. They had done an hermeneutical end run around their own traditions and the plain command of Scripture to honor father and mother.

In a similar way, this current definition of prophecy indulges in a corban-like maneuver. The sign posted on the fictional highway to Corban says it all, "Relax. Prophecy is not false after all, just immature or mistaken."

> . . . there is almost uniform testimony from all sections of the charismatic movement that prophecy is imperfect and impure, and will contain elements that are not to be obeyed or trusted. For example, Bruce Yocum, the [Roman Catholic] author of a widely used charismatic book on prophecy writes, "Prophecy can be impure—our own thoughts or ideas get mixed into the message we receive—whether we receive the words directly or only a sense of the message."[30]

The difficulty may be that today's prophecy advocates look at what is going on around them and see little possibility that true Christians may utter false prophecy.[31] The "unreliable" accommodated prophecy view, which neatly explains things "as they are" in many places at the same time, opens up the Christian assemblies to all kinds of currents and falsehoods.

Montanism in the primitive Church (165 A.D.) was eventually repudiated in part because the "new prophecy" it featured was not the same as had been existing and functioning in the Church all along.[32] A repudiation of today's fallible prophecy, i.e., the "present definition" currently in vogue, would have a healthy historical precedent. Accommodated prophecy faces a serious obstacle right here. "Fallible" prophecy in the Old Testament was "false" prophecy. The "sometimes mistaken" prophecy of the current era would have been none other than "false" prophecy in Old Testament times.

## *Endnotes*

1. Arnold E. Airhart, *Beacon Bible Commentary* (Kansas City, MO: Beacon Hill Press, 1965), vol. 9, 498.

2. Wayne Grudem, *Systematic Theology* (Grand Rapids, MI: Zondervan, 1994), 1049.

3. Wayne Grudem, *The Gift of Prophecy in 1 Corinthians* (Washington, DC: University Press of America, 1982), 95.

4. Wayne Grudem, *1 Peter* (Grand Rapids, MI: Eerdmans, 1998), 14.

5. Eldon Woodcock, personal correspondence, 1998.

6. Grudem, *Systematic Theology,* 1050-1051.

7. W. Robert Willoughby, personal correspondence, 1998, 3-4.

8. Albert Runge, personal correspondence, 1998, 1-2.

9. Grudem, *Systematic Theology,* 1032.

10. W.E. Vine, *The Expanded Vine's Expository Dictionary of New Testament Words* (Minneapolis, MN: Bethany House, 1984), 835.

11. Walter Bauer, William Arndt, and F. Wilbur Gingrich, *A Greek English Lexicon of the New Testament and Other Early Christian Literature* (Grand Rapids, MI: Zondervan, 1968), 507.

12. Woodcock.

13. C. Samuel Storms, "A Third Wave View," *Are Miraculous Gifts for Today?* (Grand Rapids, MI: Zondervan, 1996), 207.

14. Ibid., 208-209.

15. Robert L. Saucy, "Open But Cautious," *Are Miraculous Gifts for Today?* (Grand Rapids, MI: Zondervan, 1996), 127.

16. Willoughby, 2.

17. Ibid., 4.

18. Walter C. Kaiser, Jr., *Back Toward the Future* (Grand Rapids, MI: Baker Book House, 1989), 87.

19. Willoughby, 1. Willoughby cites Berkley Mickelson, *Interpreting the Bible* (Grand Rapids, MI: Eerdmans, 1963), 285, note 5 [Kramer, Rendtorff, Meyer, Friedrich, TWNT VI. 781-863] and George Barker Stevens, *The Teaching of Jesus* (New York: MacMillan, 1901), 96. Also George Barker Stevens, *The Christian Doctrine of Salvation* (New York: Charles Scribners Sons, 1917), 265, 273.

20. F. David Farnell, "The Current Debate about New Testament Prophecy," *Bibliotheca Sacra,* July-September 1992, 292.

21. Grudem, *Gift of Prophecy,* 3.

22. Ibid., 11.

23. Francis X. King and Stephen Skinner, *Nostradamus: Prophecies Fulfilled for the Millennium and Beyond* (New York: St. Martin's Press, 1994), 42-43.

24. Ibid., 56.

25. Charles F. Parham, *The Everlasting Gospel* (Baxter Springs, KS: Apostolic Faith Bible College, 1911), 55, 72, 120-121.

26. Wayne Grudem and John Piper, *Recovering Biblical Manhood and Womanhood* (Wheaton, IL: Crossway Books, 1991).

27. Grudem, *Systematic Theology,* 1050-1051.

28. Richard B. Gaffin, Jr., *Perspectives on Pentecost* (Phillipsburg, NJ: Presbyterian and Reformed, 1979), 72.

29. F. David Farnell, "Does the New Testament Teach Two Prophetic Gifts?" *Bibliotheca Sacra,* January-March 1993, 88.

30. Grudem, *Systematic Theology,* 1055.

31. Ibid., 1057.

32. Christine Trevett, *Montanism, Gender, Authority and the New Prophecy* (Cambridge: Cambridge University Press, 1996), 38.

# "The Spirit Shouted Loudly"

ONE OF THE EARLIEST KNOWN USAGES of First John 4:1-3 [in the modern era] to test for spurious . . . manifestations occurred in Britain in the 1830s during the days of Edward Irving's emphasis on the charismatic gifts of the Holy Spirit. Irvingism was a Montanistic-like spiritual gift movement in Britain in the early 1800s.

On one occasion when someone was prophesying, the spirit of the prophecy was directly challenged with the question, "Wilt thou not confess that Jesus Christ is come in the flesh?" The spirit responded loudly, "I will not!" The demon was cast out and never returned.[1]

### Endnote

1. Paul L. King, *A Believer with Authority: The Life and Message of John A. MacMillan* (Camp Hill, PA: Christian Publications, 2001), 274. (Page numbers in this and later citations refer to a prepublication manuscript. The page numbers in the published book may slightly differ.)

## Section B

# Prophecy Problems
# in the New Testament

---

### *1. Prophecy and John the Baptist*

John the Baptist announced that Jesus would baptize with the Holy Spirit and fire (Matthew 3:11). In Acts, Jesus references the great Baptist in anticipation of the events of Pentecost (Acts 1:5). When the day of Pentecost arrived and the Holy Spirit and fire descended upon the disciples, it was understood that prophecy had been fulfilled.

The words of Jesus anticipated an exact and precise fulfillment of John the Baptist's prophecy. He did not say that John had had an immature revelation or that since he was certainly a zealot his passion had overcome him and it wouldn't necessarily be exactly as John had said. There were also additional parts to John's prophecy. "His winnowing fork is in his hand to clear his threshing floor and to gather the wheat into his barn, but he will burn up the chaff with unquenchable fire" (Luke 3:17).

I know of no place in the New Testament where these pronouncements in Acts have been withdrawn. They are commonly taken to be references to the still-coming judgment day. If not, John was a false prophet. However, that he was indeed a true prophet is attested by two of the writers of the Gospels (Matthew 21:26; Luke 1:76). In fact, he was clearly a prophet of the old school, with ethical content, a messianic theme and an uncompromising attack on the establishment—which finally cost him his life. He was not an "apostle-prophet" as some prophecy advocates would surmise, and certainly his predictive prophecies are not illustrations of fallible prophecy.

This argument against the present definition of prophecy is especially significant in that John the Baptist was a bridging figure between the testaments. He was clearly a prophet and identified as such. Since the law and the prophets were until John, he could be assumed to be either the last of a long line or the first of a new era. Walter Kaiser observes,

> . . . John the Baptist was considered by Jesus to be the last of the prophets who prepared the way for the coming of the Messiah. In fact, John the Baptist formed the natural dividing point between the Old Testament prophets and those who were to come in the New Testament. . . . "For all the Prophets and the Law prophesied *until John*" (Matthew 11:13, emphasis added).[1]

Nevertheless, and important to this discussion, John the Baptist's prophecy was cited in the future tense (Matthew 3:11) and as a fulfillment on the day of Pentecost (Acts 1:5). It was prophecy in the future fulfillment mode. Prophecy as defined by the Old Testament, true and reliable, continued to be honored in the New Testament context and continued to occur (2:17-21; 11:28; 21:10).

## 2. *Prophecy and the Four Gospels*

All four Gospels reference the precise and accurate fulfillment of Old Testament prophecies. None of them provides a hint of fallible though divine prophecies still to come. If prophecy has been changed, the indicators are invisible in the Gospels.

Matthew (8:16-17) shows that Jesus' healing ministry fulfilled Isaiah's words. Jesus made clear that His capture in the garden had the intent of fulfilling Old Testament Scripture (Mark 14:49). Luke also regards prophetic fulfillment similarly, and forthrightly claims that Jesus' reading of the Isaiah 61:1-2 text in the synagogue was the fulfillment of prophetic Scripture in their hearing (Luke 4:21). Also, significantly, Jesus' anticipation of end-time events is intended to be understood as the "fulfillment of all that has been written" (21:22). And in John 19:24, where the gambling for Christ's robe fulfills Psalm 22:18, Scripture is very precise about the New Testament fulfillment of Old Testament prophecies. All these biblical examples support the traditional view of prophecy.

We must not miss Luke's reference either. As the author of Acts, he may be expected to portray prophecy in Acts as he had already done in his Gospel. To prove that prophecies may be fallible or inadequately retold is hard to establish as a view advanced by Luke. It is far, far easier to assume that Luke, even though he is Greek, continues with the Old Testament definition. There is no hint in Luke's Gospel or any other that a new, accommodated and fallible kind of prophecy is about to be introduced. To the contrary, if we concur with the structure of the canon as embraced historically by the Church, the Gospels are the first major section of the New Testament (in the canonical order at least), and it is clear that they do not contain any advocacy of imperfect prophecy. Rather, they demonstrate the opposite—that the four evangelists are repeatedly exulting over the exact fulfillment of prophecy as contained in the Old Testament and strikingly fulfilled in New Testament times.

In John's case, his apocalyptic writing called the Revelation is labeled prophecy (Revelation 1:3). Moreover, it describes what is past, what is present and what is to come (1:19). In that sense it is in part predictive prophecy with elements of both the poetic and symbolic.

And at the same time, Revelation announces curses upon those who add to or take away from its prophetic message (22:18-19). I do not see a lot of room here for immature prophecy, and there is no hint that John may have "missed it" on a few points. The claims that John makes here for the Revelation prophecy fit only the traditional definition where even the words themselves have significance and meaning.

In the end, and at best, silence about a flawed prophecy in the four Gospels and Revelation moves the conversation forward. Arguments from silence, of course, are not in themselves finally definitive.

### 3. Prophecy and Peter's Use of Joel in Acts

The accommodated definition of prophecy also flies in the face of Peter's New Testament use of Old Testament references to prophecy. When Peter spoke on the day of Pentecost, he claimed that the events that had just taken place were the fulfillment of the prophecy of Joel. It would have been a fine time to announce a new kind of prophecy, but to the contrary, he reinforced the Old Testament criteria and expectations, suggesting that prophecy was being exactly fulfilled and implicitly suggesting that still more of it needed to be fulfilled.

David Farnell sees a clear and powerful connection between Joel 2 and Acts 2, arguing that those Scriptures establish a

> fundamental continuity between Old and New Testament prophecy. . . . New Testament prophets and prophecy stood in direct line with their Old Testament counterparts who proclaimed God's message and will to the people of God. Therefore, New Testament prophecy is fundamentally a development and continuation of Old Testament prophecy.[2]

Kenneth Gentry likewise sees a strong continuity between Joel 2 and Acts 2. His argument is especially weighty since he sees Peter interpreting Joel under the inspiration of the Holy Spirit, providing an hermeneutic against which no dissent should be mounted. After all, who is going to argue with the Holy Spirit? "Thus, here we have prophecy of the Old Testament type entering into the New Testament era—and this according to Peter's divinely inspired interpretation of Joel. . . . This establishes a fundamental continuity linking Old and New Testament prophecy."[3]

We must not miss the clear statements by Joel about a much more widely diffused prophetic gift. If God's Spirit is to be poured out upon all people, and sons and daughters are to prophesy, and if indeed this happened as Peter explained (Acts 2:17-18)—and we believe it did—then there are to be far more prophets in the New Testament era. Though the numbers clearly increase, there is no divine hint or offer of allowable errors or an expected threshold of permissible immaturity. There is no suggestion that the prophecy anticipated by Joel and announced by Peter would be eroded in value and suspect overall.

## 4. Prophecy and the Book of Acts

In addition to Peter's use of Joel in Acts, there are other significant passages. In chapter 13, Elymas the false prophet is charged by Paul with making "crooked the straight ways of the Lord" (13:10, NASB). This description by Luke of Paul's appraisal of a false prophet emphasizes two words—"straight" and "crooked." The clear expectation of false prophets is that they will be crooked, not straight.

In the 21st chapter the Holy Spirit warns Paul that prison and hardship await him in Jerusalem (21:23). Those warnings—prophecies—were in fact straight and true. What the unnamed brethren warned him would happen did happen. We sometimes question Paul's response to those warnings, but he chose to ignore them and would not be dissuaded on the journey back to Jerusalem. The disciples, including Luke, gave up and resignedly said, "The Lord's will be done" (21:14).

Apparently at issue is not whether the prophecies were inaccurate or immature. They were neither. Like those of Agabus, they announced impending disaster. The disciples, including Luke, tried to talk Paul out of going, but he was not "dissuaded" (21:14). Apparently, in the mind of the apostle, warnings from the Holy Spirit through prophecy did not necessarily mandate self-protective behavioral change.

The difficulty in understanding this in the modern era may be our view of persecution. After all, could it ever be the will of God for a Christian leader to willingly put himself directly in the path of persecution? What is at issue may not be the nature of prophecy; rather, it may be that authentic warnings of the Holy Spirit were delivered to a man of God on his way to do exactly the will of God, even though it included imprisonment and death.

## 5. Prophecy and First Corinthians 14:29, 33

"Two or three prophets should speak, and the others should weigh carefully what is said. . . . For God is not a God of disorder but of peace." What does it mean to "weigh carefully what is said"? Does that biblical weighing just sweep aside fallible and immature prophecy—or is the broom for false prophecy?

The first meaning of the word "judge" (KJV) or "weigh" (NIV) (*diakrino*) is to "separate," then "to discriminate, discern and decide;" also "select" and "choose."[4] The judging Paul is calling for is a separation, a selection, a choosing. While choosing to label some prophecy fallible and some immature might be the instinct of some, the tenor of Scripture and the predominance of truth and falsehood in biblical language leads me to believe that Paul wishes the observers to distinguish between true and false.

Another factor in this discussion is the use of *diakrino* since a cognate of the word is used in Paul's description of discerning of spirits (1 Corinthians 12:11). Further, John in his first epistle (4:1-3) moves rather comfortably back and forth between prophets and spirits. Prophecy is a spirit expression, and judging prophecy is an occasion for the exercise not just of discernment (which is the possession of all Christians as they mature [Hebrews 5:14]), but is by the use of *diakrino* an implied opportunity for the use of discerning of spirits, the special gift of some Christians. While *diakrino* has other uses in the New Testament, its use in this context suggests discerning between spirits.

The word used for the disorder (*aktastasia*) that Paul wants to avoid in First Corinthians 14:33 is a strong one, "indicating great disturbance, disorder, or even insurrection or revolution."[5] That word is far too strong if all that is involved is a prophecy that is somewhat immature or unhappily and inadvertently fallible. The broom, I repeat, is for false prophecy.

## 6. Prophecy and First Thessalonians 5:19-22

"Do not put out the Spirit's fire; do not treat prophecies with contempt. Test everything. Hold on to the good. Avoid every kind of evil." This passage presents a clear biblical directive to discern. As in the case of the Corinthian assembly, the church in Thessalonica also had been having utterance trouble. They were "not to become . . . unsettled or alarmed by some prophecy . . . saying that the day of the Lord has already come" (2 Thessalonians 2:2). *Rather, they were to learn how to handle predictive false prophecy.* Note, the Thessalonians were not wrestling with immature prophecy. It was false prophecy, and we know what the falsehood was—that Christ had already come.

Because of the abuses in the Thessalonian church—many utterances apparently having no validity—there was the temptation to dismiss prophecies altogether. "Paul's negative command is in effect a positive exhortation to value and appreciate what the prophets say, and the implication is that some members of the congregation were skeptical of the value of such messages."[6] William Hendrickson adds, "[B]y means of despising prophetic utterances, their Giver, the Holy Spirit, was being dishonored."[7]

It is also possible in the Thessalonian context that Paul was including tongues and interpretation here as well, since when both are together, the result equals prophecy (1 Corinthians 14:5). In any case, because some in Thessalonica were treating prophecies with contempt, the Thessalonians were missing the edification, consolation and encouragement of the prophetic ministry.[8] Since objects are placed first in Greek to give emphasis, a proper translation would be, "Prophetic utterances, do not despise."[9]

The placement of *panta* in the Greek text is significant as well. *Panta* means "all, the whole, every, in all respects, always at all times."[10] All things are to be tested. All things are to be tried. All things are to be proved. All things are to be documented.

The verb used for prove or test is *dokimadzo*, which means "to test, to approve, to examine."[11] Grundmann emphasizes that this word is used when "attestation is an urgent question," when God's will is to be learned "by testing," and when the spirits are to be tested; it is even used when Christians are to test themselves (11:28).[12]

If we combine the force of *panta*, "all," along with the imperative form of the verb *dokimazo*, "test" and "verify," we have an exceptionally forceful statement by the apostle. How were the utterances to be tested? Whatever testing meant,[13] the result was intended to be the holding fast to that which was discerned to be good. The testing process was intended to isolate the bad so as to be able to "seize the good." In the present discussion, i.e., the viability of the current ideas of prophecy, it would be understood as requiring that one isolate the false so as to seize the true. It makes far less sense to suggest, "isolate the flawed so as to seize the perfect," or "isolate the immature in order to seize the mature." Leon Morris, aware of the "seizing the good" concept, relates *dokimadzo* to coins "that ring true, that is of the genuine as compared with counterfeit coin."[14]

Prophecies were being depreciated. Paul orders testing and proving in every case. The final verse of this test focuses on evil: "Avoid every kind of evil" (1 Thessalonians 5:22), "every evil species."[15] The searchlight here is not upon immature prophecy and hampered hearing on the part of the one who prophesies. No. Something far more sinister is threatening. Darkness and falsehood are lurking. These prophecies are not just immature, they are counterfeit, and they are evil. Moses long ago made it clear that other gods prophesy (Deuteronomy 18:20), and John in his first epistle (4:1-3) restates the Old Testament reality. *Real prophecy must be regarded as proceeding from a spiritual source, perhaps divine, perhaps diabolical.* Paul is warning against every kind of evil and counterfeit. Evil is in the crosshairs. There is poison in the pot. To suggest that fallible or immature prophecy fits here as other than false prophecy is not tenable.

## 7. Prophecy and John

Dear friends, do not believe every spirit, but test the spirits to see whether they are from God, because many false prophets have gone out into the world. This is how you can recognize the Spirit of God: Every spirit that [continually] acknowledges that Jesus Christ has come in the flesh is from God, but every spirit that does not [continually] acknowledge Jesus is not from God. (1 John 4:1-3)

In his first epistle, the aged Apostle John makes several unusual statements that bear upon the definition of prophecy. Initially, he equates prophets with spirits and makes clear that false prophets possess spirits which are not associated with the Spirit of God (4:1). Pardon the repetition, but we have just observed above that prophesying by the gods was considered a very real and terrible possibility by Moses (Deuteronomy 18:20). The potential for lying spirits to prophesy for their gods is ominously similar to this New Testament warning. *Prophecies which are not wholly true cannot be laid at the door of the Spirit of Truth. They belong elsewhere.*

Secondly, John makes clear that spirits/prophets who do not continually affirm [an exact and very specific] Jesus are not from God (4:2-3).[16] What kind of spirits do error-prone false prophets have? If the true prophets of God must continually profess a very precise formula about a very specific Jesus and His incarnation, John's advice is exceptionally narrow. Repeat, there is no wiggle room, no room for adventuresome and frivolous definitions of prophecy. In today's context, John would not be amused. He would find "mistaken" prophets "false." Moreover, he offers no such categorization under a heading of "immature" or "sometimes mistaken" prophecy. Prophets are true or false—there are no other biblical labels. What follows is plain Scripture. John is not offering yet another theological view "to be considered."

Current phenomena in the Church seem to require a definition which allows prophecy to be fallible. The emergence of "fallible prophecy" as a valid option should focus our attention on several biblical texts (1 Thessalonians 5:21; 1 John 4:1-3 and Revelation 2:2). Fallible prophecy has been redefined to accommodate it to the present phenomena which are assumed, *ipso facto*, to be from the Holy Spirit. For example, what would happen if First John 4:1-3 were applied to prophecy—i.e., directly addressing the spirit manifesting and demanding that it, the spirit, confess that Jesus Christ is come in the flesh? All that is required would be some courage and a straightforward hermeneutic—a belief that the Scripture, "Every spirit that does not confess (continually) that Jesus Christ is come in the flesh is not of God," should be directly applied. This procedure, which some have called the Ruark Procedure when applied to tongues,[17] involves exactly that. The application of direct confrontation to the spirits of tongues is widely documented by a number of authors.[18]

On occasion, this procedure when applied to tongues-speaking produces breakdowns of the pseudo-glossolalia and ends up with demonic tongues being cast out. My own experience with this procedure is that much of the time, but not always, the tongues are false.[19] In recent doctoral work and in an upcoming book, Paul King supplies at least two incidents where the Ruark Procedure was applied to prophecy. In the Irvingism incident related elsewhere in this text, the test was put to a spirit of prophecy thus, "Wilt thou not confess that Jesus Christ is come in the flesh?" The loud response was, "I will not."[20] Mary E. Barber, missionary to China, also relates an incident where "a clearly supernatural voice spoke prophetically and seemingly scripturally from the house of a deceased preacher, but was found to be counterfeit."[21]

King's work demonstrates that a number of people have written explicitly about this procedure from the time of Irvingism in the 1800s to the present. These include D.M. Panton, George Pember, Isabel Robson (the future wife of J.A. MacMillan), Robert A. Jaffray, Jessie Penn-Lewis, Paul Rader and others.[22]

Archie Ruark ministered in the early twentieth century, but the practice had emerged in the nineteenth as well. Research into other glossolalic movements would undoubtedly add more data. There is also at least one incident in Montanism that clearly indicates a testing procedure being done by the Church.[23] No doubt more research will be forthcoming. A.B. Simpson, writing before the Pentecostal movement, said this, "Let us be prepared for false spirits and let us not fear to try them, for if God is giving us any message or revelation, He will always give us ample time to be quite sure that it is of God."[24]

In summary, the Scriptures are self-evident. The Thessalonian prophecies were not to be despised; everything was to be tested and proved (1 Thessalonians 5:21). Similarly, the Ephesian church encountered some false apostles, tested them and found them liars (Revelation 2:2). If the Church today were to begin a new obedience to First John 4:1-3, there would not be any need to allow for fallible prophecy.

## Endnotes

1. Walter C. Kaiser, Jr., "Prophet, Prophetess, Prophecy," *Evangelical Dictionary of Biblical Theology* (Grand Rapids, MI: Baker Book House, 1996), 646.

2. F. David Farnell, "The Gift of Prophecy in the Old and New Testaments," *Bibliotheca Sacra,* October-December 1992, 393.

3. Kenneth L. Gentry, Jr., *The Charismatic Gift of Prophecy,* 2nd ed. (Memphis, TN: Footstool, 1989), 8.

4. W.E. Vine, *The Expanded Vine's Expository Dictionary of New Testament Words* (Minneapolis, MN: Bethany House, 1984), 610-611.

5. W. Harold Mare, "1 Corinthians," *Expositor's Bible Commentary* (Grand Rapids, MI: Zondervan, 1976), 276.

6. I. Howard Marshall, "The Epistles of John," *The New International Commentary on the New Testament* (Grand Rapids, MI: Eerdmans, 1978), 158.

7. William Hendrickson, *Exposition of Ephesians* (Grand Rapids, MI: Baker Book House, 1955), 139.

8. Ibid.

9. Ibid., 140.

10. Anonymous, *The Analytical Greek Lexicon* (London: Samuel Bagster and Sons Limited, n.d.), 311.

11. James Strong, *The Comprehensive Concordance of the Bible* (Iowa Falls, IA: World Bible Publishers, n.d.), 1381.

12. W. Grundmann, "dokimadzo," and "dynami," *Theological Dictionary of the New Testament* (Grand Rapids, MI: Eerdmans, 1985), 182.

13. K. Neill Foster, "Discernment, the Powers and Spirit-Speaking," unpublished dissertation (Pasadena, CA: Fuller Theological Seminary, 1988), 156-158.

14. Leon Morris, "1 Corinthians," *Tyndale New Testament Commentary* (Grand Rapids, MI: Eerdmans, 1983), 106.

15. Robert Jamieson with A.R. Fausset and David Brown, *Commentary, Critical and Explanatory, on the Whole Bible* (Grand Rapids, MI: Zondervan, n.d.), 392.

16. Foster, 168.

17. Dorothy Brotherton, *Quiet Warrior* (Beaverlodge, AB: Spectrum Publishing, 1991).

18. See Dickason, Warner, Birch, McGraw and others.

19. Foster.

20. Paul L. King, *A Believer with Authority: The Life and Message of John A. MacMillan* (Camp Hill, PA: Christian Publications, 2001), 274.

21. Ibid.

22. Ibid., 357-358.

23. Foster.

24. A.B. Simpson, *Christ in the Bible Commentary* (Camp Hill, PA: Christian Publications, 1994), vol. 6, 374-375.

# "I Don't Care If They Raise the Dead . . ."

FOUR OF US ANGLO TYPES had squeezed into a pew amidst a sea of multicultural worshipers at the Brooklyn Tabernacle in New York City where Jim Cymbala is pastor. The service was marvelous, the music inspiring, the sermon by a guest preacher outstanding. But a brief comment by Pastor Cymbala riveted my attention. My recall is as follows.

He was speaking about "crooked preachers" of whom there were many preying upon the city. After denouncing such preachers, Cymbala concluded by saying, "I don't care if they raise the dead—they are still crooked!"

Gradually it dawned on me that I had heard a statement that belonged in these pages.

# Section C

# More Prophecy Problems

I N THIS ONGOING DISCUSSION of Christian prophecy, the concept of fallible prophecy that proceeds from the Holy Spirit of Truth continues to be problematic. History, for example, gets twisted by today's definition.

### 1. Prophecy and Montanism

Montanism (circa 160 A.D.) was a movement led by a prophet called Montanus. Two prophetesses, who had left their husbands to follow him, were part of his entourage. The movement featured prophecies, apocalyptic behavior and feminine leadership. It was deemed heretical by the Church of its day, possibly because the prophecy was new (i.e., different than what they were used to) and the spirits were clearly in control.

The modern definition of prophecy is a de facto present-day argument for the validity of Montanism, one of the first major heretical movements in the second century of Church history.[1] Montanism was called the "new prophecy" by the early Church.[2] It was in apparent contradiction to what had gone before for more than 100 years, and the Church repudiated it. Basically a new form of the Corinthian excesses, it was eventually labeled as heresy even though Tertullian had been swept into the fervor.

Once they had been expelled as heretics, the Montanists faced a rigorous four-day procedure to get back into the Church: 1) they were made Christians the first day, 2) they became catechumens the second day, 3) they were exorcised the third day and 4) they were baptized the fourth day.[3] Why, I ask, did the early Church exorcise the Montanists? Could it be that exorcism was more than the application of an historical pattern present in the primitive Church?

Apparently the Montanistic errors had sometimes taken forms of demonization. Christine Trevett's recent and formidable work on Montanism makes it clear that Montanism was attacked by orthodoxy on two main fronts: ecclesiastical power was used to suppress it, and exorcism was repeatedly used to confront it.[4] Secular Roman power undoubtedly also helped to eliminate the remnants of Montanism.

Another worrisome factor in the present passion to de-hereticize Montanism (as evidenced by a willingness to accept "fallible" New Testament prophecy and the current description of Montanism as a "minor" heresy) is that throughout Church history the various prophecy movements of similar nature were with some exceptions deemed heretical. (For example, there were similar manifestations among the Quakers, the Cevenal Prophets in France, Edward Irving in London, the Shakers and the Mormons.[5]) It has been in uniquely pragmatic America and only through the National Association of Evangelicals that the Montanistic movements widely gained orthodoxy for the first time. That modern break with the lengthy history of the Church should be regarded with concern. (Did those who pronounced the Montanists heretical have more discernment than twentieth-century evangelical pragmatists?)

## 2. Prophecy and the Arbitrary Suspension of Scripture

The current interpretation of prophecy repeats a common hermeneutical flaw that exists today in some sectors of evangelicalism. Tongues, in such contexts, remain a sign for believers even though the Scripture says that tongues are a sign for unbelievers (1 Corinthians 14:22). The interpretation advanced says that in the case of the baptism of the Holy Spirit with a tongues manifestation, there is a difference between tongues as the evidence and tongues as a sign. By suspending Scripture, tongues become a sign for believers. Therefore, there are two or more definitions of tongues (and now two definitions of prophecy).

In like manner, the Bible asks, "Do all speak with tongues?" (12:30, Amp.). In the original language, the negative answer— "no"—is implicit in the Greek text at the beginning of the statement. Those who advocate the opposing view assume that the passage does not refer to the baptism of the Holy Spirit, but to the gift of tongues which not everyone has. Once again, the scriptural views of past generations are suspended. The fact that the view on fallible prophecy has accumulated wide support and many advocates does not validate it.

### 3. Prophecy and Delusional Thinking

The current definition of prophecy reinforces delusional thinking. Instead of accepting the possibility of having given a false prophecy—with the personal introspection, crucifixion of the self-life and the rejection of Satan that that acceptance might demand—people are encouraged to believe that they just didn't get it quite right. With this definition, any place that may have been given to the devil remains undisturbed. Such a stance is conducive to delusional thinking and behavior.

It is also in conflict with Old Testament realities. Nathan the prophet got it wrong about the Lord's intent to have David build the temple. He later had to return and correct his false message with the truth (2 Samuel 7:1-13).[6] If truthfulness and accuracy are no longer important, then even corrections and admissions of wrong-doing in this New Testament era are off the table.

The present definition of prophecy also offers freedom and licence to the self-life and to sin. Although a fudged definition of prophecy that caters to the carnal nature should not be attractive, the accommodated definition of prophecy makes it so. The carnal Christian who is prophesying would much rather be untaught or mistaken than just plain wrong—or false. Jesus' description of the end times included this statement: "Many false prophets will appear and deceive many people" (Matthew 24:11). He earlier warned, "Many will say to me on that day, 'Lord, Lord, did we not prophesy in your name, and in your name drive out demons and perform many miracles?' " (7:22). There is no hint that these evildoers are just immature or that they simply had trouble hearing the word of the Lord to them.

The "other Jesus" who harassed the early Church (2 Corinthians 11:4) had a message—but it was a delusional message suited to the pampering of the self-life. The prophecy as currently advocated is a comfortable doctrine, an attractive interpretation that eases the concerns of the heart about deception and falsehood in kingdom matters. But it flies in the face of the biblical statement that truly sound doctrine has to be endured (2 Timothy 4:3). Conversely, current prophecy teaching can be welcomed gladly. It takes the tension out of discerning between false and true (Matthew 7:15-20), out of testing the spirits (1 John 4:1-4), out of proving all things (1 Thessalonians 5:21).

## 4. Prophecy and the Church Fathers

The emerging theory about predictive New Testament prophecy also conflicts with the Didache and the writings of Eusebius and others from the apostolic Church. These early writers struggled with prophecy in their day as we do today: "As shown . . . early postapostolic Christians utilized Old Testament standards to judge later prophets. . . . The criteria set forth in the Old Testament was used to condemn the excesses of Montanus and his followers for their false or 'mistaken' prophecies."[7]

To conflict with these early writers or the Didache is not especially grievous in that these ancient documents never made it into the scriptural canon. Nevertheless, they should generally be taken as fair descriptions of views and attitudes in the early Church. As such they too make the recently advanced theories questionable.

## 5. Prophecy and Jesus Christ

There is a Christocentric element in prophecy that must be acknowledged. "The testimony of Jesus is the spirit of prophecy" (Revelation 19:10). Jesus said, "See, I have told you ahead of time" (Matthew 24:25). "I am telling you now before it happens, so that when it does happen you will believe that I am He" (John 13:19). Jesus Christ is Himself considered to be a prophet (Deuteronomy 18:15; John 1:21, 45, 6:14; Acts 3:22, etc.). He certainly did not allow Himself any inaccuracies: "It is particularly through God the Son that the prophecies of the Old and New Testaments come into their sharpest focus . . . the main line of witness of the Old Testament was to the Messiah . . . the true spirit of prophecy always manifests itself to bearing witness to Jesus."[8]

It is curious that the prophecy now in vogue is necessarily nonchristological in that it is allowed to be both inaccurate and untrue while the Son of God is none other than the Way, the *Truth* and the Life. How terrible that the prophecy as presently defined because it is sometimes false, fails to relate to Jesus Christ, the Living Truth, the prophet about whom Moses spoke (Deuteronomy 18:15). Surely it fails the christological test. If the present definition of prophecy is correct, then other possible descriptions such as "immature" and "unrefined" have to be set aside. Could it be that the right terminology is not the Spirit of Christ but the spirit of antichrist?

## 6. Prophecy and the Holy Spirit

I have alluded to this earlier, but now is the time to speak clearly. Prophecy is a gift given by the Holy Spirit (1 Corinthians 12:7-11).

Luke describes one incident thus, "The Holy Spirit said, 'Set apart for me Barnabas and Saul for the work to which I have called them' " (Acts 13:2). When Agabus made his prophecy (which some say was erroneous, though I do not), he introduced it with, "The Holy Spirit says" (21:10-11). To repudiate Agabus is to cast reflection on the Spirit of Truth.

Although A.W. Tozer was not directly addressing prophecy, he certainly expressed the heart of what I am trying to say here:

> Spiritual truth (by which I mean the disclosure of the Holy Spirit to the human spirit) is always the same. . . . The Spirit always says the same thing to whomsoever He speaks and altogether without regard to passing doctrinal emphases or theological vogues. . . . The Holy Spirit is the true conservator of orthodoxy and will invariably say the same thing to meek and trusting souls."[9]

The Holy Spirit does not speak with a forked tongue—but we know who does.

### 7. Prophecy Is Better in the New Covenant

The book of Hebrews is a remarkable document that clearly enunciates the Jewish roots of the New Testament in the Old. It also makes very clear that Jesus Christ is the better, the superior sacrifice.[10] Thirteen times the author of Hebrews uses the word "better." Please remember, if you will, that the Mosaic Covenant included clear instructions about prophecy (Deuteronomy 13 and 18). It had to be "right" under the Mosaic covenant and even if it was right, it could not draw the people away from God; if prophets did that, they were still false.

Today we are being asked to embrace fallible prophecy in the name of the Holy Spirit, all of this under the better and superior covenant of the New Testament. It does not wash. New Testament prophecy, because of the covenant under which it functions, should be better, not worse, than the prophecy that functioned under the Mosaic covenant.

## Finding a Place to Park

The inability to find a parking spot is one of the aggravations of urban life. More times than I want to remember I have found myself doing the circuit of frustration. All I lack is a place to park. What is lacking in this whole discussion about the definition of prophecy is a place to park false prophets and pseudo-prophecy.

It is further curious that in the Old Testament, even prophecy that was accurate was rejected in the end because of the intrinsic motivation of the deviant prophet (Deuteronomy 13). In the Old Testament we know that even prophets who were factually true could be rejected. But in the New Testament, where Jesus did not come to destroy the law but to fulfill it, and the expectation is obviously better things (the book of Hebrews), we are being asked to believe lesser things—that prophecy though fallible and inaccurate should still be considered a divine manifestation of the Spirit of Truth, the Holy Spirit.

The arguments for accommodated prophecy all but do away with false prophecy. At the very least, two of the major factors for determining falsehood in prophecy (accuracy and reliability) are yanked away. The Church, in one fell swoop, is being asked, informally at least, to incorporate into its body of belief a corpus of material that is not true. If this definition of prophecy is embraced, where does one put the diminished and shrunken false prophecy category? And if false prophecy is set aside as a present danger, can this broadly biblical peril be safely parked anywhere?

Today's definition of prophecy effectively disengages false prophecy as a modern possibility. If trustworthiness and truthfulness can safely be abandoned, what need is there to verify truth, or even, for that matter, consider the now remote possibility of false prophecy?

The present perspective on prophecy suggests that there are very few false prophets out there, while John shouts that many antichrists have gone out into the world (1 John 4:1).

In summary, the prophecy now advocated is not anticipated in the Old Testament nor is it enunciated among the prophets of the Old Covenant. It gets no traction in the John the Baptist account. It finds no resonance in the four Gospels. Paul's writings do not support it, and it is boxed in and negated at the end of the New Testament by the patterns of use in John's epistles and the Revelation. Finally, it relates most closely to the spirit of antichrist.

If I visit your town and announce the birth of twelve new churches, and it does not come to pass, then I need to renounce the hidden works of darkness in my life. I need to repudiate Satan's intrusion, and I need to repent thoroughly of my susceptibility to delusion. None of these acts of contrition and repentance cancels for a moment my obligation to covet earnestly the best gifts, especially prophecy (1 Corinthians 14:39).

The definition of errant prophecy must be rejected. Farnell waxes prophetic himself when he observes that the current hypothesis about prophecy should be viewed with alarm. Since prophecy has the assumption of revelational authority from the Holy Spirit, the idea of mistaken prophecy has the potential of doing untold harm to the Church.[11]

Indeed, the Christian Church is in peril of being reduced to an occult view of prophecy. T.K. Oesterreich in his classic work, *Possession, Demoniacal and Other*, described events in Tonga as follows: "False prophesies by possessed persons are also accepted without any particular scandal."[12]

We must not ever despise prophesying. But we must return to categorizing prophecy as true and false, welcoming at the same time our Lord's anathema on false prophets.

It is time for "scandal" once again to be attached to false prophecy. These are not pleasant words, and the hearers may be few. Nevertheless, if these words are truth, if they are correct, what then? Dear God, what then?

## Endnotes

1. Wayne Grudem, *Systematic Theology* (Grand Rapids, MI: Zondervan, 1994), 878.

2. F. David Farnell, "Does the New Testament Teach Two Prophetic Gifts?" *Bibliotheca Sacra,* January-March 1993, 62.

3. John De Soyres, *Montanism and the Primitive Church* (Cambridge: Deighton, Bell and Sons, 1878), 52.

4. Christine Trevett, *Montanism, Gender, Authority and the New Prophecy* (Cambridge, UK: Cambridge University Press, 1996), 36, 156.

5. F. David Farnell, "The Current Debate about New Testament Prophecy," *Bibliotheca Sacra,* July-September 1992, 296-297.

6. Walter C. Kaiser, Jr., "Prophet, Prophetess, Prophecy," *Evangelical Dictionary of Biblical Theology* (Grand Rapids, MI: Baker Book House, 1996), 644.

7. Farnell, "Does the New Testament Teach Two Prophetic Gifts?" 66.

8. Walter C. Kaiser, Jr., *Back Toward the Future* (Grand Rapids, MI: Baker Book House, 1989), 18-19.

9. A.W. Tozer, *Born after Midnight* (Camp Hill, PA: Christian Publications, 1989), 76-78.

10. Garth Leno, *Hebrews* (Camp Hill, PA: Christian Publications, 1996), 5.

11. Farnell, "Does the New Testament Teach Two Prophetic Gifts?" 88.

12. T.K. Oesterreich, *Possession: Demoniacal and Other* (New Hyde Park, NY: University Books, 1966), 279.

# 5

Tongues
and Tongues

# An Unexpected Tongue

ON ONE OCCASION in a Sunday school class I was talking about First John 4:1-3 and advising that tongues as a prophetic expression could and should be tested. A young man came up afterward.

"I speak in tongues, and I would like you to test them," he said.

We went to a quiet place and after some prayerful interchange I told him to speak in tongues and that while he did so I would ask the question, "You spirit that is now manifesting, did Jesus Christ come in the flesh?" Since he was an open-faced young man who greatly desired to serve the Lord Jesus Christ, I fully expected a positive response.

However, as he began to speak and I asked the question, his face became contorted into a most ugly expression. The tongue proved to be false. It was not from Almighty God but rather from an evil personage that needed to be renounced and repudiated. Believing as I do that in the matter of tongues "some do" and "some don't" (1 Corinthians 12:30) and that some are true and some are false, I had been expecting other than what we discovered.

Unfortunately, the young man did not agree to renounce his experience and has not yet done so, as far as I know.

# A Troubling Dissertation

AMONG THE DUSTY TOMES in the cavernous lower levels of the McAlister Library at Fuller Theological Seminary in Pasadena, California rests a Ph.D. dissertation from 1988. Mine.

One day, a graduate student found the volume with the curious title: "Discernment, the Powers and Spirit-Speaking." With his interest piqued, he began to read, but he was not prepared for what he encountered.

The man was at that point in his ministry the head of a charismatic parachurch mission. After reading the dissertation thoughtfully, he called me to ask a question: "Where can I go to have my tongues tested?" He wanted to know if I would conduct a test over the telephone. I have always regretted that I declined his request.

Though I do not recall that he gave the name of his mission, his request for privacy (which I have paraphrased) holds a powerful pathos. In an evangelical tension that almost defies description, this leader said, "The people in my mission would be appalled if they knew I was asking this question about the validity of my own experience."

I cannot tell you if the uneasiness in this man's soul was ever addressed. An immense deception may be continuing to this very day. The sadness in the life of such a person is overwhelming to contemplate. What I can tell you on the basis of strong biblical authority is that we are to "prove all things" (1 Thessalonians 5:21, KJV)—certainly not excluding glossolalia and certainly when we are leaders among God's people.

# Tongues and Tongues

T HIS CHAPTER IS NOT a great way to win friends and influence people. Perhaps, due to the very title chosen, I have already alienated several broad sectors of Christians. Among them may be those who believe that there is no such thing today as speaking in tongues. Similarly, others who accept every tongue expressed in ecstatic speech as an authentic gift of the Holy Spirit will be offended at the suggestion that there may be true and false tongues.

This chapter is included under the section, "Prophecy—A Major Understanding," for a biblical reason. Biblically speaking, tongues with interpretation (1 Corinthians 14:5) is like prophecy. For that reason, these comments fall here in connection with and in subordination to the discussion on prophecy.

## Tongues Exist

The Apostle Paul had been dramatically converted on the Damascus road and later filled with the Holy Spirit through the ministry of Ananias. Subsequently, he addresses the Corinthian church which had fallen into a pattern of abuse in the exercise of tongues-speaking. In the process, he calls upon his apostolic authority and personal experience as he admonishes them on how to handle speaking in tongues. "I speak in tongues more than all of you" (14:18), he says, obviously trying to relate to his hearers and soften the blow of what would follow.

To avoid the excesses they were experiencing, Paul lays down several regulations for public speaking in tongues: 1) only two or three may do it in any given service (14:26-28); 2) if there is no interpreter, tongues-speakers should remain silent. Those readers who question the reality of tongues will have the difficult task of relegating the corrective instructions of the Apostle Paul to marginal use or perhaps none at all. To accept it is to admit the existence of tongues and to welcome godly restraints and regulations on it.

## Paul Spoke in Tongues

Though Paul probably did not speak in tongues when he was first filled with the Holy Spirit (there is no biblical basis for that assumption), it is apparent that he later did receive the gift and indeed practiced it.

Paul was a prodigious servant of Christ and was also called the "Apostle to the Gentiles." Though he did not walk the highways and byways of Israel with Jesus and the other disciples, he was, nevertheless, prolific in his writings and, under the power and control of the Holy Spirit, the second great theologian after John in Christ's Church. He was also the first true intellectual to emerge in the early Church—and he was a tongues-speaker. He did not appear to particularly celebrate that giftedness, but he also did not appear to mind admitting that it was part of his Christian experience. Neither is there any scriptural hint that he was backing away from the reality of his own giftedness.

Paul's missionary journeys are renowned. His persecutions and sufferings are recorded in detail. And he was in the end a martyr for Jesus Christ, a man of God whose blood was spilled by a Roman ax. It occurs to me that if tongues-speaking was good enough for Paul, why is there such resistance to it today on the part of some? The ec-icities at Corinth did not cause a tongues repudiation in the life and ministry of Paul. There is no hint of embarrassment when he announced (for corrective reasons) that he was a tongues-speaker. But he was obviously hitting the brakes on tongues, not jamming the accelerator to the floor.

## Isolate and Seize the Good

Where does the concept of true and false tongues-speaking emerge in the Scriptures? Again, we turn to Paul. He made it very clear to the Thessalonian church that they were not to despise utterance prophecies (1 Thessalonians 5:19-21), and that they were not to put out the Spirit's fire (5:19). It is likely that Paul was including tongues and interpretation here as well, since when both are together, he equates them with prophecy.[1]

The Scriptures just cited imply that utterances, such as tongues and prophecy, need to be tested. The thrust and intent of this passage is to enable Christians to isolate the bad and seize the good. The object of testing is not to focus on the false, but to focus on the true. The force of the Greek words *panta* and *dokimadzo* make it clear that whatever testing is meant to be, it is intended "to isolate the bad so as to be 'able to seize the good.' "[2] Testing is to be undertaken with the expectation of good results. My paraphrase of First Thessalonians 5:19-21 is as follows: "The Holy Spirit, stop quenching. Prophecies, stop depreciating. Absolutely all utterances are to be tested and verified, so that you will be able to isolate and seize the good."

From a biblical perspective, there is no question that false prophecy and false prophets are widely referenced (Jeremiah 23:32; Matthew 7:15, 1 John 4:1-3). Similarly, since tongues-speaking is prophecy-like, it is wholly appropriate to think in terms of true and false tongues. And there is ever-enlarging literature on this matter. One of the first to go public with this concept in the latter part of the twentieth century was Gerald McGraw of Toccoa Falls College. He and a colleague, Jerry Sproul, began their investigation by applying First John 4:1-4 to glossolalia. The results were dramatic—and troubling. McGraw's two articles in *The Alliance Witness* have become foundational literature in this area.[3]

In conversation with Dr. McGraw, he revealed that the procedures for testing,[4] which have now been carried on for more than twenty-five years, were learned from John A. MacMillan, his professor years earlier at Nyack College. In fact, many who write today about these matters invariably connect to J.A. MacMillan and his renowned book entitled *The Authority of the Believer.*[5] The basic theology setting forth the deliverance ministry and the testing of spirits, including tongues spirits, was, as far as I can determine, enunciated first by MacMillan in the modern era. Recent research has demonstrated that MacMillan had learned from others.[6]

## The Canadian Connection

Dorothy Brotherton's book, *Quiet Warrior*, issued in 1991, was the life story and theological thought of Archie E. Ruark,[7] a professor both at the Prairie Bible Institute and the Peace River Bible Institute, frontier schools located in Alberta, Canada. Through fifty-five years of spiritual warfare, much of which included the confrontation of tongues manifestations, he kept detailed notes. A very high percentage of the tongues which were tested were, in his opinion, spurious.[8]

Ruark did, however, believe that there were true tongues, but as could be expected, he was not very optimistic in view of his lifelong experiences. He denied any connection to MacMillan when asked, but when he was being moved from one site to another in his old age, a copy of MacMillan's classic dropped out of his personal effects.[9] He was also ordained by the same denomination of which MacMillan was a part.

When the Brotherton book was published, some significant voices emerged to say that Ruark deserved a hearing. Paul G. Hiebert, Professor of Mission and Anthropology at Trinity Divinity School wrote, "In this groundbreaking work [*Quiet Warrior*] Ruark raises important questions and provides new insights related to the ways God, through His Spirit, works in the lives of His people. Not everyone will agree with Ruark's conclusions, but he makes an important contribution to the current debate."[10]

In like vein, Dr. Joseph C. Aldrich, at the time president of Multnomah School of the Bible, said, "The Western church is just beginning to stir over the issue of spiritual warfare and its implications. The helpful illustrations in the Ruark material make the book particularly valuable. His life and ministry demonstrate the truth of 'testing the spirits.' It is an encouraging work."[11]

Timothy Warner, a former president of Fort Wayne Bible College, concurred: "Archie Ruark discovered early that Satan's primary tactic is deception. This account [*Quiet Warrior*] of his pilgrimage into deliverance ministry through dealing with counterfeit tongues is a valuable contribution to the ongoing discussion on spiritual warfare."[12]

## The China Connection

George Birch, a contemporary of Ruark, was a former missionary of the China Inland Mission. In his book entitled *The Deliverance Ministry*,[13] he did not wholly concur with Ruark, but appeared to use what I call the Ruark Procedure, i.e., direct confrontation of glossolalia as a spirit manifestation.

In the early Church, the first major struggle after the Corinthian experience in the testing and verifying of spirit-speaking was a confrontation with one of the heretical movements, namely the Montanists. In attempting to verify what kind of spirit a certain Montanist prophetess named Maximilla had, some "were then present in order to test and converse with the spirit as it chattered."[14] Though an exorcism was not effected, it apparently was considered. We have already indicated that the Montanists had to pass through exorcism to get back into the church.[15]

These references in Church history are not yet broad enough in themselves to establish a consistent procedure, but they do buttress the plain reading of Scripture. Ultimately, research may make clear that the exorcising of Montanist spirits was the real reason why Montanists gained the heretical label.

More recent research by Paul King has shown that the concept of challenging a tongues or prophecy manifestation predated Ruark by perhaps 100 years. George Pember and Isabel Robson of the China Inland Mission, and Paul Rader of Moody Church, among others, all had similar encounters before Ruark.[16] Their concentration seemed to be on the spirit of prophecy and was, of course, prior to the Azusa Street events. The only rationale for calling the confrontation of tongues spirits the Ruark Procedure is that he appears to be the first to document his glossolalia cases over a lifetime. Had Pember, Robson, Rader or MacMillan had the same concentration on tongues over a similar period and had kept notes, we might today be calling the system the MacMillan Procedure.

The Apostle John makes it clear:

> Dear friends, do not believe every spirit, but test the spirits to see whether they are from God, because many false prophets have gone out into the world. This is how you can recognize the Spirit of God: Every spirit that acknowledges that Jesus Christ has come in the flesh is from God, but every spirit that does not acknowledge Jesus is not from God. This is the spirit of the antichrist. (1 John 4:1-3)

It cannot be disputed that Scripture clearly declares the existence of false prophets and false prophecy. Further, as observed above, tongues with interpretation is equated with prophecy (1 Corinthians 14:5).

## Lori's Story

One of the most remarkable incidents I have ever encountered took place in 1963. My wife and I, along with several other Christian workers, become involved in an extended deliverance (referred to elsewhere in this book). A seventeen-year-old girl had become profoundly demonized. Sometimes the violence was such that at least five men were required to restrain the demonic strength she exhibited. The good news is not the list of all the powers and counter-kingdom garbage to which she had submitted and which were continually being expelled. No, the good news is that she was finally delivered in the name of the Lord Jesus Christ. But there were a couple of side events that impinge on this discussion.

Early on, she exhibited tongues manifestations. Since the spirits who were speaking did not continually confess the Lordship of Jesus Christ and did not continually confess that Jesus Christ had come in the flesh, they were cast out as any other spirit of darkness. That in itself is a great story, but there's more to it. At one point, another tongue exhibited itself which sounded beautiful, even heavenly. She was singing in tongues. This time, while she was singing, she was able to confess the Lordship of Jesus Christ continually, something she was physically unable to do when she was in a normal, non trancelike condition. Every biblical test we knew was applied, and in every case the response was positive and true. The true tongue became an avenue of blessing in her life and a great encouragement in her journey out of bondage.

My conclusion, then and now, was and is that in this person both true and false tongues resided. None of the Christian workers were (are) pentecostals. None of us were (are) charismatics. And this was long before the Vineyard had emerged. All of those present were without exception sober, supernaturalistic evangelicals who were just as surprised with the evidence as you may be. Since then, I have had other Christian workers tell me that they too have seen both true and false tongues in the same person. McGraw, in fact, cites such an incident.

At that time, I had never tested any tongues, nor had my colleagues, but soon someone asked for a test. The only person from the class [who had spoken in tongues] . . . was an outstanding Christian lady—capable, talented, balanced, dependable, a soulwinner. She said she had never used her tongues except in private. As she related her spiritual experience of some years ago to my wife and me I just could not imagine that this fine believer could have a tongues demon. I told her so.

But she was not satisfied. She talked with my colleagues later. Upon testing we found a tongue quite manifestly of the Holy Spirit. But soon another tongue appeared in the same woman—a tongue that was bitter and hateful toward Christ, toward her and toward us. The true tongue was clear evidence to me that her sanctification was genuine. Yet it was undeniable that a demonic tongues spirit [also had] inhabited her.[17]

Case studies, of course, do not carry moral authority. It is dangerous to build any kind of doctrine on incidents such as I have just recounted. But—and here is the powerful fulcrum in this matter—all of Scripture affirms the polarities. As certainly as there was a Cain, there was an Abel. There is always right and wrong. God and the devil. True and false. Heaven and hell. Lost and saved. The magicians of Egypt imitated the miracles of God in response to several of Moses' encounters. We should not be surprised that Satan has confused the Church of Jesus Christ with "tare" tongues among the "true" wheat, nor that they will be together till the end.

## *Endnotes*

1. K. Neill Foster, "Discernment, the Powers and Spirit-Speaking," unpublished dissertation (Pasadena, CA: Fuller Theological Seminary, 1988), 156.

2. Ibid., 157.

3. Gerald McGraw, "Tongues—True or False?" and "Tongues Should Be Tested," *The Alliance Witness,* 1974, May 22, 8-10 and June 5, 3-6. See Appendix 3.

4. McGraw, personal conversation with the author, July 1999.

5. J.A. MacMillan, *The Authority of the Believer* (Camp Hill, PA: Christian Publications, 1997).

6. Paul L. King's doctoral dissertation identifies MacMillan's key mentor in the authority of the believer and the testing of spirits as George Pember whose commentary on First John 4:1-3 reads as follows: "The apostle is clearly legislating for those cases of prophetic utterances and speaking in tongues which were then common in the church. . . . Therefore the duty inculcated by John is that of testing the spirits of prophets, to discover whether they are influenced by the Spirit of God or by demons." This research predates Ruark by at least a generation. *A Believer with Authority: The Life and Message of John A. MacMillan* (Camp Hill, PA: Christian Publications, 2001), 274-287.

7. Dorothy Brotherton, *Quiet Warrior* (Beaverlodge, AB: Spectrum Publications, 1991).

8. Foster, 180.

9. Ruark's daughter, Eileen, confided this to the author.

10. Paul G. Hiebert as cited by Brotherton, front matter.

11. Joseph C. Aldrich as cited by Brotherton, front matter.

12. Timothy M. Warner as cited by Brotherton, front matter.

13. George Birch, *The Deliverance Ministry* (Camp Hill, PA: Horizon Books, 1988). Other authors who treat this matter include William McLeod of the Canadian Revival Fellowship, C. Fred Dickason of Moody Bible Institute, and Conrad Murrell, to name a few. Additional data on these authors is found in the bibliography.

14. G.A. Williamson, *History of the Church from Christ to Constantine* (Minneapolis, MN: Augsburg Publishing House, 1975), 220.

15. John De Soyres, *Montanism and the Primitive Church* (Cambridge: Deighton, Bell and Sons, 1878), 52.

16. King, 274-287.

17. McGraw, "Tongues Should Be Tested," 3-6.

# 6

Music

and Music

# The Red Party

IN 1990 DAVID NEFF and George Brushaber, in a significant article on British evangelicalism in *Christianity Today*, made these still-memorable and pointed remarks.

> And with regard to theology, no one puts it more directly than the genial bishop of Chester, Michael Baughen. Baughen, who succeeded Stott as rector of All Souls, Langham Place, is president of the Anglican Evangelical Assembly, an annual by-invitation-only gathering of leaders representing different dioceses, mission societies, theological colleges, and other organizations.
>
> As a bishop, Baughen must speak and act with a broad tolerance toward all believers in his 340-church diocese. . . . Yet on theological concerns he cannot remain silent.
>
> After learning that in the major charismatic songbooks only one percent of the hymns contain references to the Cross, he fears that the doctrine of the Atonement is being ignored: "I'm about to start a 'red party'—that's 'red' for the Atonement. The church has lost sight of the centrality of the Cross."[1]

Indeed, contemporary praise choruses are still almost universally devoid of references to the blood of Jesus Christ or His atonement. One pastor of a large contemporary church in California interacted with this observation by going though all the music being used by his church and eliminating music which seemed to ignore the blood of Jesus Christ.

The devil's hatred of the blood is no secret. Should we not be asking more questions?

### *Endnote*

1. David Neff and George K. Brushaber, "The Remaking of British Evangelicalism," *Christianity Today,* vol. 34, issue 2, Feb. 5, 1990, 25.

# Music of the Spirit

*by John Harvey*

AS ONE OF THOSE who has been pulled kicking and screaming into the worship emphasis of our day, I was surprised to observe that King David recognized musicians for their prophetic ministries as those who used "the harp in thanking and praising the LORD" (1 Chronicles 25:3). What is disturbing is that the musical ministries of the sons of Asaph, Jeduthun and Heman were called prophesying. That lofty term implied that the Holy Spirit was empowering their talents. It lifts their contribution beyond controversial to sacred. While we might exalt someone like Charles Wesley as a prophetic composer, it's hard for us to do so for contemporaries like Graham Kendrick, another prolific English musician ("Shine, Jesus, Shine" and many other songs). Prophetic recognition demands less criticism and more participating in what the Spirit is doing through fresh worship styles.

Music has proven to be a major minefield in most generations. Could it be that part of the cause for all the heat is that many of the musicians have indeed been prophetic? Prophets are rarely honored in their own time. The truly prophetic become lightning rods of criticism; it's all part of the role. While none of us would want to be guilty of verbal abuse of God's anointed, it is a common enough sin.

Fortunately, God gives His prophets thick skins to repel unkind words and scornful opinions. He also gives them courage to do their thing. It's not just preachers who need to be courageous, but also leaders of worship and their fellow laborers who minister in song in the power of the Spirit.

David's exaltation of the inspired musicians lifts the debate over music styles into the area of obedience, not just individual tastes. It demands a spirit of discernment rather than a vote on preferences. Our age has been blessed with more musical creativity in worship than possibly any generation before it. Is the devil the only one to be credited with the diversity and magnitude of contemporary music?

In Church history fresh and abundant music has usually been evidence of renewal for the Church. If we make it a habit of holding our ears and stoning the ministers of new songs, we are bound to include among the rejected, musical seers who have been sent to us by God. May the Lord protect us from continual knee-jerk reactions in the area of worship. The jury is still out on the claim of some that the Tabernacle of David is being restored in our day, and what is meant by that restoration is not all that certain. Nonetheless, it does seem evident, at least to this writer, that prophesying with and through music is all part of the work of God in our times, and that reality encourages even this introvert to lift up his hands in praise to God.[1]

## Endnote

1. John Harvey, "Music of the Spirit," *Alliance Life,* January 2001, 46.

# Music and Music

—————oooo@ooo————

THE ASSOCIATION OF MUSIC with prophecy is found in the Scriptures and will be cited as this chapter unfolds. But let's begin on more familiar ground.

At this point, we explore a little different and more speculative twist to testing whether a supernatural manifestation or any inspired utterance in music is from God or from the counterkingdom. If Christian music is accompanied by words that are doctrinally false, it is obvious that such music needs to be rejected out of hand. It has failed the most elementary of tests: the verbal. The problem arrives, as we noted in Chapter 1, when we are confronted with nonverbal communication, i.e., instrumental music without words *or* instrumental music which collides with wholly orthodox lyrics.

If one sees the possibility of truthful false prophets, as in Deuteronomy 13:1-3, then one must go beyond the verbal to the nonverbal. We have already discussed the dual test of Deuteronomy 13:1—verbal combined with nonverbal or nonverbal which stands alone. I would guess that not many are willing to apply such a test to music.

A common argument runs as follows: "Sound/rhythm/beat is not the important issue. It's meaning. It's what the song is saying—and the lyrics of a song's meaning are what gives us that meaning. I believe that music (particularly instrumental music) is absolutely de-void of moral qualities for either good or evil."[1]

There are several problems with assuming that only words give meaning, not the least of which is that several Scriptures are ignored, notably those which associate prophecy with instruments (1 Chronicles 25:1-3; 1 Samuel 10:5-6). Also, the first description of a false prophet shows him with flawless words—but only for a while (Deuteronomy 13:1-3). New Age radio stations which run only instrumental music seem odd, even illogical, if words alone carry the meaning in music. Musicians tell us that rhythm and tempo and mood have a great deal to say about ultimate meaning. Roberta King (Ph.D. in ethnomusicology) states that among the various cultures of the world, "each music is its own language."[2]

## Discernment Needed

It is quite obvious that discernment in these matters is sorely needed. In Paul's prison epistles especially, his passionate prayers for the development of discernment in the churches he could no longer visit is evident.

> I have not stopped giving thanks for you, remembering you in my prayers. I keep asking that the God of our Lord Jesus Christ, the glorious Father, may give you the Spirit of wisdom and revelation, so that you may know him better. I pray also that the eyes of your heart may be enlightened in order that you may know the hope to which he has called you, the riches of his glorious inheritance in the saints, and his incomparably great power for us who believe. (Ephesians 1:16-19)

> And this is my prayer: that your love may abound more and more in knowledge and depth of insight, so that you

may be able to discern what is best and may be pure and blameless until the day of Christ. (Philippians 1:9-10)

For this reason, since the day we heard about you, we have not stopped praying for you and asking God to fill you with the knowledge of his will through all spiritual wisdom and understanding. And we pray this in order that you may live a life worthy of the Lord and may please him in every way. (Colossians 1:9-10)

Beyond the obvious need for discernment, there are other principles that speak to the matter of judging between music and music. For instance, one should never be so naive as to presume that everything new is corrupt and that only the old and familiar adorns the doctrine of God. Beyond the obvious fact that everything was new sometime, biblically speaking there are going to be "new" songs (Psalm 33:3; 40:3). Possibly the greatest gospel songs, hymns and spiritual songs the world has ever known are still to come.

Sometimes objections are raised against certain instruments, but the scriptural index of instruments is immense. Boschman's references involve twenty instruments and hundreds of citations.[3]

## Three Premises

There are three premises which I wish to advance in the whole issue of appraising Christian music. While I do not offer these concepts as tests of orthodoxy, I do posit them for your thoughtful consideration.

*First, Christian music is intended to be an expression of the Spirit-filled life.* The biblical basis for this is Ephesians chapter 5: "Be filled with the Spirit. Speak to one another with psalms, hymns and spiritual songs. Sing and make music in your heart to the Lord, always giving thanks" (5:18-20).

We have a family friend who is a beautiful soloist. Although abandoned by her husband when she was pregnant with their sixth child, she managed—with the help of a caring church—to raise her children for the Lord. Through fasting and prayer, she brought them all into the family of God. When she sings, the power of the Holy Spirit is obvious. In fact, that is the most striking thing about her ministry—its awesome power. It flows from a broken heart, a broken life and a broken home.

Another couple involved in gospel singing went through serious trauma when their young son-in-law crashed his pickup truck into a concrete abutment. He perished instantly, and the vehicle burned. His beautiful young wife, their daughter, was left an expectant widow. Once the parents began to sing again after the tragedy, the message came through their broken hearts with extraordinary power. Their music had become an expression of the Spirit-filled life. Similarly, in the Welsh Revival, music anointed by the Spirit of God became a dominant factor.[4] No doubt similar statements could be made about all true revivals in the Church—one of the identifying factors is Spirit-empowered music, an expression of the Spirit-filled life.

My mind goes again to the revival in Bobo Dioulasso. By definition, the revival was a movement of the Holy Spirit. Agonizing confessions were being made. Wrongs were being made right. The church was jammed. There was a sea of radiant black faces. Hands were thrust jubilantly into the air. And the drum was pounding out its evangelistic rhythm.

Suddenly, the African evangelist sent word down to the drum. Abruptly, the sound changed. Even my North American ears could hear the difference. I guessed that the word had been: "Smarten up."

But the story does not end there. The music from Bobo was exceptionally beautiful and moving. Missionary Bob Overstreet captured some of it on tape and sent a small cassette home with me. On a Sunday morning we tucked the cassette into a book-sized player, set it on the floor about halfway down the long auditorium and plugged it into the nearest outlet. What followed surprised all of us. When the Bobo music began to play, many in the congregation began to weep. It was not the words nor the culture that moved that group to tears—for we knew neither. No, it was the power of the music. I have never forgotten that incident. It was the first time in memory that I became powerfully aware that there was music and music.

*Second, Christian music is intended to be a prophetic expression.* Although this premise is more unusual than the first, I have discovered that there is a solid biblical base for making such a statement. In the Old Testament, First Chronicles 25 is the key chapter. Heman and Jeduthun and their sons are set apart for the ministry of prophesying with harps, lyres and cymbals (25:1). Jeduthun, particularly, is referred to in verse 3 as a person "who prophesied, using the harp in thanking and praising the LORD" (see 25:3).

A similar incident takes place in the lives of Samuel and Saul. A procession of prophets, Saul was told, would meet him, and they would be playing instruments and prophesying (1 Samuel 10:5-6).

Psalms chapters 2, 16, 22, 34, 35, 41, 49, 68, 69 and 109 all contain prophecies that are fulfilled in the New Testament.[5] If the psalms are musical, as we know they are, we need not hesitate to admit that music is capable of being a prophetic expression. Ellicott wrote, "The 'psalm' as the word implies, is music with instrumental accompaniment."[6] In my opinion, Boschman may not be going too far when he suggests that the definition of prophecy is to "speak or sing by inspiration."[7] At the same time, however, the Hebrew word, *naba*, (meaning prophecy) does have an element of music in it, and musicians are sometimes referred to as prophets.[8] I am not insisting that Christian music is necessarily prophecy, only that it should be regarded as a prophetic expression.

In the New Testament, Ephesians 5:19 is translated in the Amplified version as follows: "Speak out to one another in psalms and hymns and spiritual songs, offering praise with voices (and instruments), and making melody with all your heart to the Lord." This translation seems to support our first premise—that music is meant to be an expression of the Spirit-filled life, and hints at supporting the second—that music is meant to be a prophetic expression.

Another related passage is First Corinthians 14:26 where a hymn is linked with a word of instruction, a revelation, a tongue, an interpretation. The musical expression, not commonly understood to be prophetic in nature, is associated with and put in the same list with phenomena which are known to be charismata. If Christian music in its most powerful form may be understood as a prophetic expression, then the apostolic linking of these items becomes significant. Thus, I am arguing—carefully, I trust—from clear Old Testament statements as well as from New Testament intimations, that music, both vocal and instrumental, should be regarded as a prophetic expression.

*Third, Christian music is to be judged by prophetic criteria.* How are prophecies judged? In the Old Testament, the early criteria demanded that a distinction be made between false and true. Moreover, Moses, as we have already observed, mentions the truthful false prophet ahead of the lying false prophet (Deuteronomy 13:1-3; 18:22). In the case of the truthful false prophet, all his words are true and come to pass—at least for a while. But he is not to be followed. He is false. (This also infers that time becomes an arbiter in distinguishing between true and false prophets.)

The lying false prophet is quite a bit easier to identify. He makes predictions which do not come to pass (time can be a factor here as well), and he is declared false on the basis of clear evidence. Jeremiah enumerates at least four forms of false prophecy (14:14): false visions, divinations, idolatries and delusions. The application of true and false criteria to Christian music, then, is not so outrageous as it first sounds.

The New Testament makes clear that prophecies are not to be despised, but rather to be carefully examined (1 Thessalonians

5:20-21). Two or three prophets may speak, and the others are to weigh carefully what is said (1 Corinthians 14:29). If these scriptures are to be obeyed, and if music is indeed a prophetic expression, then Christian musicians should expect the same careful examination of their music as is given to prophecy. By Old Testament criteria, music with wrong words or questionable nonverbals should be rejected.

Following New Testament criteria, consideration might involve such questions as: Is this ministry in the Spirit? Or is it in the flesh? What spirit is involved here? Do the lives of the musicians demonstrate what they are saying and playing? Prophecy, in whatever form it may take, is to be judged by those who sit by (1 Corinthians 14:29).

## "Have You Seen the Music?"

During a ministry hiatus of about one and a half years while I was writing my dissertation, my wife and I attended a certain church in southern California. We greatly benefited from and enjoyed the ministry there. The music was invariably excellent both in quality and spirit. One Sunday, however, a young woman, who had been invited to sing on the basis of a recommendation, arrived at the church. One pastor after another, we were told later, went to the senior pastor with the same question: "Have you *seen* the special music?" When she walked onto the platform, we too raised our eyebrows. The nonverbals—her demeanor and attire—were, to put it bluntly, witchlike. Since it was a difficult situation from which to retreat, the staff decided to allow her to sing.

She sang "How Great Thou Art," but the majestic words of one of the world's greatest and most-loved hymns could not save her. The dissonance between the verbals and the nonverbals was overpowering. My wife and I were appalled. The Lord's sheep, either undiscerning or just polite, applauded nicely. Later we learned that the senior pastor, after allowing her to sing in the first service, had come very close to handing her the honorarium and telling her that she would not be needed in the second. We were relieved to discover that the pastors were indeed discerning but had been caught in a trap of circumstance.

Had we been looking at music as a prophetic expression and had we been weighing it carefully, seeking to judge it by prophetic criteria, an elder might have risen to say, "Dear sister, your words are magnificent, but your spirit is wrong. Please sit down." That, of course, would have been shocking, to say the least, but immense benefit might have been derived. The Lord's people might have gained discernment, and the young woman herself might have been rescued from later problems.

## *Music from a Machine*

Let's briefly attempt to apply these ideas to electronic accompaniment. (Now I really am treading on thin ice!) We in the pragmatic West are culturally unable to resist technological advance, so-called. Singing with "canned" accompaniment has become common. The best musicians would be the first to agree that it certainly can be the expedient thing to do. But sometimes there is dissonance between the music and the lyrics, between the verbals and the nonverbals— even a slavish attention that makes it appear as though the singer is submissive to the accompaniment. How different it might be if the vocalist were accompanied by a musician who sensitively and prophetically followed the lead of the soloist—two hearts in tune with one source.

There are other unanswered questions when it comes to electronic accompaniment: Was the musician who recorded the music a believer? Was he or she ministering in the flesh or the Spirit? Was he or she full of the Holy Spirit or "high" on something else? These are uncomfortable questions.

So then, should we ban the use of electronic accompaniment? No. That is not only naive, but it also is not likely to happen. Rather, accompaniment—whether live or electronic—should come under the same biblical scrutiny as the words and the singer(s). The Scriptures clearly admonish us: "Despise not prophesyings. Prove all things; hold fast that which is good" (1 Thessalonians 5:20-21, KJV).

In this chapter, we have moved from positing Christian music as potentially prophetic and intended as a full expression of the Spirit-filled life to urging that it be judged by prophetic criteria. If prophesying may be musical, as the Scriptures indicate, we arrive at some obvious questions: Is there true and false music? Does the combination of dissonant nonverbals and "holy" words sanctify the result? Is it possible that teaming biblical messages with sensual music (or vice versa) contaminates the whole? If nonverbal communication is part of the way mankind communicates with itself and other beings—and it is—what happens when the messages are mixed? Is it flawed, or is it false?

If the premise is adopted that Christian music is intended to be a prophetic expression and therefore should be judged by prophetic criteria, the discussion moves from instruments and styles to focus on the spirit of the music as well as the words.

## Endnotes

1. Dana Key with Steve Rabey, "Tool of Satan or Tool of God?" *Contemporary Christian Music*, 1989, 24.

2. Roberta King, *Pathways in Christian Music Communication: The Case of the Senufo of Côte d'Ivoire* (Pasadena, CA: Fuller Theological Seminary, 1989), 6.

3. La Mar Boschman, *The Rebirth of Music* (Springdale, PA: Revival Press, 1980), 79-85.

4. Leona Choy, *Powerlines* (Camp Hill. PA: Christian Publications, 1990), 225-229.

5. Boschman, 37-38.

6. Charles John Ellicott, *Ephesians*, volume 8 (Grand Rapids, MI: Zondervan, n.d.), 51.

7. Boschman, 91.

8. R. Laird Harris, Gleason L. Archer and Bruce K. Waltke, *Theological Wordbook of the Old Testament* (Chicago: Moody Press, 1980), 545. See

also William Gesenius, *Gesenius' Hebrew-Chaldee Lexicon to the Old Testament*, trans. Samuel Prideaux Tregelles (Grand Rapids, MI: Baker Book House, 1979), 525-526. *Naba* means 1) "To cause to bubble up," hence to "pour forth words abundantly," as is done by those who speak with ardour or divine emotion of mind. (Literal root meaning—it is an onamatopoetic that sounds like what it means—*naba*, to bubble.) 2) To speak (as a prophet) by a divine power, to prophesy. 3) To sing holy songs as led by the Spirit of God, to praise God. 4) To sing as seized by a divine impulse, to praise God. 5) To act as if mad (of false prophets).

# 7

# Revelation
# and Revelation

# Look at the Picture

*by Richard H. Harvey*

I WAS DELIGHTED WHEN I was asked to serve on the board of trustees of LeTourneau College, Longview, Texas. Richard LeTourneau, the president of the college, had meant much to me and the Southwestern District [of which Harvey was superintendent] through his wise counseling. I felt the invitation would give me the opportunity to at least show a little appreciation. . . .

One day, at a specially called meeting of the board, Richard informed the trustees that because of his father's ill health he had no choice but to assume the leadership of the LeTourneau Corporation and that someone else would have to be appointed to take the responsibility for the college.

A nominating committee was appointed. Its nominee was Richard Harvey. I was stunned. My reaction was instantaneous.

"I can't, gentlemen. This is not my field nor experience. Besides, this is largely a technical school, and I know nothing about engineering. I have a job, too, from which I can't conscientiously resign because no one can be elected to take my place before next fall, a year from now."

All my speeches were ignored. I was decreed elected, and Richard LeTourneau and Richard Harvey were to work out the difficulties.

After consultation with our denomination officials . . . , it was determined that for one year I would maintain both positions, . . . and that we would live in Longview. Thus from Monday morning until Friday noon, I served the college. On Friday afternoon, the college furnished a plane and pilot, and on Friday evening, Saturday and Sunday I served the district. Every evening after 10:00 I called my secretary in Dallas, the mail was read to me and answers were dictated over the phone. . . .

I had been at LeTourneau College only a couple of weeks when there was a breathing spell at the office. I reached for some of the books in the pile on my desk which Richard LeTourneau had put there that I might familiarize myself with the many aspects of college administration.

I scanned a few until I came to a little book describing [an organization of] America's small colleges and universities. On the first page was a list of those who were members; our college was listed.

I thought, *I'd better discover what the organization is all about.* So I fingered through the pages with one thought, *I'll return to this when I have more time.*

I laid the book aside. But a strong impression came over me to pick it up again. I have learned to obey the "inner voice of the Spirit."

About one-third of the way through was a picture of the organization's full-time director. I read the caption under the picture, then began to thumb through the pages again.

The impression came again, "Look at the picture. Read the caption carefully." I did.

Again, "Read it carefully."

Again I read it carefully and laid the book down.

Then there was a knock on my office door—a man had come directly, not through the secretary. When I saw him, I responded, "Good morning, Dr. _____."

"How do you know me?" (He almost lost his balance standing there.) "You have never seen me before, have you?"

"No, I have never met you either. Sir, I don't think you would understand if I tried to explain."

"You're new here, aren't you?"

"Yes, sir, I am pinch-hitting for Richard LeTourneau."

"But I want to know how you knew who I was. No one knew I was coming here. I didn't know myself until I was flying over Longview and decided to stop for a few minutes. I met no one on the journey or on the campus."

I saw I was going to have to give an explanation.

"Just before you came in, sir, I was talking to God and seeking guidance for the day. An inner urge led me to read your little book on America's small colleges and universities."

"Oh, so you're one of those religious crackpots."

"Yes, sir, I'm in that classification." I explained how I was led to pick up the little book after laying it aside. I told him how God had stopped me at his picture and how He had guided me to reread the paragraph under the picture. I then quoted it practically word for word.

"You must be one of those religious fanatics like my daughter. She got religion at one of Billy Graham's meetings."

"Yes, sir, that is exactly the same thing I have. Both your daughter and I have the same Christ."

The incident seemed to keep him from leaving. He hung around all day. We went to lunch together. Before the day was over, I had prayed with him. He left with his eyes full of tears. His parting words were, "Dr. Harvey, I'm convinced there must be something real to this religious bit."[1]

## *Endnote*

1. Richard H. Harvey, *70 Years of Miracles* (Camp Hill, PA: Horizon Books, 1992), 169.

# Seeing but Not Believing

*by L. David Mitchell*

OUR SECOND DAUGHTER, HELEN, had a friend at university, Meg, who would suddenly look up and say, "So-and-so will knock on the door." A few seconds later, the rat-a-tat would echo down the hallway. Meg would [also] tell fortunes for other women and sometimes be right in many details, to her "client's" amazement. Sometimes she would be quite wrong. There was no dependability, but some people were fascinated and often came to her for advice.

Helen arranged a picnic when I could meet Meg. Casually, I said to her, "I hear you have an interesting gift." When she replied with a nod, . . . I asked her where she thought it had come from. "It came from God," she said, for she was a keen member of a Christian church.

To my question, "Do you enjoy this gift?" Meg answered, "No. I would rather I did not have it, but I suppose it must be for someone's good, mustn't it?"

Meg admitted that when clairvoyant thoughts came into her mind she did not know whether to speak about them or not. Sometimes they were ugly and menacing, or they could be happy and pleasing. Sometimes the thoughts were accurate . . . and sometimes hopelessly incorrect. On balance, she would be very happy if God would take the gift away from her.

I asked if her mother had the same ability. "Oh, yes! And my grandmother, too." . . .

When I suggested that the fortune-telling spirit might not be from God, but from the devil, Meg perked up visibly. "You mean, I *should* get rid of it? How can I do that? I have had it as long as I can remember."

After some teaching, Meg gladly confessed her sin and renounced the devil and her evil family inheritance. I prayed with the authority Christ has given to the church, and she was delivered. Meg jumped to her feet and ran off, dancing. "I'm free!" she sang, "I'm free.". . .

Then I met Phyllis, a hairdresser who loved her work, and whose customers loved her. She would often get pictures in her mind about a client and tell them what she saw. When she told a woman something that only the woman knew, her customer would be amazed, and ask for more insights. Gradually Phyllis built up a clientele which valued her almost as much for her fortune-telling as for her hairdressing. . . .

She came to me one day to tell me of her "gift," and her desire to be rid of it. Now she knew Christ in an intimate way and had found how totally trustworthy and consistent God is. The psychic "gift" she had inherited from her mother was tawdry and darkly offensive to her spirit.

She related one frightening experience she had had while doing a customer's hair. Suddenly, she had "seen" the woman's husband and son in a head-on collision at a precise bend in a certain country road. Knowing that this could be a "false prophecy," she had held her tongue, not wanting to alarm her client. A few days later a head-on accident claimed the lives of the two men at the exact spot she had envisioned.[1]

### Endnote

1. L. David Mitchell, *Liberty in Jesus* (Edinburgh: The Pentland Press, Ltd., 1999), 71-72.

# Revelation and Revelation

T HE PLACEMENT OF THIS CHAPTER in this book may seem curious. Why, you may ask, enter into a discussion of the spiritual gift of revelation here at the end of a lengthy multi-chapter discussion on prophecy? The reasons are biblical (1 Corinthians 14:6, 25, 30). Revelation is closely associated with prophecy in the biblical text.

It was 1971, and revival was blazing in the city of Saskatoon. One of the key pastors in that event, the Rev. Walter Boldt, was scheduled to speak at a Christian Conference on Business which I had arranged in another city. Thirty or forty participants were registered. Before the day arrived, Boldt called to ask if he could change the topic from business to revival. I agreed. He told me later that he would have canceled had I not concurred.

## Take the Chair

The conference did indeed become a conference on revival. In one session, as had been the custom in the Saskatoon happenings, a chair was placed in the middle of the room. As Pastor Boldt preached, I remember only that I could not stop weeping. When the invitation was given, there was only one in the group who responded to "take the chair" and receive the ministry of the revival team. It was I. As the brethren prayed over me, I was conscious of a deep working of the

Spirit of God in my heart. Curiously, ever since that day there have been times when the Lord seems to show me things in prayer. They often relate to future ministry, and for that reason I now call the manifestation "revelation."

For example, some years back I was heading for a day of preaching at a site in Côte d'Ivoire, Africa. As I prayed about it, I "saw" the blessing of the Lord descending upon a group of people that included me. We were outside under a big tree. However, when we arrived at the location, there was a church building and benches within. It did not appear that we would be assembling under a tree. Then, as the service time drew near, I watched in amazement as the benches were dragged out and placed under a tree. It was there later that evening that the blessing of God fell.

On yet another occasion, in the Philippines, as our revival teams headed toward Manila, in prayer I "saw" the interior of the church to which we were ultimately headed. It had a balcony, a feature almost unknown in the churches in the Philippines at that time. But when we arrived, there was the balcony, and there, likewise, the blessing of God.

## A Road Going North

Now, fast-forward from 1972 to 1988. I had just completed my doctoral work at the School of World Mission in Pasadena, California, and my wife and I were waiting on the Lord for His direction in our lives. What would the next step of ministry be?

One of the options was the presidency of my alma mater, Canadian Bible College and Canadian Theological Seminary. I was one of several candidates, so it was certainly not a sure thing. But as I prayed, I "saw" a pathway, flat on the top, sloped up on each side, leading north from California to Saskatchewan, Canada, where the institutions were located. Further complicating the situation, the next day I saw on the front page of one of the sections of the *Los Angeles Times* a picture of the beveled path I had "seen" the day before. As events unfolded, there was only one problem—God was not directing us to Saskatchewan! Someone else was chosen to lead the schools. Instead, we moved east to Pennsylvania, to the ministry of Christian Publications.

In the more than twelve intervening years, both my wife and I have been confirmed in our gifts and ministries many times by many people. We discovered God's will for this time in our lives. That road "picture," reinforced by the prestigious *Los Angeles Times*, was false. It was false revelation and false information, a delusion of Satan and perhaps a concoction of the self-life—real, but false.

## Proof of Authenticity

"What shall I profit you unless I speak to you . . . by revelation? . . . Whenever you come together, each of you . . . has a revelation" (1 Corinthians 14:6, 26, NKJV). The context of this passage is Paul's discussion of prophecy. While I am less than willing to call prophecy and revelation the same, as do some who tend to want to fudge on the specific biblical definition of prophecy, the idea merits some consideration.

The events at that business/revival conference caused me to search the Scriptures regarding revelation. I found my answer in First Corinthians 14. It has to do with the Greek word that is translated "revelation." This word projects the idea of little visions, little pictures which, according to Paul, the Holy Spirit gives to spiritually receptive people. At least that helped me make sense of what was happening in my life. It was the plain application of Scripture to personal experience. But let's step back a bit and remind ourselves that personal experience, even my own, or more directly, especially my own, is no proof of authority or authenticity. The only question that matters is, "What do the Scriptures say?"

*Apokalupto* has the meaning of "to take off the cover, disclose, reveal." *Apokalupsis* means "disclosure: appearing, coming, lighten, manifestation, be revealed, revelation."[1] What is being said here can also be applied to the spiritual gifts of the word of wisdom, the word of knowledge, the discerning of spirits and other revelatory aspects of the work of the Holy Spirit. Revelation can be part of the Christian experience (1 Corinthians 14:30), but it is clearly subject to analysis and restraint (14:29). This book, *Sorting Out the Supernatural,* has one main point—there is false, and there is true. We must not be so naive as to think that there are no false revelations. In this Corinthian passage, revelation appears to be part and parcel of prophecy. In fact, in verse 30, the reference to revelation is sandwiched between other teachings about prophecy.

In categorizing the spiritual gifts listed in First Corinthians 12:8-11, Carson writes as follows: "This issues in the following division: the word of knowledge and the word of wisdom lie in the intellectual arena; faith, healing, miracles, prophecy [and revelation] and distinguishing of spirits are grouped separately, perhaps linked with special faith, the lead item in this division; and tongues and the interpretation of tongues, in a category by itself."[2]

## The Revelation Connection

Carson goes on to observe that there is overlap. Prophecy has intellectual characteristics as well.[3] I wish to follow his lead by suggesting that various of the spiritual gifts may involve revelation, particularly the word of knowledge, the word of wisdom, the discerning of spirits and (as in our immediate discussion) prophecy. The imparting of information is part of all of these expressions and perhaps others. I am not saying that other gifts do not include the impartation of information. Could not a gift of healing include information about how to pray in certain situations and for certain cases? I think so.

Nevertheless, for our purposes here, my proposition is that revelation (a form of prophecy according to Carson), may be true, and it may be false. Prophecy is to be "carefully weighed" (see 1 Corinthians 14:29). *Diakrino* is the Greek word used here. It has root meanings (from *anakrino*) of examine, scrutinize, even to hold a preliminary examination, expecting more to follow. In First Corinthians 14:29, regarding oral testimony, the word is used of discerning what is of the Holy Spirit.[4] Strong asserts that *diakrino* means to separate thoroughly.[5]

"Prove all things," said Paul in a context relating to prophecies and utterances (1 Thessalonians 5:21, KJV). *Dokimadzo* (proving) is a word derived from assaying, from metallurgical processes, and is used *with a view to approval*.[6] The expectations are positive, rather than negative, but the possibility of inauthenticity and rejection is present.[7] When we relate this information to the current definition of prophecy and indirectly to revelation, the results are not happy. They do not project the idea of acceptable alternatives such as fallible prophecy or immature utterances. Rather, they suggest true and false, rejection of and separation from faulty material. These words, *diakrino* and *dokimadzo*, so often used in Scripture, suggest falsity and inauthenticity more than they suggest immaturity and innocent deviance, if there is such a thing. Arguing for expressions of fallible prophecy gifted by the Spirit of Truth sounds most like spiritual naivete.

## Getting Tough

John Brevere's book, *Thus Saith the Lord*, is one of the toughest yet to emerge on false revelation. He is relentless in his attack against false prophecy, labeling it in some cases a curse of divination that needs to be broken.[8] Unfortunately, he still includes a definition of prophecy which is layered and allows for prophecy from the Holy Spirit, who is the Spirit of Truth, to be less than 100 percent accurate.[9] This reveals a severe paradigm blockage typical in many evangelical minds, a blockage which will not allow prophecy to be challenged directly and authoritatively. This accommodation to error, so prevalent in some movements, is still to be challenged forthrightly. If Brevere is representative of charismatic trends in this area, then tougher stances may be in the offing.

One of the authors Brevere cites admits that on one occasion several Christian workers began

> telling funny stories about false prophecies. As I [Brevere] listened and laughed, I saw that it had become common practice to ignore, or at least take lightly, many of the people "speaking in the name of the Lord." We had all learned to hold our tongues and be gracious. Everyone told of receiving notes, participating in meetings and actually encouraging people in prophetic words, *knowing they were not genuine* [emphasis added]. . . .[10]

Such behavior is appalling. That it is admitted and published is a harbinger of hope.

Another hopeful sign is found in *Blessing the Church?* by several influential charismatic leaders in Britain. They are protesting unfulfilled prophecies and the charismatic departure from the authority of Scripture, particularly such statements as these:

> "Don't let the Bible get in the way of the blessing."

> "Some of you Bible-lovers need to put it down and let God work on you."

> "The Bible has let us down. It has not delivered the numbers we need."[11]

In summary, revelation, like prophecy, sometimes originates from the Holy Spirit of God and sometimes it doesn't. Two other sources are possible—the devil or the uncrucified self. Revelation, like prophecy, must never be assumed to be true without diacritical testing. And surely that testing is enabled by the Bible.

## *Endnotes*

1. James Strong, *The Comprehensive Concordance of the Bible* (Iowa Falls, IA: World Bible Publishers, n.d.), Greek, 14.

2. D.A. Carson, *Showing the Spirit: A Theological Exposition of 1 Corinthians 12-14,* (Grand Rapids, MI: Baker Book House, 1987), 37.

3. Ibid.

4. W.E. Vine, *The Expanded Vine's Expository Dictionary of New Testament Words,* edited by John R. Kohlenberger, III (Minneapolis, MN: Bethany House, 1984), 306-307.

5. Strong, Greek, 1252.

6. Vine, 63-64.

7. Gerhard Kittel and Gerhard Friedrich, editors, *Theological Dictionary of the New Testament* (Grand Rapids, MI: Eerdmans, 1985), 181-182.

8. John Brevere, *Thus Saith the Lord?* (Lake Mary, FL: Creation House, 1999), 90.

9. Ibid., x.

10. Ibid., 16.

11. Clifford Hill and Peter Fenwick, David Forbes, David Noakes, *Blessing the Church?* (Guildford, Surrey, UK: Inter Publishing Service, 1995), 51.

# Part III

# Nine Other

# Polarities

THE FIRST MAJOR SECTION of this book dealt with the givens, the controlling factors which must be in place before any effort is made to sort out the supernatural.

The second section explained the various expressions of prophecy and related matters.

Now, in this third section, we will attempt to illustrate how the sorting principle plays out in various spheres of Christian experience and reality.

Once the key definition of prophecy is established, there are additional realities which relate to that primary issue. The following have been chosen from among a larger number to illustrate the single thrust of this book.

Since these pages are about the wheat and the tares, then consideration of these realities is an exercise in tare inspection, a limited observation only, according to Matthew 13:41. The final sorting of both people and things, according to Jesus, awaits another day.

No attempt is being made to be exhaustive; hopefully rather, a principle has already been established and will be sufficiently emphasized in these pages so as to make the single teaching of this volume abundantly clear: There are polarities in kingdom matters. Recognizing these polarities expands the base of discernment in one's life.

**Polarity 1:** *Worship and Worship.* Aaron's sons offered strange fire and were judged. This is one of the most powerful passages of Scripture illustrating true and false worship.

**Polarity 2:** *Signs and Signs.* The events involving Moses and the magicians of Egypt provide clues for discerning true and false in such incidents.

**Polarity 3:** *Healing and Healing.* A number of authors recognize the healing power of Jesus Christ as well as animistic counter-kingdom healing.

**Polarity 4:** *Deliverance and Deliverance.* Jesus' own words illustrate the possibility of deliverance apart from authentic faith, as do the actions of the sons of Sceva and deliverances in the major religions of the world—imitations of the authentic deliverance in the name of Jesus Christ.

**Polarity 5:** *Jesus and Jesus.* Second Corinthians chapter 11 is the key passage in confirming the possibility and frequency of "Jesus" spirits.

**Polarity 6:** *Anointing and Anointing.* Unction is the property of false prophets as well as true. The meaning of the word "Christ" is the key.

**Polarity 7:** *Providences and Providences.* A variety of incidents, both biblical and contemporary, will be examined in an effort to provide guidelines for determining true and false.

**Polarity 8:** *Falling and Falling.* "Falling under the power" and "being slain in the Spirit"—what do they mean, and how may the true and the false be distinguished?

**Polarity 9:** *Revival and Revival.* Brownsville, Toronto, the Hebrides, the United States, Western Canada. What characteristics accompany true and false revivals?

# 8

# Worship
# and Worship

# Tozer on False Worship

I HAVE A CD-ROM that at the touch of a button zips through the works of A.W. Tozer. Imagine being able to examine forty-five books and booklets of the great author in seconds. Imagine my surprise to find that Tozer on only one occasion combined the words "false" and "worship." What a statement on bloodless worship it turned out to be!

The first false worship is Cain worship, which is worship without atonement. This kind of worship rests upon three basic errors. One is the error that assumes God to be different from what He is. He who seeks to worship a God he does not know comes without having first been cleansed by the coals from off the altar. But this kind of worship will not be accepted by God.

The second error is that man assumes he occupies a relation to God which he does not occupy. The man who worships without Christ and without the blood of the Lamb and without forgiveness and without cleansing is assuming too much. He is mistaking error for truth and spiritual tragedy is the result.

The third error is that sin is made less serious than it is in fact. The psychologists and psychiatrists and sociologists . . . that have come in over the past years have taken the terror out of sin. To worship God acceptably we must be freed from sin. Cain worship is worship out of an unregenerate heart.

. . . But also we must worship Him in truth. Now the worshiper must submit to truth. I can't worship God acceptably unless I accept what God has said. . . . Before my worship is accepted I must accept what God has said about Himself. We must never edit God. We must never apologize for God. No man has any right to get up in the pulpit and try to smooth over or amend anything that God has said about Himself. . . .

Then I must believe whatever God says about sin. Here's another place where the psychologists and psychiatrists have done us great injury. They have euphemized sin. They call it a guilt complex. I believe our trouble these days is that we've listened to the blandishments of these children of Adam and that we're afraid to see anybody get on his knees and really get scared.

Some of you have no doubt read of Peter Cartright, the Great Methodist preacher who lived a century or so ago. Well, Peter was quite a preacher, an ignorant fellow, but God was on him. They tell how he once went to a conference and preached. The conference was in the charge of a little fellow from a seminary and of course Peter had little time for those boys. When Peter gave the invitation a lot of men came including a big logger, a great big brawny fellow with monstrous ape-like arms, a huge fellow. He came down to the front and threw himself down and began to pray.

He'd been a sinner and he told God about it loudly, which scared this little seminary student half to death. He ran to him and said, "Compose yourself, brother, compose yourself." Peter Cartright pushed him aside, slapped the big logger on the back and said, "Pray on, brother, there's no composure in hell where you're going." Finally, the man saw the goodness of God and the power of the cross, and the grace of God reached down and saved him. He leaped to his feet with a howl of delight and looked around for someone to hug and the first fellow he got hold of was the little seminary student. He picked him up and went dancing around at the top of his voice. It was hard on the young student's dignity, but perfectly right nevertheless.

Now it is possible to have religious experience without Jesus Christ. It's not only possible to have religious experience, it is possible to have worship without Jesus Christ. . . . Cain had a religious experience, but God did not accept him.[1]

### *Endnote*

1. A.W. Tozer, *Worship: The Missing Jewel* (Camp Hill, PA: Christian Publications, 1999), CD-ROM/false worship/acceptable worship/par. 5.

# Worship and Worship

---

T HE ASSUMPTION AS WE BEGIN this chapter is that authentic
Christian worship should be supernatural in its expression.
Paul makes it clear that Old Testament events are to encourage and warn the Church (Romans 15:4; 1 Corinthians 10:11). A
prime biblical example is the profound drama found in Leviticus 9.
Like a book, Leviticus chapter 9 has an introduction, a body of information, a succinct conclusion and a fascinating appendix. On our
way to sorting out worship and worship, let's check out some brief
excerpts from this amazing passage.

> ". . . today the LORD will appear to you." . . . Then Moses
> said, "This is what the LORD has commanded you to do, so
> that the glory of the LORD may appear to you." . . .
>
> Then Aaron lifted his hands toward the people and
> blessed them. And having sacrificed the sin offering, the
> burnt offering and the fellowship offering, he stepped
> down.
>
> Moses and Aaron then went into the Tent of Meeting.
> When they came out, they blessed the people; and the
> glory of the LORD appeared to all the people. Fire came out
> from the presence of the LORD and consumed the burnt
> offering and the fat portions on the altar. And when all the

people saw it, they shouted for joy and fell facedown. (9:4, 6, 22-24)

## The Introduction and the Promise

"For today the LORD will appear to you" (9:4). What an introduction! What a promise! God's glory is coming! Can you imagine being in a gathering where word came from the Lord that He would appear to you that very day?

After more than forty years in Christian ministry, I remember only once when God promised me such a visitation. I was preaching at a frontier church in an isolated village in the province of British Columbia. As a result of those few days of teaching, correction had come to the church, and it pulled back from embracing an heretical direction. One day, the Lord gave me a promise: "Tomorrow [I] will do amazing things among you" (Joshua 3:5). It was one of those times. God intended to do something for His glory. And He set the timetable.

The next day, dinnertime came and went but nothing happened. The evening service came. I preached as usual. Nothing extraordinary took place. But after the service, as a group of us were chatting in the foyer, a man we knew to be a recent convert walked through the front door. He had previously undergone an operation which had locked one knee into place. His leg had become permanently stiff. He told us that that very day he had been to his doctor who now informed him that the other leg would have to be "done" too. As a new Christian, he was facing great trauma. In that state of mind, he had come to the church.

As news of the situation spread through the group, one of the elders, the pastor and I were each drawn as if by a magnet to his side. Sensing compassion for this young believer, we reached out and placed our hands on his knee and began to pray. Not yet acculturated to the evangelical habit of closing one's eyes during prayer, he watched these strange proceedings. As we prayed he could feel things going back into place in his knee. In my mind, it was clear that the Lord had stretched forth His hand to do wonders among us on the very day He had promised.

Similarly, in Leviticus, the Lord God promised to appear to His people and show them His glory. That was the agenda for the day, the divine introduction to a never-to-be-forgotten experience.

## Not Only What, but How

The body of this Leviticus 9 "book" is found in verses 2-6 where Moses gives instructions—precise instructions with a precise goal: "This is what the LORD has commanded you to do, so that the glory of the LORD may appear to you" (9:6). Moses has left no misunderstanding about the path that must be followed if the people want to see the glory of God. Such a pathway is of immense significance. If the Westminster divines are correct—and the chief end of man is to glorify God and enjoy Him forever—then this passage is pivotal in the kingdom. The path, an unfolding of a series of sacrifices, is crucial to the understanding of our present-day longing to see and experience the glory of God.

Sacrifices must be made. They anticipate the coming of the Lamb of God, the revelation of His glory (John 1:29) who Himself was the sacrifice slain from the foundation of the world (Revelation 13:8). This Leviticus passage is both christological and theological in its anticipation: These Old Testament sacrifices anticipate Christ's ultimate sacrifice on the cross—and they have significance to us who live in this twenty-first century.

## The Sin Offering

God, being holy, must deal with sin. He cannot overlook it. It must be addressed. Blood must be shed if sins are to be remitted (Hebrews 9:22). There are no shortcuts to the glory of God. Sin separates. It must be faced and dealt with if true worship is desired. It occurs to me, if I may leap ahead for a moment to the appendix of this levitical "book," that Nadab and Abihu did not take time to deal with sin (Leviticus 10:1-3). They supposed that they could rush precipitously into the presence of a holy God without dealing with sin. Not so. Not then. Not now. Not ever. There are good biblical reasons for some "high" Protestant churches prioritizing the communal confession of sin before other elements in the worship service are introduced.

## The Burnt Offering

Further, the Israelites were to offer not only a sin offering but also a burnt offering (9:3). The specifics of these offerings intrigue me. In the case of the burnt offering, the ram was to be without defect; and the list of the people for whom it was to be offered was specific—it was for Moses and Aaron, his sons and the elders of Israel—first a sin offering and then a burnt offering.

The leaders were required to offer a bull, a more serious and expensive offering. Followers were allowed to offer a goat. But the procedure was the same—deal with sin, *then* consider such matters as sanctification (setting apart) and consecration (giving up). The burnt offerings followed, and they were totally consumed. It was the custom for the Levites to receive parts of various offerings for their support and sustenance. Not so with the burnt offering. It was burned until nothing was left. This, in brief, was the Old Testament pathway to the glory of God—first, sin had to be dealt with, and beyond that were the matters of sanctification and holiness—total and complete.

*Sorting Out the Supernatural* is being written as the twenty-first century dawns. My perspective from this point in time is that evangelicals have lost their sense of sanctification, of separation from sin. We no longer are a distinct, set-apart people. Not surprisingly, we have developed a form of godliness devoid of power (2 Timothy 3:5). A kind of evangelical itch has spread among us, and no one seems to know the cure.

Where might that cure be found? I believe it is here on the pathway to the glory of God. Sanctification is ignored at great peril. "Without holiness no one will see the Lord" (Hebrews 12:14). Any theological paradigm that has no place for Spirit-empowered holiness and the fullness of the Holy Spirit is inadequate. A.W. Tozer allowed that no one was ever filled with the Holy Spirit who didn't know it.[1] After the sin offering comes the burnt offering—the life of self dead and gone, burned up, totally consumed on the altar of sacrifice—all this on the way to the glory of God!

## A Fellowship Offering

Next, Moses makes clear, was the fellowship offering, the sacrifice of a ram. It speaks of relationships, vertical (to God) and horizontal (to people). Notice again—for the third time in these offerings blood is shed.

Every once in a while we puny humans get into controversy with God Almighty. Sometimes we even get angry with God and, like Jonah, sulk and pout around the kingdom. It is interesting to note that Jonah's marvelous experiences in ministry did not keep him from anger at Jehovah when Nineveh was not destroyed after all (Jonah 4:1), and the resulting rupture in Jonah's relationship with the Creator of all the universe is clear.

Many years ago I wanted to buy a publishing operation. The Lord's answer to me was a clear and unequivocal "no." I was angry. Angry with God. But today, in God's time, we are fully involved in the publishing ministry. I am ever so glad to be over that foolish response to not being able to have my own way. I also know that God will not bless me if He regards iniquity (and anger is certainly iniquity) in my heart (Psalm 66:18). God forgave me long ago. He knows what Moses was like, and He knows what we—you and I—are like. He provided the fellowship offering for Moses, and He provides it for us too. We must be "thoroughly right with God," as Finney used to say. The longer I know God, the more I want to be thoroughly and fully and always right with Him. There must be nothing between my soul and the Savior. One of the reasons is that such a stance is one of the milestones on the path to true worship and to the glory of God.

With the primacy of the vertical relationship in place, fellowship with other people becomes of the essence. It is the warp and woof of the tapestry on which God's glory is displayed. Being rightly related to others is an extremely important kingdom condition. Without both strands, there is no weaving together, no integration of the earthly and the heavenly. "Confess your sins to one another, and pray one for another, so that you may be healed" (James 5:16, NASB).

There was once a preacher that I didn't like. He didn't like me either. But during revival days in Western Canada I went to my brother. "Please forgive me. I haven't loved you as I should have," I said. His forgiveness was strong and warm, and the relationship was healed. Yes, the fellowship offering too comes before the revelation of the glory of God.

A lady in the Philippines once told me, "I squint whenever I go to church." The reason? "The other lady." She was afraid she would see her! But, thank God, reconciliation came, Filipino style, at 5 o'clock one morning. It is for reasons like these that the fellowship offering follows the burnt offering and the sin offering. Aaron's sons, Nadab and Abihu, had no time for the fellowship offering. Being right with other people was not on their list of priorities. They were so absorbed with having fire, any kind of fire (Leviticus 10:1), that they brushed right past the fellowship offerings of right relationships with God and others.

## The Grain Offering

The grain offering suggests a process of planting and nurturing for an abundant harvest, i.e., involvement with God's plans and purposes, a disposition to do His will. It suggests a whitened harvest where the reapers are few. It suggests that prayer should be offered so that the Lord of the harvest will send workers into the fields

(Luke 10:2). It also suggests that the Great Commission (Matthew 28:19) is part of the pathway to the glory of God. If the nations truly shall declare the glory of God (Isaiah 66:18-19), then the Lord of the Harvest must be honored, obeyed and worshiped.

Notice that the grain offering is mixed with oil (Leviticus 9:4). Oil is a symbol of the Holy Spirit. The Holy Spirit's presence is related to the glory of God. He wants Spirit-empowered service rather than self-empowered service. With God, it's His way or no way. True worship—and therefore service—is wrapped around the work of the Holy Spirit. Authentic worship is worship in Spirit and in truth.

Prose fails us here. Israel, Moses and Aaron were in a state of anticipation and exhaustion. The sacrifices had been made. The obediences had been completed. Perhaps the whole nation was holding its breath. The conclusion to our levitical "book" is predictable: "Moses and Aaron then went into the Tent of Meeting. When they came out, they blessed the people; and the glory of the LORD appeared to all the people. Fire came out from the presence of the LORD and consumed the burnt offering and the fat portions on the altar. And when all the people saw it, they shouted for joy and fell facedown" (9:23 24).

Moses' description of this event seems almost understated. The truth was that holy exuberance had enveloped the whole people. The grand objective of the appearance of God's glory had been achieved (9:6). And what's more, authentic, true worship of God had been achieved. It came God's way, in God's order.

But there is more to the story.

## The Unfortunate Appendix

A fitting conclusion to this book was the arrival of the glory of the Lord. That is how it was supposed to be. But appended to the story, interrupted by a man-made chapter division, is the story of Nadab and Abihu. These young men were undoubtedly witnesses of all that had taken place. They had observed the prodigious work of their father, Aaron, in the presentation of the various offerings. They had grown up knowing the proper sequence. They knew the path to the glory, but they had their own plans, their own agenda, their own lust for fire.

Contrary to God's command and in circumvention of His mandated (and bloody) process, they took their censers, put fire in them, added incense, and offered unauthorized fire before the Lord. The result was not the presence and glory of God. Rather, fire came out from the presence of the Lord and consumed them, and they died before the Lord (10:1-2).

Can you imagine it? The two sons of the respected high priest falling down dead before the whole congregation? Why was the punishment so swift and certain? Answer? They had affronted both the holiness and the honor of God. The Scriptures tell us that Aaron, who had just lost two sons in one bold stroke of divine judgment, was silent (10:3). What was there to say before a holy God whose worship had been defiled? Nothing.

The conclusion is this: False worship cannot be tolerated. When offered in the Old Testament era, it was summarily judged.

What does this all mean for us? Do these Old Testament principles and procedures apply to us today? I believe they do. Let's conclude this chapter by looking briefly at the parts of the process that Nadab and Abihu ignored.

## Bloodless Worship

These men ignored the cross, the blood. False worship is not only worship of other gods, but, as it is defined in Leviticus 9 and 10, it is a substitute bloodless adoration which ultimately brings glory to Satan and not God Almighty. In the Christian context we must not ignore the cross. "The preaching of the cross is to them that perish foolishness; but unto us who are saved it is the power of God" (1 Corinthians 1:18, KJV). Bloodless worship is false worship.

For the first 300 years of the Christian church, the "preliminaries" of worship services addressed the sins of the people and the need for cleansing and forgiveness. I ask you, how long is it since you have been in a service where acknowledgment and confession of sin or sins have been urged before or as part of the call to worship? The prodigious labor of Moses and Aaron and all the priests to offer the appropriate sacrifices were in one deliberate stroke eliminated by Nadab and Abihu. The barrels of blood so diffusely spread around the camp of Israel were not important to Aaron's rebellious sons.

## Samuel's Corollary

There is a dramatic passage in Second Samuel 6:13 which is the scriptural corollary to Leviticus 9. The ark of God has been taken in battle and is now being returned to Israel.

The phrase "the Ark of God" reminds many of us of David's unbecoming dance. But the real focus should be on the oft-overlooked prior verse. When those who were carrying the Ark of the Lord had taken six steps, David sacrificed a bull and a fattened calf (2 Samuel 6:13). Commentators, including Keil and Delitzsch, will not insist that this sacrificial event took place more than once, but they do observe that it could have been repeatedly enacted.

> These words are generally understood as meaning that sacrifices of this kind were offered along the whole way at the distance of six paces apart. . . . And even the immense number of sacrificial animals that would have required is no valid objection to such an assumption. We do not know what the distance really was: [but] . . . it was not so much as ten miles . . . so that a few thousand oxen and the same number of fatted calves would have been quite sufficient.[2]

It could be argued that the penalty of Perrez-Uzzah's death (2 Samuel 6:6-7) had been so extreme that David might well have decided that sacrifices every six steps would be the safest procedure.

Had I been David, I would not have been taking any chances. We do know that the journey was concluded with the final sacrifice of "seven bullocks and seven rams" (1 Chronicles 15:26, KJV).

The overall conclusion is inescapable. Bloodless worship which skirts the requirements of the remission of sin, holiness and sanctification is false worship. Worship which fails to honor God is false worship (Leviticus 10:3). Worship which attempts to manipulate or imitate the holy fire of Almighty God is false worship.

The holy fire revealed to Moses and Aaron, as well as to the entire nation of Israel, was nothing less than the revelation of the glory of God. To assume, as did Nadab and Abihu, that God's glory can be managed or manipulated by false fire is anathema. As A.B. Simpson so lucidly writes,

> The true fire is kindled at the Altar of Sacrifice. The false fire ignores the blood. There is much religious fire today which is merely the so-called "enthusiasm of humanity," or the emotion stirred by eloquence, art or zeal for some human cause and selfish interest. It is not enough to believe in the Spirit, for spiritism and spiritualism all do this; *but the true Spirit always comes in association with the blood* [emphasis added].[3]

The glory of God rests only where the blood of the crucified One has been applied.

### Endnotes

1. James L. Snyder, *In Pursuit of God* (Camp Hill, PA: Christian Publications, 1991), 45.

2. C.F. Keil and F. Delitzsch, *Commentary on the Old Testament* (Grand Rapids, MI: Eerdmans, 1980), volume 2 [4th of the ten], 335.

3. A.B. Simpson, *When the Comforter Came* (Camp Hill, PA: Christian Publications, 1991), 118-119.

# 9

Signs
and Signs

# Sequentially Fulfilled Signs

A SIGN, BIBLICALLY DEFINED, is a supernatural event which demonstrates spiritual power. For instance, at Bethlehem the angel of the Lord announced to the shepherds, "And this shall be a sign unto you; Ye shall find the babe wrapped in swaddling clothes, lying in a manger" (Luke 2:12, KJV). Jesus referred to the sign of Jonah (Matthew 12:39-40), and Paul warned the church against false signs (2 Thessalonians 2:9).

Old Testament prophecies of things to come, especially the sequential prophecy concerning Tyre in the book of Ezekiel, is strikingly illustrated by Walter Kaiser's comments reproduced here. After listening to him at the Evangelical School of Theology in Myerstown, Pennsylvania in the fall of 1999, I discovered his written text of the same material in my own library.

> Ezekiel 26:7-14 is an excellent example of this [sequential] category. This prophecy warned that many nations would come against Tyre; however, the focus of the prophecy was on Nebuchadnezzar's destruction of the mainland city of Tyre on the coast of the Mediterranean Sea. Suddenly in the midst of the prediction, there is a sudden switch from the third person masculine pronoun "he" and "his" to the third person plural "they."

Some have contended that since Nebuchadnezzar was frustrated because he was unable to capture the people of Tyre who merely moved from the mainland city to an island one half mile off-shore, that this was an indication that the prophecy was unfulfilled. But it is not an example of an unfulfilled prophecy, for it was fulfilled sequentially.

After the Babylonian nation worked its destruction of the mainland city in the 580's B.C., Alexander the Great came along in the 330's B.C. and finished the rest of the prophecy by throwing the "stones, timber and rubble" of the city that Nebuchadnezzar had destroyed "into the sea" in order to build a causeway from the mainland out into the Mediterranean Sea to the island city and capture the city. The prophecy was fulfilled, but it was fulfilled sequentially.[1]

## Endnote

1. Walter C. Kaiser, Jr., "Prophet, Prophetess, Prophecy," *Evangelical Dictionary of Biblical Theology,* ed. Walter A. Elwell (Grand Rapids, MI: Baker Book House, 1996), 646.

# Familian of Caesarea

## (circa A.D. 200)

"[A] CERTAIN WOMAN APPEARED here, who having represented herself as being ecstatic, presented herself as a prophetess and thus acted as if she were filled with the Holy Spirit. Moreover, she was so driven by the impetus of the chief demons that for a long time she disturbed and deceived the brotherhood by performing certain marvelous and portentous deeds. She also promised to make the earth tremble, not that the demon had power so great that on his own he could move the earth or shake the elements, but that sometimes an evil spirit by his foreknowledge and perception of a future earthquake, pretends that he will cause that which he has seen will occur. By these lies and boasts he had subjected the minds of individuals so that they obeyed him and followed wherever he was commanded and led.

"He also made that woman walk barefooted through frozen snow in harsh winter. She was not bothered in any way or injured by that activity. She also used to say that she was hurrying to Judea and Jerusalem, making out as if she had come from there.

"The demon also duped a presbyter named Rusticus here, likewise also another who was a deacon, so that they had sexual relations with that same woman. This was discovered a little later, for suddenly one of the exorcists appeared to her. He was a good man and one who always lived well in respect to religious discipline. This man, incited by the exhortation also of many brothers, who, themselves also being brave and worthy of praise, supported him in the faith, raised himself up against the evil spirit to conquer it.

"The spirit, by subtle intrigue, had predicted a little earlier that some adverse and faithless tempter would come. Nevertheless, that exorcist, inspired by the grace of God, bravely stood his ground and showed that spirit, which was previously thought to be holy, to be most wicked."[1]

Further, it is the opinion of an exceptionally knowledgeable writer and Montanistic scholar, Christine Trevett, that based on the Familian account, the woman succumbed to exorcism.[2]

### Endnotes

1. Ronald E. Heine, *The Montanist Oracles and Testimonia* (Macon, GA: Mercer University Press, 1989), 104-105.

2. Christine Trevett, *Montanism, Gender, Authority and New Prophecy* (Cambridge: Cambridge University Press, 1996), 171.

# Signs and Signs

---

T HE STORY OF KING OLAF TRYGVESSON of Norway (circa A.D. 995) is a fascinating one. Apparently he was in danger of mutiny from his own soldiers, but a seer who had been blessed by the God of the Christians warned him about the impending mutiny. The king would survive, the man said, and afterward he would be baptized. The events as predicted did come to pass, and King Olaf was dramatically converted and baptized.

Later, in the South Orkney Islands, King Olaf began his missionary career. "I want you and all your subjects to be baptized," he told the local leadership. "If you refuse, I will have you killed on the spot, and I swear that I'll ravage every Island with fire and steel."[1]

When one potential victim/convert was about to escape, Olaf "hurled a tiller at the young man, striking him on the head and killing him instantly,"[2] and when a slave offered the head of an enemy Olaf had been pursuing, "Olaf thanked him, gave him a gold ring, and then had him beheaded."[3] What today would be called "power encounters" leading to the turning of entire peoples to the name of Jesus Christ seem to have worked rather well in mid-career for Olaf, the murdering missionary.

This true account should give pause to today's missiologists who write breathlessly of power encounters taking place around the world where whole peoples are apparently turning to Jesus Christ. Is anyone listening when we suggest here that there may be power encounters and power encounters? A supernatural event in itself must not lead us merrily on our way to questionable theological conclusions. Murderers do not inherit the kingdom of heaven, nor do they possess eternal life (1 Peter 4:15; 1 John 3:15), baptized or not, prophesied to accurately or not.

## Signs in Scripture

There is a sense in which "signs and signs" is the essential idea of this book. When one begins to search the Scriptures for signs, the obvious place to start is Egypt (Exodus 7) where Moses, followed by the local magicians, performed several of them.

The prophet had God-empowered ability to perform miracles, but the magicians of Egypt also had power. It was not from God. This entire book emerges from this idea: *Expressions of divine power may sometimes be duplicated or imitated by occult means.* Moses and Aaron performed signs before Pharaoh. The magicians of Egypt followed suit, doing the same things but with a different power-source. However, the battle didn't last long. The magicians managed to duplicate (or is it imitate?) only the first three miracles. It all came to an abrupt halt when Aaron threw down his staff before Pharaoh (7:10), and it became a serpent. When the magicians of Egypt tried to duplicate the feat, "Aaron's staff swallowed up their staffs" (7:12).

The scene must have been dramatic indeed, and the process time-consuming. (How long would it take for one snake to devour several others?) Certainly, they had time enough at least to assimilate the significance of God's overwhelming power. (I'd like to imagine that Aaron's rod became a boa-like snake, the kind that lies like a log on a road. The magicians' snakes, I think, were like the pencil-like poisonous ones that make life miserable in Africa. In my mind's eye, I see the Lord's snake gobbling up the others in record time.) Following this dramatic display of divine power, a third encounter follows. The plague of frogs is unleashed by Moses' command and Aaron's rod (8:6). The magicians counter (8:7). The supernatural, still not limited only to God's servants, is also being exhibited by the Egyptians.

The first three miracles of the contest (7:14-24) are done—and God wins! Then Moses orders Aaron to stretch out his staff over the waters of Egypt. When he strikes the Nile, "all the water was changed into blood" (7:20). "But the Egyptian magicians [do] the same things by their secret arts" (7:22). Following that, as we know, Pharaoh's heart is hardened (7:22). The plague of gnats follows. God tells Moses to tell Aaron to stretch out his staff, strike the dust of the earth and "throughout the land of Egypt the dust will become gnats" (8:16). It happens! "But when the magicians tried to produce gnats by their secret arts, they could not" (8:18).

But that isn't the end of the contest. The succeeding plagues—flies, death to livestock, boils, hail, locusts, darkness and finally the destruction of the firstborn—all continue to flow through God's servants. Issued by God's command, carried forward through Moses and Aaron, the miraculous acts of divine judgment and persuasion continue, apparently without duplication or imitation by the magicians of Egypt. After being unable to duplicate the fourth sign, they finally capitulate: "This is the finger of God," they say (8:19). From that point on the magicians of Egypt fade from the scene.

An intriguing final statement in the matter comes from God just before the plague of hail. Jehovah makes clear to Pharaoh what He is doing: "But I have raised you up for this very purpose, that I might show you my power and that my name might be proclaimed in all the earth" (9:16). There is no more mention of the Egyptian seers in the Exodus account. Their significance has evaporated; their power has been demonstrated as being both inferior and limited. *Nevertheless, the Scriptures admit their supernatural ability.*

Here is a fascinating paragraph from a classic work, *Christian Counseling and Occultism.*

In the Old Testament the conviction already prevails that the nature of a sign . . . is not ambiguous. The Israelites knew that anything surprising and fascinating could originate from other powers than God. It could be the work of magicians or some other elohim-powers; indeed, God could even permit some dangerous person to succeed in performing a miracle, in order to put His people to the test. In the New Testament the situation is even more precarious. For the word *semeion* is sometimes used of divine miracles (Mark 16:17; John 2:23; 4:54; 6:2; 9:16; 11:47; Acts 4:16; etc.), but sometimes also of demonic miracles (Matthew 24:24; Mark 13:22; 2 Thessalonians 2:9; Revelation 13:13; 16:14; 19:20). This double meaning of the term shows the difficulty of evaluating signs . . . the sign is in itself no indicator of the origin which inspires it. It requires the word of God as its interpreter and formal principle.[4]

Twenty-seven years after the citation above, Gregory Harris convincingly argues the same thing:

Strikingly the words used for the miracles of Christ and the apostles are also used of the miracles performed in the Tribulation by those in allegiance with Satan . . . the emphasis placed in the next verses [2 Thessalonians 2:9, 10] on "deceit" and "lie" indicate that these should be viewed as miracles leading to the acceptance of the lie associated with the claims of the man of lawlessness.[5]

If we are paying attention at all, we will soon figure out that there are signs and signs, miracles and miracles. In David Thompson's *Beyond the Mist* is a current-era account that could probably be duplicated in any country in the world. He is describing the worship of Bwiti, a spirit god of Gabon, Africa.

> Bwiti's worshipers learned that their god would materialize at their gatherings if they danced to the pounding of the drums. They learned that Bwiti was pleased when they sang or chanted songs praising his power and greatness over and over until their minds were numb.[6]
>
> When the *ngangas* [witch doctors] and their followers submitted their bodies to Bwiti and drank moderate quantities of *iboga* [fermented drink], the spirit enabled them to perform unbelievable acrobatic feats, sometimes leaping five, even six feet up into the air from a standing position. Men almost routinely walked on live coals without burning their feet. There were other bizarre demonstrations of superhuman power involving the reproductive organs best left undescribed. During these seances, it became commonplace for Bwiti to appear as a shimmering, pale form. When Bwiti was pleased, he gave the *ngangas* the power to perform public miracles, such as causing it to rain on only one house at a time or making tongues of fire appear in the air.[7]

Though apparently there were no resurrections of the dead among the followers of Bwiti, Dr. Thompson describes a levitation procedure that accompanied burials.

> Bwiti obscured that failure [to raise the dead] by staging a spectacular miracle during a Bwitist's funeral. When a great Bwitist lay dying, he could request to be carried to his grave, not by his fellowmen but by Bwiti himself. . . .
>
> As the tempo of the drums increases, the men dance, encircling the body. They sing and dance in unison, calling on Bwiti to come and carry the body to the grave. The

singing and dancing last for hours, but the men show no signs of fatigue. Suddenly, the pitch of the drums changes and the air becomes electric. As on cue, the dancers turn towards the lifeless body and without touching it extend their hands. The body stirs, then stiffly rises, lifted by an invisible power that seems to emanate from the dancers' hands. Holding their fingers inches from the body, the men move trancelike down the torch-lit path leading to the cemetery some fifty yards from the village. Supported by nothing visible, the body moves through the village and down the path between two rows of men, floating in the air until the group stands at the foot of the open grave.

At this point, Thompson, a highly credentialed and skilled surgeon from America, can hardly restrain his amazement.

What follows is impossible to attribute to anything but the supernatural. The drums pound with new intensity. Waving their hands rhythmically toward the dead man's head, the Bwitists [without touching] stand the body upright. With every change in position the drums renew their intensity. Still suspended in air, the body turns until its back is to the grave. With one final, almost unbearable paroxysm of the drums, the Bwitists lower the body until it hovers parallel to the ground. Hands still extended, [and still not touching it] the Bwitists lower the body into the grave until it settles firmly on the bottom. When it is over, the exhausted pallbearers barely manage to stagger back to the village before falling onto their mats. It will take days for them to recover.[8]

Before moving on to supernatural sign manifestations from Almighty God, I must pause to explain that now in Gabon the power of

Bwiti has been broken throughout the country, broken by the preaching of the Christian gospel and the message of Jesus Christ. When I returned for a second visit there a few years ago, the only way to describe what was happening then is that the Gabonese were rushing pell-mell into the kingdom of God. Explosive church growth was taking place in a nation once so very dark.

## Signs in Pennsylvania

Now, on the positive side, one of the most helpful and trustworthy books on miracles I have ever encountered is Richard Harvey's *Seventy Years of Miracles*. It is filled with remarkable incidents, including this one.

> On July 5, 1905, in a tumbledown shack that was called a parsonage, in Grove City, Pennsylvania, a cross-eyed, tongue-tied "blue" baby was born to Emma and Henry Harvey. The parents were told that it was only a matter of hours before the baby would die.
>
> Not convinced, the father went immediately to God in prayer, "[E]ven though the physicians said it was impossible for us to have another child, You have given us one. Would You reveal to us what You have to say concerning our son?" Then, for an answer, he went, as usual, to God's Word.
>
> In Psalm 118, verse 17, God gave him this promise: "I shall not die, but live, and declare the works of the LORD." As far as that young father was concerned, it was a definite promise to him that the child would live and serve the Lord. And my father was right—because over 70 years later, here I am! . . .
>
> When I was 11 months old, I contracted double pneumonia and whooping cough. A nurse who was visiting the home and assisting my mother came and told my father

that I had died. Father said, "Don't tell his mother. He's not dead." He knelt by my crib and reminded God of His promise until he was satisfied that God had answered prayer and the crisis was past.

When I was about a year old, my parents were sure I was cross-eyed. It was not just a weakness, but something that looked permanent. So one day they clasped hands over my crib and laid their hands on me and asked God to straighten my eyes. And He did it! (I'm homely enough now, but I'm sure I must have been far worse as a cross-eyed baby!). . . .

Before I was four years old, a nurse visited our home. My parents said to her, "Our son seems to have normal intelligence." (Now, you may doubt that and think it parental prejudice, but that's what they said.) "But Richard won't talk. We can't get him to say anything." I hadn't even said, "Mama" or "Daddy." Instead I had sounds for everything I wanted.

The nurse looked into my mouth and said, "Reverend Harvey, your son is very badly tongue-tied. There is a string at the roof of his mouth, as well as under his tongue." When she left, my mother and father knelt beside me, laid their hands on me and prayed. Again my father quoted the promise, "I shall not die, but live, and declare the works of the Lord." He prayed, "Lord, You said not only that my son would live and not die, but that he would declare the works of the Lord. He cannot declare Your works with his tongue tied."

God loosed my tongue. Sometimes I think He did too good a job—for it has many times gotten me into trouble! I began to speak at four years and some of my relatives said I made up for it in the next two years.[9]

The most recent edition of Harvey's biography includes on its cover an artist's rendition of the following incident taken from a newspaper photograph at the time.

During our time in Chicago, *The Tribune* ran a full-page ad about a boat excursion on Lake Michigan. I looked at that ad with great longing. Both my brother and my mother watched me as I stared at it.

"Dick, you'd like to go on that boat, wouldn't you?" Lynn asked.

"I sure would," I replied.

"I'll tell you what I'll do," he said. "We'll put a bank on the table and all of us will put our spare cash into it. The night before the boat sails, we will open the bank. If there is enough for all of us to go, we'll go, and if there isn't enough for all of us to go, then none of us will go. Is this a fair agreement?"

I agreed it was. I was willing to grasp at any hope at all. . . . We all did our part in putting what we could into the bank on the table.

As a boy, it was difficult for me to wait for the opening of the bank. The occasion is still fresh in my memory: I can see my brother trying to use a knife to slip the coins out of the acorn crockery bank and because of the slowness of the process, finally taking a hammer and smashing it, causing the money to roll on the table. I was very excited as I watched him count it. And I was heartbroken when he announced it was $1.77 short.

It was more than I could take. I ran out of the house and went behind an old barn that was still at the back of the property and there I burst into tears. When I got control of myself, I returned to the house and my brother said, "Dick, I think we'd better stick to our agreement. We can't go on the excursion, but tomorrow you and I will go down and watch the big boat sail."

The next morning Lynn and I got up early. After he had done some chores, we took a streetcar to the Chicago Loop. We stood on the bridge at a good vantage point to observe all the excitement on the pier below. The flags were flying, the band was on the ship's deck playing, and many, many people were waiting to board the ship.

The gangplank was lowered and the chain let down. The people poured onto the boat. In a short time the bell sounded, the whistle blew, and the chain was pulled across the gangplank.

Many of those left behind were very disappointed. Such cursing and swearing I had never heard before. As I remember, one man was permitted to crawl under the chain and go up the gangplank. The bell on the ship rang once again, the whistle blew, the gangplank was pulled aboard, and the ropes to the pier were loosened.

And then, before our eyes, that giant ship, the *Eastland,* tipped over in the Chicago River. Something had happened on shore that had caused the ship's passengers to rush to one side. About the only ones saved were those who had been on the top deck. Many of these crawled to shore over the bodies of those beneath them.

Soon, men were piling human bodies on the pier like one might stack boxes. The city sent dump wagons pulled by horses to carry the corpses to the funeral parlors.

God's act of withholding $1.77 had almost certainly saved my life.[10]

There are many other similar stories from the life of Richard Harvey. I knew him well. And loved him greatly. His death at eighty-six was a profound personal loss. David Thompson I know also. He is a career missionary, a skillful surgeon and a godly man. I believe that these true accounts serve to drive home a vital lesson. There are two sources in the supernatural realm, and they are not always so easily categorized as the examples I have chosen. That is why we must be sure—repeat, sure—which kingdom is staging the event. "Test everything. Hold on to the good" (1 Thessalonians 5:21). As one of my friends says, "Either the Lord is leadin' or the devil is dealin'."

## Endnotes

1. James Reston, Jr., *The Last Apocalypse* (New York: Doubleday, 1998), 22.

2. Ibid., 24.

3. Ibid., 25.

4. Kurt Koch, *Christian Counseling and Occultism* (Grand Rapids, MI: Kregel Publications, 1965), 272.

5. Gregory Harris, "Satan's Deceptive Miracles in the Tribulation," *Bibliotheca Sacra* 156, July-September, 1999, 311.

6. David Thompson, *Beyond the Mist* (Camp Hill, PA: Christian Publications, 1998), 18.

7. Ibid., 19.

8. Ibid., 25-26.

9. Richard H. Harvey, *70 Years of Miracles* (Camp Hill, PA: Horizon Books, 1992), 29-31.

10. Ibid., 35-38.

# 10

Healing

and Healing

# Cancer—A Healing Encounter with God

*by Timothy Owen*

IN THE FALL OF 1958, my senior year at Wilson High School in Portland, Oregon, I noticed that the lymph nodes in my neck were swollen. My parents and others noticed it too as the swelling increased. I went to our family doctor, a general practitioner, for a diagnosis. He thought it was just the result of an infection that would soon pass.

My sister provided baby-sitting for a family, the father/husband of which was an internist. One evening when he came to pick up my sister to do some baby-sitting, he gave me a cursory exam. He was concerned, and so he requested that I come in for an appointment with him in his office the next day.

A biopsy was performed soon thereafter. The results were positive. I had Hodgkin's disease. The doctor ordered a schedule of radiation treatments. As I began to undergo these treatments, I was warned not to allow any trauma to the radiated areas. Before being diagnosed with this cancer, I was on the wrestling team which I, of course, had to quit. However, perhaps because I was in denial and certainly being careless, one day after school, as I was watching the wrestling team, I gave in to the temptation to wrestle a little bit.

Soon the cancer metastasized, spreading throughout my body. I had swollen lymph glands in every location where they existed—including elbows, armpits, knees and, most critically, my chest. I also began to experience other symptoms such as night sweats, severe weight loss and increasing pain. Gradually I reached the point where I was critically ill.

My parents, long-time members of a church with good teaching on divine healing, called for the elders of the church to anoint me and pray for me. They also called in other pastors and evangelists to pray for me.

My sense of the spiritual significance of this event was small. As far as I was concerned, I was just sick and bewildered about it. I don't remember praying much about it or struggling with God or even having a fear of death. I did take comfort in my belief that I wasn't the only one who had gone through this kind of thing. Others had been able to handle it; I could too.

I have often wondered if perhaps God was using this more in my mother's spiritual life at the time than in mine. I do remember her being in great turmoil and in much prayer about this situation. I really see her as the main player, spiritually, in this whole scene, with my having a supporting role.

Again I was admitted to the hospital. The doctors had to use very strong medication to alleviate my pain and allow me to sleep. Every morning I would awaken, step on the scales and find myself another five pounds lighter. The doctor prescribed a dose of primitive chemotherapy called Nitrogen Mustard. One dose was administered. My condition worsened.

I hated being in the hospital and convinced my mother to persuade the doctor to let me go home. My mother told me later that she and the doctor had had a conversation about my prognosis. It was Wednesday, and he predicted that by the weekend I would be in a coma, at which time an ambulance would transport me back to the hospital where the medical people would care for me until I died.

But mother had heard from God. He wanted to heal me. "Doctor," she said, "God is going to heal my son."

The doctor, being a wonderful man but an agnostic, patronizingly responded, "That's fine. You hang on to that faith. You're going to need it."

Mom said, "No, God's going to heal him."

I was overjoyed to be back in the comforts of home and out of the sterile, lonely hospital with its tasteless food. I immediately began to heal. I ate lots of mom's great meals and began to gain weight. The symptoms of night sweats and pain left. That Sunday I went to church and the next day, Monday, I returned to school. My classmates and teachers were delightfully surprised to see me.

Three weeks later I wanted to go skiing on Mt. Hood with some of my friends, and my mother allowed me to go. Though several of these friends later came down with the flu, I stayed healthy!

I was not strong enough to try out for the track team that spring, but I gradually regained my strength. I could feel the cancer being flushed out of my body. That summer I worked on my dad's construction project. In the fall, I went off to college in Southern California and played on the football team.

One day the coach called me in to tell me he couldn't let me play. He had been reading through the players' files and discovered I had had cancer. I was very disappointed. I decided to make a deal with him—I would go to the American Cancer Society office in Los Angeles and have a physical. If they would clear me to play, then I would play. He agreed.

I went to the clinic; they examined me and could find no evidence of cancer, so they gave me permission to play football. Still my coach was not convinced. So I went to the City of Hope, a hospital that specializes in cancer treatment. While I was there, the doctor in charge called my mother to verify my story. After she affirmed my history, the doctor exclaimed, "I want to tell you, Mrs. Owen, that I have larger lymph nodes than he has. I can't believe this, except for God!"

Needless to say, his exam also cleared me to play. I had a great season.

The doctor had said that due to the treatments I had undergone, I would likely be sterile. Later, when my wife, Edie, gave birth to Randy, our firstborn, my mother called the doctor to tell him the good news. The doctor's response was, "Well, maybe he never had cancer."

If I didn't have cancer, I was surely very sick with something life-threatening. It was more than a bad case of the flu! If I didn't have cancer, what did I have? Further the doctor had consulted with a team of doctors concerning my case. Did they all misdiagnose it?

I didn't come to realize the full spiritual significance of the illness until later. After I was healed, I had a fear of recurrence. The doctor told me this fear was called "sophomore's disease." He said that it is the sophomores in medical school who study pathology, and each night they are convinced they have the disease they studied that day!

So with anything unusual I felt physically, I feared the cancer was returning. At such times when this occurred and I was in a bad place spiritually, I would fear facing God and would confess my sin, repent and live righteously. However, when the threat passed, I would revert to my sinful pattern. This was my spiritual lifestyle until I was twenty-eight.

By then I was a seminary graduate, licensed in The Christian and Missionary Alliance and serving as a youth pastor in an Alliance church. I was also married and had a one-year-old son. Spiritually, I had hardened my heart against God and His call to righteousness. I did so because I didn't believe I could, or He could, or anyone could ever deliver me from the power of sin. So I lived a hypocritical life, presenting myself as a good Christian on the one hand and living a secret life of concealed sin on the other.

God, in His goodness, dramatically interrupted that pattern. In January of 1970, symptoms appeared, indicating the return of the cancer. A big lump swelled on the side of my neck. Night sweats and fevers were common. My family doctor, knowing my health history, said the Hodgkin's disease was back. I went through the same repentance pattern as before. When the biopsy report said the mass on my neck was merely a nerve tumor and that I did not have cancer, I went back to my sin.

Then one evening—March 23, 1970, to be exact—I was at home with my wife and son. I was reading a book when I felt a strange sensation in my head. I feared it was a brain hemorrhage. I was certain I was about to die. I reasoned that it was too late to call a doctor or get to the hospital. Nobody could help me. This was different than cancer. This threatened immediate death.

Today if this were to occur, I believe it would be diagnosed as a panic attack. In 1970, that diagnosis was not common. In any case, I was sure I was going to die very soon.

I hadn't prayed in a long time. I thought about whether I believed God existed. I concluded that I did. I wondered what He would do when I died and faced Him, which I thought was coming very soon.

I remembered back to some Scriptures I had memorized as a child. "If we confess our sins, he is faithful and just and will forgive us our sins and purify us from all unrighteousness" (1 John 1:9). I thought of how undeserved it would be for me to be able to be forgiven just before I died, but I didn't want to face the alternative. So, with a little faith, I confessed my sin, until then hidden, and hoped for forgiveness.

By then, my wife knew that something was wrong. I asked her to call an ambulance. I remember thinking that she could pay for it with the death benefit from my life insurance. The ambulance transported me to the hospital. My senior pastor and his wife met us there.

The doctor examined me and could find nothing wrong. He asked if I had been experiencing any stress in my life. I replied that there was nothing more than usual. We went back home. I was still convinced that my life was about to end. The pastor and his wife met us back at the house, had prayer with us and left.

At the same time, I made a very significant decision. With a great sense of peace flooding my heart, I decided that I would confess my sin, my hypocritical life, to Edie. I had just confessed it to God. I was about to die. What did I have to lose by confessing it to my wife? I felt that I owed her honesty.

As I confessed my sinful life to her, she too had a profound spiritual experience. She had been praying that night. Until then, she had feared my death from cancer and didn't want to lose me. By the time 1970 came around and we had been married seven years, she concluded that she could do without me!

I had abused her, not physically, but emotionally and spiritually. I was overbearing and argumentative. Being a better arguer than she was, I was able to talk her into and out of things that she knew better than to do or not do. I had manipulated her to the point that she had lost all self-confidence.

So, that crucial night, she prayed, "Lord, take him. I can live without him, and I want to live for You."

When I didn't die as I told her I was going to do, she concluded that God hadn't answered her prayer. But when I confessed to her, she experienced the presence and love of God in a brilliant and dynamic way that completely filled and inspired her. God reminded her that He would take care of her in *any circumstance, and she marks that night as a most important spiritual turning point.*

We went to bed and fell asleep. I didn't expect to wake up. In fact, I was counting on not waking up. I had confessed my sin to God, reasoning that I could afford to do so because I wouldn't have long to live. For such a short span of time, I could live a holy life—but if I had to live for another day or week or more, I knew I could not be holy that long. Then I would be back to despair!

I woke that next morning. I was confused. I just did the rote things. I got up, prepared for and went to the office to work. All the while I was wondering about what I would do when a temptation came along. I knew I would sin again. I had never successfully resisted sin in certain situations, and I knew I would fail again.

Sure enough, midway through the morning I needed to run an errand. Along the route, I faced a temptation. I was very frustrated. I knew it would happen again! And so I angrily said to God, "Here I am, facing temptation. Last night You tricked me into confessing my sin with the hope of death. Now I am still alive, and I have to face this! I cannot be responsible for this temptation. I cannot bear it! It's Your problem!"

I can't vouch for the theological accuracy of that prayer, but I believe that God heard my heart cry of desperation and delivered me. The next thing I knew, the temptation was gone. It had not turned to sin! For me, this was a first-time experience! I was so profoundly struck by it that I had to pull over to the side of the road and think about it for a while.

As I did, I retraced the events of the recent hours. I concluded that God had broken me and forced me into an impossible situation that caused me to be desperately dependent on Him. When I cried out to Him, He gave me power over the sin. In the next hours and days, I searched the Scriptures for an interpretation of this experience. I realized that God had filled me with His Spirit. He was empowering me to live righteously.

From then on, every time I faced temptation I began to repeat that pattern of desperate prayer and was thereby enabled to overcome. God was giving me lessons on walking in the Spirit. Romans 7, 8 and 12 and Galatians 5 were becoming my experience.

Meanwhile, my wife was undergoing her own transformation, learning anew to live for God. We didn't know what was ahead, but we were excited and ready for whatever came. This experience transformed our marriage, our ministry and our lives.

In retrospect, as I consider this sequence of events in my life, I believe that God had it all arranged in order to glorify Himself in my life. Now I know at least some of what God planned when I came down with cancer in 1959.

## Postscript

My son, Randy, is a medical doctor. He received his undergraduate training at Seattle Pacific University, his medical training at Columbia College of Physicians and Surgeons in New York City, which is the oldest medical school in the nation. He completed his residency in General Surgery at Einstein Medical School and Hospital in the Bronx and is now a Fellow in head and neck surgery at Montefiore Hospital in that same borough of New York City.

Due to his involvement in head and neck surgery, he questioned me about my health history, in particular regarding the Hodgkin's disease, and asked if I could procure a copy of my medical records for him to study. After some delay, my oncologist found the records.

Randy asked him about the diagnosis, extent of involvement, prescribed therapy and outcome. The biopsy report detailed the measurements of the swellings. There was a formal diagnosis of Hodgkin's disease due to the presence of Reid-Sternberg cells.

Randy was stunned. The doctor said the prescription for therapy was to apply 1200 rads of radiation therapy to the right side and 900 to the left. He reported that upon receiving the radiation, I went into crisis with metastasis throughout my body. The nodes in my abdomen were so large that they were manually palpable.

Randy asked the oncologist, "Don't you think it is remarkable that my father survived this disease?"

After a pause, he responded, "Yes."

Randy asked further, "If a patient came into your office today and presented these symptoms, even with the current therapies, what chance of survival would you give him?"

After some thought the doctor replied, "Oh, five percent or less."

I had never had medical confirmation of my disease and healing before this. All I ever heard was from my mother passing on information she received. I am very encouraged by this development. It defines the work that God did. My healing was indeed a miracle![1]

## Endnote

1. Timothy Owen, *Cancer—A Healing Encounter with God* (Camp Hill, PA: Christian Publications, 2001). The booklet also appears in *Healing Voices* (Camp Hill, PA: Christian Publications, 2000) as "God Healed Me of Hodgkin's Disease."

# The Wart Remover

*by Charles Hill, as told to George McPeek*

MY STEP-GRANDFATHER WAS A WART REMOVER. He used his powers on many different people, but especially on his grandchildren. When I was ten years old, I had warts all over my right hand, probably a dozen or more—between my fingers, on top and underneath. The doctor tried ointments and other treatments. At one point my hand was bandaged for two months. Nothing worked, so my mother and father took me to my grandfather.

He was a strange man, and I didn't like to be around him much. One time, he took me for a walk in the forest, when he pushed a stick in the ground, but left half of it sticking out. "Now watch as the devil pulls it down," he said. And sure enough the stick began to sink into the ground all on its own until it disappeared.

Another thing I remember about my grandfather was his superstitiousness. Once when he was driving me somewhere, a black cat ran across the road in front of us. Grandfather slammed on his brakes and turned around so the cat would not cross his path. He told me it was very bad luck if that happened.

When we got to my grandfather's place, he sat down on the sofa. "Do you want those warts?" he asked.

"No, I don't," I said.

"Do you want me to have them?" he asked.

"Yes," I answered.

At that point, he rubbed both hands all over my right hand where all the warts were. He made sure to touch every one with both hands. Nothing happened right away, and I was a bit disappointed. But the next morning when I woke up, the warts were gone. Full of excitement, I ran to my mother with the news.

"I knew he could do it," she said. He did the same with other relatives, including my mother, a niece and a first cousin.

In 1965, Grandfather had a cerebral hemorrhage and was taken to the Veteran's Hospital in Louisville, Kentucky. I was a junior in high school at the time. We got a call that he was dying, so our whole family drove down to see him one last time. By that time, he already had been in a coma for three days. When we got to the hospital, we walked into his room as a family. He was motionless. I placed my right hand on his, and it moved under my touch.

The next morning he passed away. About thirty minutes later, the nurse took my parents, my sister and me into the room to be with him. When we got to the edge of the bed, we looked at his hands. They were covered with warts which had not been there before.

The nurse sort of screamed and ran from the room. In a few moments, the doctor hurried in to check out her report. He couldn't explain it. The medical records showed he was admitted without warts, but when he died, they were all over his hands.

Mother said, "Every wart he ever took from you kids he got back." She was a strong believer in the occult and was involved in witchcraft and fortune-telling, so this seemed logical to her.

As for Grandfather, he would never tell how he removed warts. He said if he gave away his secret, he would lose the power.[1]

### Endnote

1. Transcribed and edited by George McPeek from an interview with Charles Hill, conducted on November 22, 2000.

# Healing and Healing

M Y PURPOSE IN THIS CHAPTER is not to enumerate the ways in which true and false spiritual experiences are to be discerned, but to demonstrate sufficiently well so as to be convincing, I hope, that there are polarities in healing as well as in the other areas already considered.

For as long as I can remember I have always believed in divine healing. Ever since I began to know anything about the Bible, I have believed that God can and does heal the sick. That belief, however, was a mile wide and an inch deep. I had no immediate expectation that I myself might ever see something so marvelous and miraculous as divine healing. It was, in my mind, for other people and places.

Then came my preparation for ordination. I was obligated to read, among other things, A.B. Simpson's *The Gospel of Healing,* and to provide the ordaining council with a written review. It became a life-changing event. For the very first time I began to dare to hope to believe that Jesus Christ still healed in the here and now. It was a fresh and powerful realization.

The Scriptures are clear. In the Old Testament, God announces Himself as "the LORD, who heals" (Exodus 15:26). The psalmist too sees Jehovah as the forgiver of every iniquity and the healer of every disease (Psalm 103:1-3). Isaiah, the prophet, anticipates the cross of Jesus and makes clear that with His stripes we are healed (53:4-5).

In the New Testament, Jesus heals the sick on every side, and His healing ministry is linked to Isaiah's prophecy (Matthew 8:16-17). The apostles, like their Master, drive out demons and heal the sick (Luke 10:1). Peter stretches forth his hand to the man crippled from birth and heals him in Jesus' name (Acts 3:1-6). James invites the sick to seek the healing ministry of the elders and affirms that the prayer of faith will save the sick (James 5:15). These were the things I was learning as I prepared for ordination.

Moreover, during that same time period, I was pastoring a small church. One of my parishioners was a country storekeeper who had begun attending the services. Though his wife was 200 miles away in a hospital, he unhesitatingly asked prayer for her. I remember the two of us standing among the grain sacks of his warehouse praying for his wife to be healed. The news a short time later was fabulous—she had dramatically recovered after our prayers. For me, it was the first inkling that the Holy Spirit was still able to work in this powerful way.

On another occasion in a subsequent pastorate, a woman came to me one Saturday.

"Pastor," she said, "would you pray for me?" She showed me her eczema-covered hands. I reached for my copy of *The Gospel of Healing*, gave it to her and advised her to prepare herself for the communion service on the following day when the elders would be available for prayer.

Sunday came. After celebrating the Lord's Supper, we invited those who wished prayer for healing to come and sit on the front pew. She was one of the first to come. We gathered around and prayed simply, without ostentation or demonstration of any kind, a quiet, plain request about an obvious need.

We were not prepared for what happened. As soon as the "amen" Susan began to wave her hands around excitedly. The ec- instantly disappeared! The young people from the choir around to take a closer look. One dear saint told me later that after witnessing that event she had not been able to sleep the entire night. When Susan showed me her hands the next day, the skin was as fresh and smooth as a baby's.

In yet another incident, a friend named Duane and I had driven 100 miles or more over tortuous terrain to a wilderness settlement to minister to the Cree Indians of Northern Alberta. In the very first service we prayed for a boy whose jacket covered a twisted arm. They told us that he had been born that way. The next day, the arm was straight, and the boy, about eleven years old, was shaking every hand in sight with the arm that had been crooked the night before. During the long ride home, I could think of nothing else than that young boy's miracle.

I believe in divine healing!

## Other Healings

Let's look at healings in other contexts. The account that follows is particularly significant to me in that I know the son of W.G. Weston and have no doubt about the authenticity of the events described below.

"God has done a creative work in my body." The following is a testimony written under that title by Rev. Harold M. Rhoads, Jr., published in 1943.

> At the age of five I was stricken with pleuropneumonia, and was unconscious for almost two weeks. There was absolutely no hope for my recovery. The trained nurse, who was caring for me, had packed her things and was ready to leave, as I was expected to be dead by the following morning.
>
> Our family physician, Dr. P. Brooke Bland, a noted specialist in Philadelphia and vicinity, made a call at midnight and discovered a slight change for the better in my condition. If I continued to improve, he said, he would have to

operate, which he did. He removed two ribs and two quarts of pus-congestion from my pleurisy sac, and drained the same through a rubber tube which was in my side for six weeks.

The doctor stated it would be a miracle if I lived to be twenty-one, and if so I would always have weak lungs and probably develop tuberculosis. A year ago, at the age of thirty-six, a life insurance doctor examined me and stated that my lungs were perfect and no trace of tuberculosis could be found. Seldom do I contract even a cold. Only God spared my life, for His purposes, from this serious illness.

Less than a year later, overnight I was stricken with infantile paralysis. My body was paralyzed so I was unable to move my head from one side to the other, or to move my fingers. A specialist was called, and he stuck his scarf pin into the sole of my foot. I felt it but could not move away. Since I had not lost the sense of feeling they gave me a slight chance of recovery, but doubted if I would ever walk again.

Up to this time my parents were not Christians. . . . They did everything that possibly could be done for me, going to great expense to try various helps. My condition improved and soon I was strong enough to sit on the floor, and thus I learned to creep the second time. Gradually I could walk by holding on to various pieces of furniture in the room. Later I walked with crutches, using both at first, then with one and finally without the aid of anything.

My father, having been converted in "Billy" Sunday's Philadelphia campaign, learned of the Hebron Tabernacle whose pastor at that time was Dr. F.H. Senft. My father took me to special meetings there which were being conducted by that godly . . . preacher, "Daddy" E.M. Collette.

His preaching encouraged my faith. Soon after these services, Warren Collins, a lay-preacher conducted meetings and gave his testimony as to how God had healed him of a throat goiter. I was anointed that evening, and my left ankle (which was so deformed that holes were worn through the side of the shoes at the ankle bone quicker than through the soles, because my foot dragged on the pavement with every step) immediately straightened up, and has remained straight to this day. My left leg, which was three-fourths of an inch shorter than the right one grew one-half inch in several weeks and my limp was greatly reduced.

God did great and mighty things in those meetings. My noted improvement, and my photograph, were included with other testimonies of healing and miracles in *The Philadelphia Inquirer*.

Six years ago I attended the Summit Grove Camp Meeting in New Freedom, Pennsylvania, where W.G. Weston was the evangelist. One night he told of a girl in Atlanta, Georgia, whom God had wonderfully healed. Her case was similar to mine in that there was not much sinew or muscle on one hip. My left hip was much smaller than the right one and each time I purchased a suit of clothes the tailor had to alter the trousers by removing a piece of material from that side so they would not look baggy or bulky.

Brother Weston prayed that night that God would do a "creative" work of healing in my body, causing muscle and sinew to develop on that hip. I trusted God for this healing. Several years later I purchased a new suit at the same department store and had the same tailor examine the trousers I had bought. He exclaimed that they fitted me perfectly, different from any that I had ever bought before.

I stepped on the scales and discovered I had gained considerable weight, the majority of it being on that left hip. Since that time I have gained about thirty pounds and am stouter than I have ever been.

My heart is full of praise and gratitude to God for sparing me from death's door and doing for me all that He has done.[1]

To rehearse the acts of God is an inspiring and powerful enterprise. But there is another kind of healing. Those who say that all healing is from God are, at the least, naive. Satan has his ways as well.

John L. Nevius, in his classic book on demonization in China, narrates a pagan observer's account of demonic healing obviously not from God Almighty.

The demon often bade us [the observer and others] not be afraid of it, saying it would not injure us, but that, on the contrary, it would help us in various ways; that it would instruct me in the healing art, so that people would flock to me to be cured of their diseases. This proved to be true; and soon from my own village the people came bringing their children to be healed by the aid of the demon. Sometimes it would cure the sick instantaneously, and without the use of medicine. . . . Many diseases were not under its control, and it seemed as if it could perfectly cure only such as were inflicted by spirits . . . the demon said he had many inferior spirits subject to him. . . . It was through his assistance I should grow more and more skilled in healing diseases.[2]

Healing is a human passion in a sick world. No one, or at least very few, want to be ill. Healings *do* take place. I do not wish to debate that point. The reality of supernatural healing is assumed in the title of this book. How one might decide the source of physical healing is a book-length endeavor in itself. The major goal of these pages will be accomplished if the reader comes to the conclusion that there is indeed supernatural healing that emanates from not one, but two sources.

To the best of my knowledge, the illustrations I use from personal experience are authentic. The point is to realize at the deepest level that Satan heals too! It is the profound difference between these two classes of healings that I am attempting to portray in this chapter. A well-known author provides a classic case of demonic healing in the following incident, using what may be called "white magic."

A woman who was seriously ill lay in hospital suffering from shingles and leg ulcers. Her condition was so critical that the doctor ordered a nurse to remain by her bedside for the whole night. It was expected that she would die. Sitting next to her, the night nurse heard the patient begin to whisper, "Nurse, you can help me. Nurse, you can help me." The nurse felt afraid, but the woman kept on, "Nurse, you can help me." In the end the nurse asked the sick woman, "What do you want me to do? How can I help you?" The woman began to get excited and said to the nurse, "Put your hand on my legs and make the sign of the cross over them three times, then say the name of the Trinity and repeat the verse I will tell you." The night nurse was now even more frightened, but at that moment the doctor walked by the ward. Asking what she ought to do, the doctor replied, "Oh, do what she asks you. It might even help her. There's no hope for her from the medical point of view." She returned to the bed. Immediately the patient began to encourage her again to begin the charming process. Finally the nurse did what she asked, and made the sign of the cross three times over her body, murmuring the names of the Trinity and the spell she had been told. The patient relaxed. She could rest. The nurse, however, was suddenly overwhelmed by a tremendous agitation and fear.

In the days that followed the medical staff was astonished. The open ulcers on the woman's legs closed up almost at once, and within five days all symptoms of her illness had completely disappeared. The doctor who knew about the charming kept the incident to himself.

Today, six years have passed since the woman was healed, but the nurse who attended her has never been at peace since. She cannot pray. She cannot listen to the gospel without feeling a sense of disgust. She often feels as if she is in a daze, that she cannot concentrate properly, and she now suffers from a number of emotional disturbances. Because of her condition she came to see me in order to get some help through counseling. In her own mind she traces every one of the physical and emotional disturbances back to the night during which she sat with the woman. Without realizing it she had used white magic in order to heal the woman's complaint.[3]

This author's view (above) is that such healings carry with them an engramm,[4] a transference of evil upon the human psyche. The reason for including this story is that it is a supernatural healing *not* from the Lord Jesus Christ.

Similarly, the nineteenth century in America was much given over to spiritism which included automatic writing, apparitions, levitations and yes, physical healings.[5] Because occult power is one of the universal realities in this world, such incidents could be multiplied from every corner of the world. My purpose is not to do so, but to draw attention to the fact that supernatural healing can come from the darkness as well as from the Light of the World, Jesus Christ. Recognizing polarities such as these immediately expands the base of discernment in a life.

I would be remiss if I concluded this chapter without at least referencing one additional reality. Healing from an alternate Jesus or from the Virgin Mary is not healing from Jesus Christ, the Son of God who came in the flesh. Healings that emerge from pseudo-Christianity are among the most difficult to recognize and categorize. Still, the principle remains: There are polarities in supernatural healing, and we forget it at our peril.

## Endnotes

1. David J. Fant, *Modern Miracles of Healing* (Harrisburg, PA: Christian Publications, 1943), 101-103.

2. John L. Nevius, *Demon Possession and Allied Themes* (Grand Rapids, MI: Kregel Publications, 1894), 25-26.

3. Kurt Koch, *Demonology, Past and Present* (Grand Rapids, MI: Kregel Publications, 1973), 119, 122-123.

4. Ibid.

5. Merrill F. Unger, *Biblical Demonology* (Wheaton, IL: Scripture Press, n.d.), 161.

# 11

Deliverance
and Deliverance

# Demons in Gabon

*by Richard H. Harvey*

IN GABON WE SAW an outstanding example of the deliverance Christ can bring to a person who is possessed by demons. The victim's name was Edward. He was a young man, highly educated by Gabonese standards, and the superintendent of that nation's second largest school system.

Edward's troubles began when he became angry at his school board (which was directed by an American Mission) for rejecting his request for some desired equipment. Refusing to accept the board's explanation, Edward became bitter, resigned all his church responsibilities and eventually ceased to attend services. He also became sick.

Whatever his sickness was, he grew worse. He visited the community doctor, but the doctor could not help him. Edward then went to Libreville to the large government hospital. They could do nothing for him either.

He was forced to resign his position with the schools. Edward's parents, who were pagans, pressured him into taking a fetish. He took it and hid it secretly. Soon he became involved in former heathen practices and living as he had before he became a Christian. One day he went to a nearby village and secretly took a second wife, but let her remain in the village with her tribe. His health continued to deteriorate, and it soon was evident that he had gone insane. The Christian leaders all pronounced him demon possessed.

One day, Edward seemed to be rational for a few hours. He called his wife, who had remained true to God and to him during this terrible time, and explained to her all the things he had done, confessing his sin and adultery. He said to her, "I don't want to die with all these sins on my heart. Will you pray that God will heal me long enough that I can make things right before I die?" They prayed together, and he confessed his sins to Christ and sought forgiveness. But Edward went back into that terrible state of insanity.

After a couple of days, he awoke quite normal and immediately started out to fulfill his promises to God. He asked forgiveness of many he had wronged, restored some things he had stolen, returned to the village where he had the second wife and released her, satisfying both her and her parents according to their custom. Then he returned to his former state of insanity—only worse than before. His body grew weaker and his ravings increased.

One day in a rational moment, he called his wife to his side. "I believe God has accepted me, but if you could get some ministers, men of God who have faith, to come and pray for me, I believe God would heal me."

The very next day the missionary and I, unaware of the situation, drove into the village where Edward lived. The same day, the pastor of the local church returned from his vacation, and the district's national evangelist also arrived in town unexpectedly. Four ministers in town at the same time was not unusual, but God was arranging it all.

As soon as Edward's wife heard this, she sent a messenger for the four of us to come to their house on the hill. We learned that Edward's relatives from all over Gabon, including an uncle who was a notorious witch doctor, had come to the home for his death. We suggested that the wife bring Edward to the pastor's hut.

Soon we saw them coming down the hill. Edward was being led like a child. He was a sight—frail, dirty, his hair matted and unkempt, his fingernails like claws and his eyes staring and wild. His wife sat him on one of the few chairs in the hut and stood by his side with her hand on his shoulder to keep him under control.

We had a session of prayer for ourselves, asking God to cleanse our hearts from all sin, known and unknown. Then the missionary said, "Mr. Harvey, the pastor and evangelist wish you would direct the procedure."

From past experience I knew that singing is many times helpful in deliverance from demon possession. I also knew that there are certain songs that demons abhor—songs of praise to God, songs about the blood of Christ and songs about the name of Jesus. As we sang, Edward began to foam at the mouth and grew violent. Each of us prayed for him, and the demons were commanded to come out. Edward managed to get away from those who were holding him. He slid under the table and lay stiff in the center of the room.

We sang again. He screamed the most horrible scream I have ever heard. Once more, in the name of Jesus I commanded the demons to come out. They did so, but with a struggle that left him as dead. His wife was frightened—she thought he had died.

"Oh, no," I said, "he will be all right." That day I was grateful for every experience I had ever had in casting out demons.

Edward soon opened his eyes and crawled out from under the table. His eyes were clear. He stood and raised his hands toward heaven and cried out, "I'm free, I'm free! Thank God, I'm free!" Then he noticed his wife. He threw his arms around her and hugged and kissed her (a very uncommon practice for an African, as they seldom show affection in public).

Edward then tried to run his hands through his matted hair. He looked himself over. "I need a bath and a haircut. Oh, please excuse me." With his wife he walked up the hill. He returned in about a half hour so clean I would hardly have known him.

But that was not all. On his return, he asked the pastor to call the village together at the church. It was not necessary—the drums had already spread the news, and people came from everywhere. Edward stood and told his story, asking them for forgiveness and promising to make everything right that he had not settled previously. . . .

A public evangelistic meeting was held in the village that very night, and many turned to the Lord.[1]

### Endnote

1. Richard H. Harvey, *70 Years of Miracles* (Camp Hill, PA: Horizon Books, 1992), 189-194 (edited).

# The Jewish Exorcist

THIS INCIDENT IS TAKEN FROM the writings of T.K. Oesterreich. It is not a Christian exorcism, but is an example of the exorcisms that take place in most, if not all, the religions of the non-Christian world. Since it is remarkably like what I myself have seen in the Christian context and in the literature with which I am familiar, I believe it has the ring of authenticity.

A demonized young woman (a *dibbuk*) is seated in public view before a large audience. The demon is manifesting itself.

A murmur arose: "The rabbi is coming."

The crowd drew aside respectfully for the new arrival. A short, rotund little man came in sight, dressed from head to foot in white. Around the long white silk *taler* which fell to his feet was swathed a wide white sash, and his head was covered with a white silk *steimel* (fur-trimmed hat). The full cheeks hung like peaches [on] his face with its complexion of mingled blood and milk, while long bushy eyebrows overhung his eyes. . . . He entered at a run, chanting Hebrew verses, and followed by a secretary and servants . . . the rabbi began his address. "In the name of the 42 letters of the God with long sight, which indeed has no end; in the name of the lesser and greater celestial families; in the name of the chiefs of the bodyguard: Sandalfon, Uriel, Akatriel and Usiel, in the name of the potent Metateron surrounded with strength . . . I adjure thee, abject spirit, outcast from hell, to reply to my words and obey all commands!"

"Wilt thou or wilt thou not reply?" resumed the rabbi, making as if to strike the girl with the *loulaf*.

"Do not strike me!" implored the man's voice. "I will reply."

"What is thy name?"

"Christian Davidovitch."

Insulted by the Christian name, the rabbi spat out a response.

"I would know thy Jewish name." It was, as it turned out, Sarah.

. . . The rabbi changed colour and shook with rage and excitement . . . seized the *loulaf* and struck the girl violently in the face with it. Then an incredible thing happened: the girl had freed her hands with lightning speed and before anyone could prevent her she dealt the rabbi two resounding boxes on the ears.

A panic followed. The frightened crowd uttered cries and oaths, storming and weeping with excitement. Never had the like been seen. Nevertheless, strong arms had seized the sick girl. The rabbi struck her so furiously with the *loulaf* that her face streamed with blood; she collapsed with a terrible cry and became unconscious. At this moment a noise was heard at the window as if it had been struck by a small stone. Everyone rushed towards it and discovered in one pane a hole of the size of a pea through which aperture the spirit had fled. The girl was carried out.

They [the observers] all believed in the existence of the *dibbuk,* they had seen the spirit come out, they heard the impact on the window and seen the hole in the pane.[1]

Oesterreich finally observes, "This narrative, which offers in other respects no peculiar psychological feature, leaves the noise and the hole in the window unexplained."

## *Endnote*

1. T.K. Oesterreich, *Possession Demoniacal and Other* (New Hyde Park, NY: University Books, 1966), 208-210.

# Deliverance and Deliverance

———— ·····◦◉◦····· ————

T HE NEW TESTAMENT IS VERY CLEAR that Jesus Christ confronted the kingdom of Satan and drove out demons. The Synoptic Gospels of Matthew, Mark and Luke are filled with accounts of Jesus' conquest over dark powers. Nowhere is this more dramatic than in the exorcism of Legion that inhabited the man described in Mark 5:1-20. Even the residents of the area knew this man's story. He was an evil institution.

Throughout the entire scriptural account, evil spirits are malevolent powers who are in constant collision with the kingdom of God. These personages were not only consistently confronted by Jesus Christ but also by the seventy disciples He sent forth. They too discovered that the spirits were subject to them through the name of Jesus (Luke 10:1-20).

After Jesus was resurrected from the dead and received into heaven, the ministry of deliverance continued. When Philip the evangelist preached, the evil spirits left screaming (Acts 8:7). Later, Paul at Philippi drove a python spirit out of a teenage girl who had fortune-telling capacities (16:18). Clearly, the driving out of evil spirits accompanied the preaching of the gospel.

In the early Church, too, the phenomenon continued. In Ramsay MacMullen's *Christianizing the Roman Empire, A.D. 100-400,* a secularist viewpoint, he suggests that the primary factor in the

Christianization of the Roman Empire was the overwhelming significance of casting out demons. All other factors were secondary.[1] "The manhandling of demons—humiliating them, making them howl, beg for mercy, tell their secrets and depart forthwith—served a purpose quite essential to the Christian definition of monotheism: it made physically (or dramatically) visible the superiority of the Christian patron Power over all others."[2]

If we wished to take the time and space, we could provide abundant evidence to substantiate that the phenomena of deliverance persistently recurred through the centuries of Church history. Martin Luther was no exception. Though he seemed loathe at times to engage the demons directly, in his advice to a pastor who was experiencing poltergeist phenomena in his home, his remarks are clear: "Let Satan play with the pots. Meanwhile, pray to God with your wife and children and say, 'Be off, Satan! I'm lord in this house, not you. By divine authority I'm head of this household, and I have a call from heaven to be pastor of this church.' "[3]

The reality is that delivering people from demons is part of the Christian ministry experience. It is possible because Christians are indwelt by Jesus Christ who is in them (Colossians 1:27). In addition, Christians are seated with Jesus Christ in the heavenlies (Ephesians 2:6). He triumphed openly over all the dark powers at the cross and made a spectacle of their overthrow (Ephesians 1:22; Colossians 2:9-15). I have witnessed such phenomenon many times. It has a persistent and pernicious sameness to it. In fact, I see no true hope at all for the demonized apart from the ministry of Jesus Christ. He is the Deliverer—the only true Deliverer.

Another pastor and I were counseling a teenage boy. When we suggested the possibility of some kind of bondage in his life, he discounted the idea. Nevertheless, at some point in the conversation, I quietly began to address the spirits we knew were there: "Come out of him in the name of Jesus Christ. Is Jesus Christ Lord? Did Jesus Christ come in the flesh?"

Suddenly, the boy's voice changed and became more guttural. The answers now were, "No, no, no." As we persisted, suddenly the demonic bondage gave way. Rather gently, the teenager toppled off the organ bench on which he had been sitting. He stayed there on the floor for a short time, then seemed to recover. It was as if he had just run a marathon race. He was exhausted.

The pastor asked me: "What did you do?"

"Nothing!" I replied. "This was nothing more than the authority of the believer."

But this chapter is about deliverance *and* deliverance. Jesus said, "Watch out for false prophets. . . . Many will say to me on that day, 'Lord, Lord, did we not prophesy in your name, and in your name drive out demons . . . ?' Then I will tell them plainly, 'I never knew you. Away from me, you evildoers!' " (Matthew 7:15, 22-23).

This passage suggests that the apparent driving out of demons is not necessarily a work of Jesus Christ—or His followers—only. In Matthew 12:27 Jesus asks His critics, "And if I drive out demons by Beelzebub, by whom do your people drive them out?" In this case also, the apparent driving out of demons was taking place but not in the name of Jesus Christ. The critical question is: Were the demons really driven out? Can demons drive out demons? Can demons be truly driven out by any other than the Lord Jesus Christ?

If we move on to the book of Acts, we are introduced to the seven sons of Sceva and Paul's confrontation with them:

> Some Jews who went around driving out evil spirits tried to invoke the name of the Lord Jesus over those who were demon-possessed. They would say, "In the name of Jesus, whom Paul preaches, I command you to come out." Seven sons of Sceva, a Jewish chief priest, were doing this. One day the evil spirit answered them, "Jesus I know, and I know about Paul, but who are you?" Then the man who had the evil spirit jumped on them and overpowered them

all. He gave them such a beating that they ran out of the house naked and bleeding. (Acts 19:13-16)

Clearly, Paul had a ministry of deliverance, but there is another kind. Verse 13 in this passage says that these men had been going around driving out demons. How so? Certainly it was not originally in the name of Jesus Christ, but apparently by another method and perhaps in another name. *Authentic exorcisms are Christian only.* John Nevius' classic work on demon possession makes reference to non-Christian Chinese who were exorcists. Apparently they had to be male—and muscular—to prevail in the battles into which they fell: "Weak people cannot do these things; hence all of this class [of exorcists] are men in the strength of manhood."[4]

Clearly, they were not exorcists of the Christian faith. They were something else. Quite an extensive study could be made of exorcisms which exist in the various religions of the world.[5] All religions seem to have them. Animists certainly do. The Jews certainly did. One author mentions exorcistic practices among African tribes, Malay tribes and Islam.[6] And yet another author reminds us that

> many Christians use particular . . . [manifestations] to test the presence of the Holy Spirit, for these are easily applied. Some look for . . . [tongues], others for healings, miracles, ecstatic experiences and resurrections from the dead [and probably deliverances from demons]. But all of these are found in other major religions of the world and in tribal animism. . . .
>
> There are numerous testimonies of healings and other miracles performed by the Virgin of Guadeloupe, . . . Tirupathi Venkateswara in South India, Voodoo spirits in Latin America, the Buddha and many other gods, spirits and healers.
>
> Even the use of the name "Jesus Christ" is no test of the presence of the Holy Spirit. This name is widely used in

South American spiritism and in syncretistic Hindu-Christian movements in India. . . .[7]

Nevertheless, Satan's house cannot be divided against itself (Matthew 12:25-26). Every single deliverance that is not in the name and power of the Lord Jesus Christ is no more than the movement of soldiers in the army of Satan from one division to another. True deliverance is found in the Savior alone. Repeat, Satan's house is never divided against itself.

Today, in Christian contexts, there are pseudo-deliverances taking place on every side. In a western city, a certain man launched a "deliverance ministry." He was under no pastor's supervision and seemed to gravitate particularly toward young believers. After his ministrations, these new Christians were invariably worse off than before. It probably could be said that rather than ministering deliverance, he was loading up the victims with evil. This conclusion has been substantiated by several people who knew of this "ministry."

## The Marks of Authentic Deliverance

If true deliverance exists, certainly the opposite—false—must also exist. This, of course, is to understand what the Bible had been telling us all along: Even in deliverances, false and the true exist. What, then, are the marks of true deliverance from demonic powers? Let me posit the following for your careful consideration:

1. In true deliverances, the evil power is expelled. An alternate occult bondage is not substituted for the previous bondage,[8] nor does a Satanic feint[9] suffice. Even the relaxation of Satan's grip for a while to imitate release and freedom is not valid. To merit the term "true" the deliverance must be total and enduring

2. In true deliverances, Jesus Christ and no other is the deliverer. The absolute uniqueness of Jesus Christ, the Son of

God, precludes prayers to angels or saints or gods or to another "Jesus" or even to the Virgin Mary.

3. In true deliverances, the kingdom of God advances, and the kingdom of darkness is broken down against its will by the power of Jesus Christ.

4. In true deliverances, ministry is in and through the Name and work of the Lord Jesus Christ who came in the flesh. No other Jesus will do.

5. In true deliverances, all glory redounds to the Lord Jesus Christ.

6. In true deliverances, against the will of the Prince of Darkness, the victims find complete freedom in Jesus Christ.

Such deliverances do take place. Thank God for that. Hopefully, as the return of Jesus Christ comes ever nearer, such authentic deliverances will occur more frequently on every side, exalting the name that is above every name—the Lord Jesus Christ.

## *Endnotes*

1. C. Peter Wagner, *Confronting the Powers* (Ventura, CA: Regal Books, 1996), 100.

2. Ramsay MacMullen, *Christianizing the Roman Empire A.D. 100-400* (New Haven, CT: Yale University Press, 1984), 28.

3. Frederick S. Leahy, *Satan Cast Out* (Edinburgh: Banner of Truth Trust, 1975), 114.

4. John L. Nevius, *Demon Possession and Allied Themes* (Grand Rapids, MI: Kregel Publications, 1894), 71.

5. Ibid. The book as a whole demonstrates this point.

6. T.K. Oesterreich, *Possession, Demoniacal and Other* (New Hyde Park, NY: University Press, 1966), 134, 233, 244-245, 273.

7. Paul G. Hiebert, "Discerning the Work of God," Unpublished paper (Pasadena, CA: Fuller Theological Seminary, n.d.), 6.

8. Kurt Koch, *Christian Counseling and Occultism* (Grand Rapids, MI: Kregel Publications, 1965), 8.

9. Matthew Henry, *Matthew Henry's Commentary* (New York: Fleming H. Revell Co., 1721), no page numbers, commentary on Luke 11:17-27.

# 12

## Jesus and Jesus

# "And Who Are You?"

IT IS SAID THAT in the Middle Ages a devout Christian monk saw a vision of Jesus Christ. He was enraptured. The vision was clear and powerful, and Jesus began to instruct the monk as to what he was to do.

The monk listened attentively and worshipfully. Then, as he was about to obey the Jesus Christ he was seeing in his vision, he abruptly asked, "And who are you?"

Instantly the vision ended. The pseudo-Christ was gone.

# An Imaginary Christ

*by A.W. Tozer*

TO FOLLOW CHRIST IN COMPLETE and total commitment means that there must be an *intellectual attachment* to Christ. That is, we cannot run on our feelings nor on wisps of poetic notions about Christ. There are a great many bogus Christs among us these days, and we must show them for what they are and then point to the Lamb of God that taketh away the sins of the world.

John Owen, the old Puritan, warned people in his day, "You have an imaginary Christ, and if you are satisfied with an imaginary Christ you must be satisfied with an imaginary salvation."

In finality, there is only one Christ, and the truly saved man has an attachment to Christ that is intellectual in that he knows who Christ is theologically. For you know there is the romantic Christ of the romance novelist and there is the sentimental Christ of the half-converted cowboy and there is the philosophical Christ of the academic egghead and there is the cozy Christ of the effeminate poet and there is the muscular Christ of the all-American halfback. But there is only one true Christ, and God has said that He is His Son.[1]

## *Endnote*

1. A.W. Tozer, *Total Commitment to Christ: What Is It?* (Camp Hill, PA: Christian Publications, 1995), 5-6.

# Jesus and Jesus

W HAT DO WE MEAN BY "Jesus and Jesus"? Centuries ago, Paul asked the same question: "Have you Corinthians received 'another Jesus'?" (2 Corinthians 11:4, author's paraphrase). Some indeed had, and some indeed have received another Jesus. Such was the case in a meeting in which I participated. At one point, a woman seeking help was overcome by a spirit which identified itself as "Jesus." This Jesus threw her on the floor and bragged through her mouth that it had the control of a certain congregation in a certain city. Was this the true historic Jesus? Obviously not. This Jesus spirit was driven out in the name of the Lord Jesus Christ.

McGraw cites a similar incident: "When the deliverance session was later conducted we encountered a spirit named Jesus. He hated the Lord Jesus Christ."[1] Paul King, in his doctoral work on the life of J.A. MacMillan, likewise recounts an incident in which an alternate Jesus was part of an occult mosaic:

> Under the influence of a spirit, [the person in bondage] engaged in automatic writing, inscribing a perfect circle on a sheet of paper. In spite of their efforts [MacMillan and others], she did not want to give up talking to her  
> mother. . . . She kept repeating that she wanted to be "

sus girl." MacMillan noted that though she claimed to be a "Jesus girl" she did not mention the name of Christ. He discerned that she had been infested with a false "Jesus spirit." (2 Corinthians 11:4)[2]

An early missionary to China describes a similar situation: "One of the stages of deliverance for Joan was the emergence of a Jesus spirit."[3]

To have a solid base for the assertion that there is one true Jesus and many false Jesus spirits, however, we must move beyond contemporary testimonies to the Scripture. Jesus Himself warned that false Christs would come (Matthew 24:24). And the Apostle John observed that many antichrists had ventured forth (1 John 2:18). In what is certainly the key passage (2 Corinthians 11:3-5), an amazing description of an alternate Jesus emerges.

> . . . I am afraid that just as Eve was deceived by the serpent's cunning, your minds may somehow be led astray from your sincere and pure devotion to Christ. For if someone comes to you and preaches a Jesus other than the Jesus we preached, or if you receive a different spirit from the one you received, or a different gospel from the one you accepted, you put up with it easily enough. But I do not think I am in the least inferior to those "super-apostles."

## Another Jesus

Observe first that this alternate Jesus is preached (11:4). Somehow we would imagine that a pseudo-Jesus might exist off in a corner somewhere. "Not so," says Paul. Rather, he is preached. Not only is there a "gospel associated with this Jesus spirit," but also it is being preached—and accepted. The false Jesus spirit is being received (11:4). The false gospel is being promulgated. The most painful com-

mentary about the spiritual state of the Corinthians was their susceptibility to this false Jesus. He went down very well. "You put up with
it easily enough," Paul notes (11:4). Apparently, this false Jesus is attractive and easy to take, making few demands. That flies in the face
of scriptural teaching which proclaims that sound doctrine has to be
"endured" (2 Timothy 4:3, KJV). The true word of God has an edge
to it. The Corinthians, Paul alleges, had fallen for a smooth-talking
Jesus from another kingdom. He was being preached, and he had his
own gospel—but he was another Jesus.

Those involved in spiritual warfare readily attest that Jesus spirits
are frequently encountered. The incident related at the beginning of
this chapter was one of three such deliverances during a week-long
camp meeting. Later, as I was sitting in a class under the tutelage of a
veteran China Inland Mission regular, Dr. Arthur F. Glasser, I heard
him say something that I didn't know anyone else had said or
thought before. His observation, as I remember it, was, "There is
something wrong with all this 'Jesus' talk." That statement concurred
with the sentiments of my own heart. When the name of Jesus is
used, I wait for further definition of which Jesus is being talked
about. Glasser's remark revealed that I was not alone, that others too
were aware of what might be called the "Jesusization" habit of many
who embrace the evangelical label.

## Weeping Blood

Similarly, in the Roman Catholic Church, there sometimes are Jesus phenomena. A Fox television network broadcast a program on
July 29, 1999 that demonstrated rather well that a statue may weep
actual human blood. (According to the documentary, female blood
emerged from a clearly male statue of Christ. That would not only be
plausible, but would make sense since Jesus had no earthly father.
According to Fox, the blood sample stood up to DNA analysis, and
the MRI process affirmed no tampering with the statue.[4] Koch, of
course, labels stigmata as occult phenomena.[5])

The same program concluded with a televised stigmata experience in Bolivia which again demonstrated the before-and-after scars on the woman suffering the stigmata. That blood proved to be human both before and after the phenomenon occurred. The woman appeared to go through a corresponding crucifixion-like agony when the stigmata were appearing on her hands and feet.[6]

What is one to say about this? It does appear to demonstrate the supernatural. That it derived from God Almighty and His Son, Jesus Christ, must be questioned. Roman Catholicism persists in the worship of Mary even though the Scriptures are clear that Jesus Christ is the only mediator between God and man (1 Timothy 2:5). The mass, too, is a reenactment of the death of Christ, whereas the Bible affirms that Jesus Christ *once* suffered and that His sacrifice is a completed work (1 Peter 3:18). On the video, it appeared that a Roman Catholic priest could "bring on" the appearance of the stigmata by passionate praying to Mary.

There were also prophecies uttered by a Jesus in this incident, duly caught by the Fox television cameras.[7] But was it the Lord Jesus Christ of the New Testament and the Apostles' Creed? My best guess would be probably not. Add to this mix the phenomena of exorcisms which have occurred, freeing individuals from Roman Catholic spirits in the name of the Lord Jesus Christ. (This incident does not imply that there are no true believers in Roman Catholicism.) My wife and I both witnessed and were participants in a deliverance in which such spirits, twenty-seven of them, were cast out of one person in the name of the Lord Jesus Christ. As they exited, the demons repeatedly cried out, "Hail, Mary! Hail, Mary!" to which the Christian workers sang, "All hail the power of Jesus' Name!" After a period of struggle, they left the young woman and were sent to the abyss in the name of the Lord Jesus Christ.

John's writing is precise: "Every spirit that does not acknowledge [this] Jesus is not from God" (1 John 4:3). There is strong textual evidence that a very specific Jesus is intended. Not just any Jesus will do.

Clark says, "There is a definite article before the name Jesus: *the* Jesus. This could be strengthened to 'this Jesus,' the one mentioned as having come."[8] Hobbs, citing another author, translates as follows: "the aforementioned Jesus."[9] Again, George C. Findlay's comments are among the most precise: "The article *ton* before *Jesus* is well established, and gives point to the shorter reading: 'Every spirit which does not confess *the Jesus* in question—*the* Jesus of the Church's faith and the Apostle's testimony [is not from God].' "[10] The possible implication here is that this Jesus to whom John refers is a very specific Jesus, readily distinguishable from all others.

## Severing Jesus

Further, there is an alternate rendering of this verse which is extremely fascinating. "Every spirit which *severs* Jesus is not from God" (see 1 John 4:3, Amp.). I have elsewhere entered into an extensive discussion of this variant rendering,[11] but, to state it clearly, there are strong arguments for this text (1 John 4:3a) to say, "Every spirit which severs [or looses] Jesus is not from God." Knowing the "Jesusization" that exists in evangelicalism, and knowing the evangelical habit of truncating the title of the Lord Jesus Christ and severing the qualifying modifiers from Jesus' name, all too often just saying "Jesus," surely the question needs to be asked: Why do we so often sever or cut off various parts of the title and the name of the Lord Jesus Christ?

At the same time, I argue emphatically for the right of every Christian to address our Savior as He is repeatedly addressed particularly in the Gospels—as Jesus. But I am uncomfortable when His lordship, messiahship and anointing are all by habit severed from His name and He is only intermittently given His full title as found in the epistles. The question must be asked: Is the frequent "Jesusization" of the name of the Lord Jesus Christ an indicator that an alternate Jesus is being referenced?

## A Sensuous Jesus

While at a camp meeting, we began to counsel a woman who was a friend of our family. She had picked up a spirit, which turned out to be a sensual Jesus (by its own admission), in a charismatic Anglican context. When we spoke or prayed together, she would sometimes involuntarily slump to the ground under the power of this entity. Attempts to set her free were ineffective.

Finally one day, the three of us met in our motor home, and the struggle for her liberation continued. In the middle of the struggle, I became aware of sin in my heart. Specifically, it was the love of money. When I quietly confessed that sin to the Lord, the pseudo-Jesus suddenly left the woman. There was instant deliverance.

The exit phenomena were so dramatic that both my wife and the other lady turned to me and demanded to know what I had done. As you might guess, I didn't want to tell them. But I finally did. As camp director, I scheduled what we called "check nights" to assist in the raising of the budget. Thursday was the chosen night, but when this woman's husband announced that he would be leaving the grounds on Thursday, I protested inwardly, "No, he can't go on Thursday. We need his check." Those covetous thoughts had grieved the Holy Spirit. Once my sin was confessed, however, the "sexy Jesus" departed abruptly. Obviously, it was another Jesus, not the Lord Jesus Christ.

## The Apostles' Creed

This controversy, these experiences and these texts turn my attention to the Apostles' Creed, which poetically identifies exactly which Jesus is under consideration. Could it have emerged in a day when the Church was struggling with the things with which we struggle today? Let me remind you what the creed says:

I believe in God the Father Almighty, maker of heaven and earth. And in Jesus Christ His only Son, our Lord, who was conceived by the Holy Ghost, born of the Virgin Mary, suffered under Pontius Pilate, was crucified, dead, and buried; He descended into hell; the third day He rose again from the dead; He ascended into heaven and sitteth at the right hand of God the Father Almighty; from thence shall He come to judge the quick and the dead.

I believe in the Holy Ghost, the holy catholic [universal] Church, the communion of the saints, the forgiveness of sins, the resurrection of the body, and the life everlasting. Amen.[12]

Sometimes in our worship services, I fear, we do not find the Jesus of the Gospels and the New Testament, the Jesus of the Apostles' Creed. We find, instead, an entertaining Jesus, a sensual Jesus, a deceiving Jesus who has not come in the flesh and who is not God.

## Endnotes

1. Gerald McGraw, "Tongues Should Be Tested," *The Alliance Witness,* June 5, 1974, 5.

2. Paul L. King, an e-mail to the author, July 13, 1999.

3. George Birch, *The Deliverance Ministry* (Camp Hill, PA: Horizon Books, 1988), 11-12.

4. "Science Test Faith," Fox television, July 29, 1999.

5. Kurt Koch, *Demonology, Past and Present* (Grand Rapids, MI: Kregel Publications, 1973), 120.

6. "Science Test Faith."

7. Ibid.

8. Gordon H. Clark, *First John* (Phillipsburg, NJ: Presbyterian and Reformed Publishing, 1981), 124.

9. Herschel H. Hobbs, *The Epistles of John* (Nashville, TN: Thomas Nelson, 1983), 101.

10. George C. Findlay, *Fellowship in the Life Eternal* (London: Hodder and Stoughton, 1909), 316.

11. K. Neill Foster, "Discernment, the Powers and Spirit-Speaking," unpublished dissertation (Pasadena, CA: Fuller Theological Seminary, 1988), 169-174. See Appendix 2.

12. "The Apostles' Creed," *Hymns of the Christian Life* (Camp Hill, PA: Christian Publications, 1978), 666.

# 13

## Anointing and Anointing

# The Clinton Anointing

THE ADVERTISEMENTS HAVING PIQUED my curiosity, I read *Bill and Hillary: The Marriage*.[1] I found the reading an unpleasant experience, but I also found something that I had not expected, something that was worrisome, even profoundly disturbing. President Bill Clinton, throughout his career (if the biographers are to be half believed) has been able to exert an unusual, even inexplicable power over people. During the time that Newt Gingrich was Speaker of the House in the U.S. Congress, he admitted that he feared to go one-on-one with President Clinton because he was so persuasive.

That power, so inexplicable in view of the various scandals of his administration, is a worrisome illustration of what a "counter anointing" is all about. The anointing that finally comes from the counter-kingdom to rest upon the world's great Antichrist will have powerful influencing elements in it. This may be one of the first times in recent history that a political leader has exhibited an "anointing" which is at once impossible for the secular mind to explain and difficult for the nonspiritual mind to comprehend.

### Endnote

1. Christopher Anderson, *Bill and Hillary: The Marriage* (New York: William Morrow and Company, 1999).

# A Charismatic Church
# Becomes a Bible Church

"HE HAD THE ANOINTING." That was the testimony of Pastor James Wigton's peers according to his own testimony. But events finally demonstrated that the anointing was an anti-anointing, an in-place-of anointing.

Back in the 1970s Pastor Wigton had a group of about thirty persons in his charismatic prayer group, all of whom had experienced tongues. However, prophecies were being uttered among his people which were not coming true. That made him uneasy. He had also read my book, now called *The Third View of Tongues*.[1] He had particularly noted that repetitious commanding was often part of the deliverance context (Mark 5:8).

Hesitantly, he began to test the various glossolalic gifts in the group. He even tested his own wife's tongue with Greek which she did not know. The tongue was spurious. Ultimately, through testing, all thirty persons were shown to be exhibiting false tongues.

When Pastor Wigton asked a discerning counselor to come and drive out all the evil powers in his group, the person declined. Instead, in a series of renunciations and repudiations—apotropaic renunciatory acts, based foundationally on the authority of the believers themselves—the whole group was set free of its bondage.

(Though this was prior to Neil Anderson's emergence onto the scene, the methodology now might be termed a truth encounter.) The once-charismatic group became a Bible Church.[2]

## *Endnotes*

1. K. Neill Foster, *The Third View of Tongues* (Camp Hill, PA: Horizon House Publishers, 1975).

2. K. Neill Foster, "Discernment, the Powers and Spirit-Speaking," unpublished dissertation (Pasadena, CA: Fuller Theological Seminary, 1988), 166, 175, 199, 222.

# Anointing and Anointing

—————⋅⋅⋅✦⋅⋅⋅—————

T HIS CHAPTER COULD JUST AS EASILY be called "Christ and Antichrist," for after all, as we shall see, the name "Christ" means "anointed one." But that is not quite the message I wish to convey. Rather, it is the anointing itself to which we will turn our attention. It is in the anointing that the true and false emerge.

As a young pastor, I was profoundly influenced by E.M. Bounds' book, *Power Through Prayer*.[1] As revealed by brief annotations in the flyleaf, I know that I read it twice in 1959 and not since then until 1998 when I was in process on this book. I discovered in the third reading that I have over the years been profoundly shaped through what I read more than forty years ago. In those pre-ordination days, I carried away from Bounds a passion to be a preacher with anointing. That has been my goal however imperfectly it may have been pursued and experienced. Whether or not the anointing has been there is for others to say.

What do I mean by "anointing"?

> Unction [anointing] is that indefinable, indescribable something which an old, renowned Scotch preacher describes thus: "There is sometimes somewhat in preaching that cannot be described either to matter or to expression, and cannot be described what it is, or whence it cometh,

but with a sweet violence it pierceth into the heart and affections and comes immediately from the Lord; but if
there be any way to obtain such a thing it is by the heavenly disposition of the speaker.[2]

Charles Spurgeon, often called "the prince of preachers," likewise
focused on the anointing preachers should enjoy:

> One bright benison [blessing, benediction] which private
> prayer brings down upon the ministry is an indescribably
> and inimitable something—an unction from the Holy One.
> . . . If the anointing which we bear come not from the
> Lord, we are deceivers, since only in prayer can we attain
> it. Let us continue instant, constant, fervent in supplica-
> tion.[3]

One denominational district superintendent would sometimes ex-
claim the following after he felt that he had preached without the
anointing, "I didn't have much snow under my runners tonight."
Spurgeon recognized the same unhappy possibility: "I wonder how
long we might beat our brains before we could plainly put into words
what is meant by preaching with unction. Yet he who preaches knows
its presence, and he who hears soon detects its absence."[4]

Recently I said to a young preacher, "In all your getting, get unction." I thought I was quoting a certain author, but, regardless of the
source, it was good advice. The alarm of my soul, however, is that,
although this anointing of the Holy Spirit is available through the
Lord Jesus Christ, there are also powerful anointings which seem divine but are false, issuing from an alternate Jesus who only curses
the True Redeemer.

The confusion is endemic. The previous chapter about Jesus and
Jesus is but the antechamber to this discussion. The Old Testament
provides the background to the anointing that would come in the
New Testament era.

The ordinance of anointing with oil was one of the most common and significant ceremonials of the Old Testament. The leper was anointed, the tabernacle was anointed, the priests were anointed, the prophets were anointed, the kings were anointed, the guest was anointed. It was the special symbol of the Holy Ghost and the dedication of the person anointed to His service and possession.[5]

What does the New Testament have to say about anointing? Obviously, it proclaims the anointed One, the Christ. Paul says, "Now it is God who makes both us and you stand firm in Christ [the anointed One]. He anointed us, set His seal of ownership on us, and put His Spirit in our hearts as a deposit, guaranteeing what is to come" (2 Corinthians 1:21-22).

Who is this Christ, the anointed One? The New Testament clearly and extensively defines Him:

- Jesus Christ is the Lamb slain from the foundation of the world (Revelation 13:8). In the beginning was the Word, and the Word was with God, and the Word was God (John 1:1).

- The Word became flesh and lived among us. Jesus Christ was God incarnate (1:14).

- The Holy Spirit, sent from God for the occasion, for a specific purpose, anointed Him to preach liberty to the captives (Luke 4:18).

- Jesus Christ went about doing good and healing all that were oppressed of the devil (Luke 6:17-19; Acts 10:38).

- He suffered under Pontius Pilate and was crucified outside the gates of Jerusalem (Matthew 27:24-31).

- After three days, He rose from the dead by His own power (1 Corinthians 15:4).

- He was seen by many witnesses in His resurrected state (15:6).

- He ascended into heaven to take His place at the right hand of the Father (Acts 1:9; Ephesians 1:20; Colossians 3:1).

- Through the cross, the resurrection and ascension, He assumed authority over every power of every kind (Ephesians 1:21; Colossians 2:15).

- Incomprehensibly, believers are seated with Him there at the right hand of the Father (Ephesians 2:6).

- Believers are in Christ, and He is in them. Indeed, it is "Christ in you, the hope of glory" (Colossians 1:27). In Christ all the fullness of the Godhead dwells bodily and believers have been given fullness and completeness in Christ who is the head over every power and authority (2:9-10).

- This Christ will return in glory, bringing His saints with Him (Acts 1:11; Matthew 24:30-31).

The early Christians formed various creeds to say the same thing in a much more memorable form. The Apostles' Creed, mentioned earlier, is more than just a formulation or statement about the identity of Jesus Christ. It identifies and sets apart the real Jesus Christ from all antichrists.

An antichrist is far more than an imposter, far more than some deluded soul who thinks he is Jesus Christ. To catch the full weight of the word "antichrist," we need to remember that Christ means essentially "the anointed One."[6] When we are thinking about Jesus Christ, we are thinking about one who has been anointed. And, when the Scriptures speak of antichrists, we should be careful not to be swayed by our knowledge of English or perhaps the Romantic languages of

Spanish, French and Italian. *Anti* means far more than "against." It also means "instead of"[7] and "in place of."[8] Hence, an antichrist has an "in-place-of anointing." This alternative anointing, alternative unction, is what distinguishes an antichrist from Christ. As Jesus Christ was anointed by the Holy Spirit, an antichrist has an anointing from the unholy (false) spirit—Satan himself.

We must not envision the antichrist necessarily as a surly antagonist of Jesus Christ, at least on the outside. Rather, he may be suave, smooth, entertaining, enlightening and illuminating—all that and more—yet crowned with an unction that does not come from God.

The Corinthians, you remember, ran into "another Jesus" who, as we have noted, "went down rather smoothly" (2 Corinthians 11:4, author's paraphrase). Such an antichrist mixes large amounts of truth with occasional error and acts out his nature, flashing his wares—subterranean giftedness given to him from Satan—along with an alternate anointing. Such a Jesus has a gospel—but it is not *the* gospel. It is a twisted and distorted message.

Nowhere is this "instead of" concept clearer in the New Testament than in First Timothy 2:6 where Paul specifically says that Jesus Christ gave His life a ransom (*antilutron*) for many. The use of *anti* as a prefix in the Greek text is striking. A ransom is commonly understood as being something "instead of" or "in place of." It was Jesus' life instead of, in place of, the penalty of God's judgment.

> So long as we mentally associate all antichrists with the Antichrist, we will miss the point of John's warning. We will completely miss the whole thrust of John's words unless we see the religious [anointing] aspect of the Antichrist.
>
> A christ is literally "an anointed one." An antichrist, then, simply has an anti-anointing. . . . We must not say that the anti-anointing is phony. It is as real as it is possible to be. But it is an anti-anointing, a substitute anointing, a demonic anointing. It is against Christ and His kingdom.[9]

All I can add is that we must, repeat, *must* remember that antichrists have an "instead of" anointing. The question, then, when encountering persons who apparently have an anointing, is always this: Where does this anointing come from?

## Endnotes

1. E.M. Bounds, *Power Through Prayer* (London: Marshall, Morgan and Scott, Ltd., n.d.).

2. Ibid., 89.

3. Ibid., 84.

4. Ibid., 87.

5. A.B. Simpson, *The Holy Spirit* (Harrisburg, PA: Christian Publications, n.d.), 76.

6. W.E. Vine, *The Expanded Vine's Expository Dictionary of New Testament Words,* John R. Kohlenberger III, editor (Minneapolis, MN: Bethany House Publishers, 1984), 50.

7. Ibid., 53.

8. Gerhard Kittel and Gerhard Friedrich, editors, *Theological Dictionary of the New Testament* (Grand Rapids, MI: Eerdmans, 1985), 61.

9. K. Neill Foster, *The Discerning Christian* (Camp Hill, PA: Christian Publications, 1981), 95.

# 14

Providences
and Providences

# The Phone Call

*by Marilynne Foster*

IT WAS THE SPRING OF 1967. My husband, Neill, had been a travel-
ing evangelist for several years when we sensed that a change was
coming in our ministry. As mentioned elsewhere in this book, he
agreed to take a pastorate, but having felt uneasy, requested that he
be relieved of the commitment. The questions now were what, where
and when?

After the birth of our third child, Jeff, in May—a brother for Tim,
seven, and Donna, three—we moved out of our house, stored our
furniture, moved in with my parents and waited for whatever God
had in mind for us. One very hot June evening, within days of when
we would leave for summer ministries, we went for a drive down to
Riverside Park to cool off and let the children play in the pool. After
a pleasant and refreshing evening, we took our place in a parade of
cars leaving the park.

Moving along at a snail's pace, we spotted a friend's car coming toward us. We stopped side by side to greet them, and the conversation quickly turned to our still empty and unsold house. The upshot
of that one- or two-minute conversation was that the couple in that
car bought our house. We were grateful for God's providence, but
our future was still uncertain.

After a busy summer, we traveled north to spend some time with my husband's extended family and to try to further discern God's will for the immediate future. One of the options we had discussed was to go to language school to learn Spanish. My husband felt that that would expand the possibilities for evangelistic tours overseas. The downside of language study was that he had once been advised by a high-school French teacher that he might as well quit the class since he was going to fail anyway. Apparently learning foreign languages was not one of his strong points!

One day, driving down the hill to have prayer with a pastor friend, he heard an inaudible (or was it audible?) voice say, "You can't learn Spanish!" It appeared to be a confirmation of what he already knew. However, the more he thought about it, the more he questioned the source of the voice. Was it God speaking, or was it the devil? He came to the conclusion that it was *not* God.

Logic kicked in. As Billy Sunday once said, "I'm in favor of everything the devil's against and against everything the devil is in favor of." My husband decided that if the devil was telling him he couldn't learn Spanish, then that was exactly what he was going to do! With uncharacteristic boldness, he returned home to announce to one and all that we were going to learn Spanish.

Given the date—about August 10—and the miles from any language school—at least several thousand—it seemed like an impossible dream. But God had spoken. He called our denominational headquarters. Someone there informed him that the options were a school in Costa Rica (quite improbable at that late date) and another in Edinburg, Texas.

My husband got the number and phoned the Rio Grande Bible Institute and Missionary Language School in Texas. The response was both encouraging and discouraging. There would be no problem registering—we would be accepted sight unseen because of our denomination affiliation—but there were no accommodations left on campus for a family of five. Now what? Was studying Spanish God's will or wasn't it? With a youthful brashness that now makes us shake our heads, he decided to write a letter to the registrar's office to tell them that we were coming anyway and that we would worry about accommodations once we got there (which would be about the time school was scheduled to begin).

The next day, with the letter hardly yet stuffed in a post office mail bag, we received a phone call from the registrar saying that there had been a cancellation and that there was a brand-new fully furnished three-bedroom apartment waiting for us, plus on-campus nursery care for our two preschoolers. Within days, our green Rambler was loaded, and we were on our way south.

More than thirty years later, we view that "providence moment" as a major turning point in our lives. God used it to open up ministry to the world. Since then, we have also studied French in Europe, which further enhanced such opportunities. Discerning between providences and providences was a major factor in finding God's will for our lives.

# Providencies and Providences

I T WAS JUNE, 1988. I had just graduated from seminary a second
time (second seminary!). It was Sunday morning, and we were
on our way to Canada for the wedding of my nephew, Kevin.
Heading north along Interstate 5 in California, as we approached the
San Francisco exit, our 1981 Oldsmobile (that we had bought because of its "mint" condition) suddenly began to show itself ordinary
after all. In fact, noises—very loud noises—began to emerge from
under the hood. I tried to limp along at least into Oakland so that we
could hear our son-in-law preach.

It was not to be. My wife finally won the debate about whether
we should turn off or not, and I eased into a small town called Dub-
lin. I had not really noticed it on previous trips, but fortunately
there were a number of repair shops, and it was also well populated
with car agencies.

We pulled into the first station. The mechanic knew immediately
what was wrong. It was not good news. It would take several days to
fix the problem (we didn't have several days to spare), and it would
cost plenty. The decision was made. We would buy a new car. There
simply was no time to do anything else.

As we began our Sunday morning itineration around the car lots, I
asked the first salesman if there was any establishment we should

avoid. He advised that the Nissan agency was in financial trouble and that we had best not go there.

So we started the rounds. It was a long and frustrating day filled with disappointment, ambivalence and pangs of conscience because of the day on which it was being undertaken.

About 4 o'clock, we decided to drop in at the Nissan agency. Never thinking that I could afford a new Maxima, I began looking at the secondhand ones. By this time, the salesman had arrived. He asked me if I would be interested in buying a new Maxima if he could get the price down to where I could handle it.

"Sure," I responded.

He led me over to the spot where two new Maximas were parked. Seemingly within seconds, the sticker price dropped dramatically. The one we liked best was "loaded." I knew as the price plummeted that he was getting close to what we might be able to manage.

By this time my daughter and son-in-law had arrived, so we men made our way to the small cubicle that all car dealerships seem to have. This one was surrounded by glass on three sides. As we sat there dickering, suddenly there was an earthquake—5.0 on the Richter scale, centered at San Jose, a few miles away.

By this time the salesman knew I was a preacher. So as the cubicle creaked and groaned, he said, "There's your sign. Buy the car." I declined. (As you probably have discerned by now, I have never been much into signs, and I wasn't then.) I had also informed the dealership that there was something drastically wrong with my wounded Oldsmobile. They plainly did not want to know the details and brushed my information aside.

Nevertheless, the decision was to "sleep on it." I am sure the salesman thought he would never see us again. My wife claims that he was almost crying as we drove away. That night in Oakland, I remember looking out the window from the third floor apartment and thinking to myself, "If the earthquake hits again, we'll end up over there." There were no more tremors that I knew about.

The next morning when we rose, both of us knew that we were going to buy the car. We had not discussed it; we just had come to a mutual conclusion without talking. It was one of those nonverbal things.

So I filled out a check for a round number, nearly $400 less than the final price of the day before. With check in hand, we returned to the Nissan dealership.

"Here it is. Take it or leave it," I said, having learned that little trick from my dad. That last several hundred dollars must have pushed them over a precipice of some kind. They plainly were not happy. Finally, reluctantly and somewhat disgustedly, they agreed.

I then proceeded to tell them that there was no money in the account on which I had written the check and that they would have to wait till Wednesday to cash the check. Again, they agreed. That Monday afternoon, we unloaded our 1981 Oldsmobile and surrendered it to the graces of the dealership. We put our baggage in the new white Maxima and headed for the Canadian border. All the dealer had left was a check that was useless until Wednesday.

Those who have heard me tell this story have observed that driving away in a new car with a still useless check in the hands of the car dealer is the most dramatic part of the story. The check did clear in due time—and we had a brand new car, plus an amazing story to tell.

But there were things that bothered me. Why did it have to happen on Sunday? Was it really God's providence? I have a Presbyterian streak in me that wants no commerce on the Sabbath! I also knew the biblical account of Jonah. When he started running away from God, a ship was waiting for him—in the wrong place at the wrong time. I couldn't decide whether this "Sunday Maxima" was a gift from God or a ship going to Tarshish.

My wife knew the vacillation of soul I was feeling.

"Quit fussing," she said, "and accept it as a graduation present from God." Weeks later a pastor friend pondered my quandary and said, "I believe it was a gift from the Lord. Accept it that way."

I was at peace. But my wife keeps wondering why our lives just can't be ordinary. I'm not sure I can answer that, but knowing there are providences and providences makes one careful and cautious, as it should.

## Biblical and Historical Examples

The word "providence" refers to a set of circumstances that are so highly unusual that they suggest the direct intervention of God in human affairs so as to secure a surprising or unexpected result. Examples abound, both biblical and historical.

- The life of Job began to unravel when Satan sent a wind sounding very much like an earthquake (Job 1:19).

- Elijah, too, was witness to an earthquake, "but the Lord was not in the earthquake" (1 Kings 19:11, Amp.).

- When Jesus rebuked the waves, the suggestion from the Greek *seismos* in the text is that behind the storm was an earthquake that needed rebuke (Matthew 8:23-27; Mark 4:36-41),[1] an earthquake with origins in the nether world.

- When Jesus died, there was an earthquake (Matthew 27:51). There was another earthquake that shook the prison that kept Paul and Silas. It clearly was from God Almighty and was used to trigger the release of the apostles (Acts 16:25).

- Historically, the Azusa Street movement of 1906 comes to mind. Events in the revival coincided with and were punctuated by the San Francisco earthquake.[2] It was as if the Almighty said, "These events are the mighty work of my Holy Spirit," or at least that would be the impression since providences are often taken to be evidences of the expressed will of God. For some, the San Francisco earthquake which rattled all up and down the west coast was an emphatic and divine witness to the authenticity of the Azusa events.

- Similarly, in recent years, John Wimber welcomed a prophet by the name of Paul Cain to the West Coast. When he arrived, his coming was also punctuated by an earthquake.

> In November 1988 Paul Cain gave a prophecy to Jack Deere for Wimber, saying that there would be an earthquake in Southern California the day he [Cain] would arrive to meet Wimber for the first time. This would be a smaller one and a large one would take place elsewhere in the world the day after he left Anaheim. The first earthquake took place near Anaheim on the day he predicted. He left Anaheim on December 7. The large Soviet-Armenian earthquake occurred on December 8.[3]

Obviously Paul Cain was a man of God whose very arrival in Los Angeles was confirmed by nature itself. Or was he? Apparently not. Wimber finally separated himself and the Vineyard from Prophet Cain as errant and strange. But note, even if Cain was indeed a false prophet, as Wimber may have believed, his arrival had nevertheless been punctuated by an earthquake as he predicted. My point is that there are providences and providences. Discerning between them is not always easy, as is evident in this next illustration.

In John Wimber's own ministry there was an event in which tongues were manifested in his assembly. The manifestation left him deeply troubled. Was this of God, or was it not? Carole Wimber tells the story.

> On Mother's Day of 1981 we had a watershed experience that launched us into what today is called power evangelism. At this time John invited a young man who had been attending our church to preach on a Sunday eve-

ning. By now we had grown to over 700 participants. The young man shared his testimony, which was beautiful and stirring, then asked for all the people under the age of twenty-five to come forward. None of us had a clue as to what was going to happen. When they got to the front, the speaker said, "For years now the Holy Spirit has been grieved by the Church but He's getting over it. Come Holy Spirit."

And He came.

Most of these young people had grown up around our home—we had four children between the ages of fifteen and twenty-one. We knew the young people well. One fellow, Tim, started bouncing. His arms flung out and he fell over, but one of his hands accidentally hit a mike stand and he took it down with him. He was tangled up in the cord, with the mike next to his mouth. Then he began speaking in tongues, so the sound went throughout the gymnasium [where they were meeting]. We had never considered ourselves charismatics, and certainly had never placed emphasis on tongues. We had seen a few people tremble and fall over before, and we had seen many healings. But this was different. The majority of the young people [over 400] were shaking and falling over. At one point it looked like a battlefield scene, bodies everywhere, people weeping and wailing, speaking in tongues. And Tim in the middle of it all babbling into the microphone. There was much shouting and loud behavior!

John sat quietly, playing the piano and wide-eyed. Members of our staff were fearful and angry. Several people got up and walked out, never to be seen again—at least they were not seen by us.

But I knew God was visiting us. I was so thrilled because I had been praying for power for so long. This might not have been the way I wanted to see it come, but this was how God gave it to us. . . . I asked one boy, who was on the floor, "What's happening to you right now?" He said, "It's like electricity. I can't move." I was amazed by the effect of God's power on the human body. I suppose I thought that it would all be an inward work, such as conviction or repentance. I never imagined there would be strong physical manifestations.

But John wasn't as happy as I. He had never seen large numbers of people sprawled out over the floor. . . . He spent that night reading Scripture and historical accounts of revival from the lives of people like Whitfield and Wesley. . . . But his study did not yield conclusive answers to questions raised from the previous evening's events. By 5 a.m. John was desperate. He cried out to God, "Lord, if this is You, please tell me." A moment later the phone rang and a pastor friend of ours from Denver, Colorado was on the line. "John," he said, "I'm sorry I'm calling so early, but I have something really strange to tell you. I don't know what it means, but God wants me to say, 'It's Me, John.' "[4]

That day, John Wimber, by his wife's testimony, crossed a rubicon: He accepted the providence as from God. Whether it had divine origin or not may still be disputed by some, I suppose, but the Vineyard movement emerged out of Wimber's acceptance of that providence. For some, the existence of the Vineyard is proof enough that the providence was from God. For my part, questioner that I sometimes am, an "it's me" response would not have been enough. I would have wanted to ask, "And who are you?"

Many times, on a lesser scale than the Richter, similar events take place. Good people observe unusual events in a spiritual context and suppose that those providences are the obvious proof of theological orthodoxy and right doctrine. But is that an accurate conclusion? Biblically speaking, the answer must be "no." The Scriptures say, "The coming of the lawless one will be in accordance with the work of Satan displayed in all kinds of counterfeit miracles, signs and wonders, and in every sort of evil that deceives those who are perishing" (2 Thessalonians 2:9-10).

The true criteria by which any providence must be judged are those enduring principles relating to morality, uprightness, character and the final fruit which heaven will reveal. The question is not: Are there miracles and providences? Rather, the question is: Does this minister travel with his own wife and does he pay his bills? Do godly lives and relentless holiness back up the supernatural claims?

## Contemporary Events

One of the phenomena of contemporary literature is *The Celestine Prophecy*.[5] An examination of its content reveals the author's fascination with the serendipities of life, with what we are calling here providences or special encounters. Most everyone has them, and the tendency is to give life significance to them. Author Redfield does that in his Celestine series. There is no hint of *divine* providence in his novel, only the fascination with unexpected and unpredicted events of various kinds. It never seems to occur to anyone that such encounters might be good or evil—possibly from God or possibly from Satan—and if from the counterkingdom, a source of deception and delusion.

During the process of writing this book, I received a manuscript that basically embraced and advocated the Toronto Blessing.[6] The author argued passionately and at great length for the providences which "led" him to go to the Toronto event for the first time. The point I am making here is simply that in the cases of *The Celestine Prophecy* and the Toronto Blessing, the arguments are similar, even identical—the first claims *profound* (unassigned) significance to unusual events; the second claims *divine* (assigned) significance to unusual events. The question apparently was never asked: Are these providences from Almighty God or from another source?

## *Endnotes*

1. J.R. Goff, Jr., "Charles Fox Parham," *Dictionary of Pentecostal and Charismatic Movements* (Grand Rapids, MI: Zondervan, 1988), 660-661.

2. G. Bornkamm, VII, *"Seismos,"* *Theological Dictionary of the New Testament* (Grand Rapids MI: Eerdmans, 1985), 1014-1015.

3. Terri Sillivant, "Paul Cain's Ministry: Recent Manifestations of the Spirit" (Grace City Report: Special Edition, n.d.), 6, 15. Varied perspectives on these events exist.

4. John Wimber and Kevin Springer, *Riding the Third Wave* (Basingtoke, Hants, UK: Marshall Pickering, 1987), 45-46.

5. James Redfield, *The Celestine Prophecy* (New York: Warner Books, 1993).

6. An unpublished manuscript submitted to Christian Publications, August 1999. See also Robert J. Kuglin, *The Toronto Blessing: What Would the Holy Spirit Say?* (Camp Hill, PA: Christian Publications, 1996).

# 15

Falling
and Falling

# Edwards' "Very Frequent Thing"

JONATHAN EDWARDS WAS AT ONE TIME the president of Princeton University. His ministry was blessed with one of the mightiest outpourings of the Holy Spirit that has ever taken place on this continent.

In speaking of it, he says,

> It was a very frequent thing to see a house full of outcries, fainting, convulsions and such like, both with distress and with admiration and joy. There were some instances of persons lying in a sort of trance, remaining for perhaps a whole twenty-four hours motionless, and with their senses locked up, but in the meantime under strong imaginations, as though they were to heaven, and had there a vision of glorious and delightful objects.

He says, in speaking of a revival in Scotland in 1625, that

> it was a frequent thing for many to be so extraordinarily seized with terror in the hearing of the word, by the Spirit of God convicting them of sin, that they fell down, and were carried out of the church, who afterward proved most solid and lively Christians. . . . [1]

## *Endnote*

1. J.A. Wood, *Perfect Love,* abridged by John Paul (Kansas City, MO: Beacon Hill Press, 1944), 114.

# Smelling Like Brenda

THE BROWNSVILLE OUTPOURING in Florida featured the falling phenomena. One citation is quite evocative, and if true, casts doubt upon some of the events at least. The text below, derived from apparently unedited audio/video material is awkward, but revealing.

> But one of our worship team ladies that fell in my arms—long after revival broke out a lady came up to me during the revival and she said, "Brother _____, your wife is so sweet. She sings so good in that worship team."
>
> And I thought, *Worship team?*
>
> She said, "You know, the black-headed one that was laying in your arms up there on the platform."
>
> I said, "That's not my wife."
>
> She said, "It's not?"
>
> She just fell out under the fire too and just happened to land in my arms. And so I said, "Lord, this don't smell like Brenda here."[1]

Without commenting definitively on the larger series of events at Brownsville, could the incident cited here be a manifestation of the Holy Spirit?

## *Endnote*

1. John Kilpatrick, *In Times Like These*, videotape (Pensacola, FL: Brownsville Assembly of God, 1996), May 30.

# Falling and Falling

I N THIS CHAPTER WE ARE TALKING about what is commonly called "falling under the power." I must confess that I am not a happy writer. I don't want to write about true and false in this area since even the idea of "true" falling offends my sense of propriety and probably my pride (which God has determined to resist ahead of time—1 Peter 5:5). However, to follow the inner mandate and to handle this book with integrity, falling as a religious and spiritual phenomenon, like many other things, must be divided into true and false.

Indeed, so influential a figure as John Wimber said this,

> There's no place in the Bible where people were lined up and Jesus or Paul or anyone else went along and bopped them on the head and watched them go down, and somebody else ran along behind. Can you picture Peter and James—"Hold it, hold it, hold it!"—running along behind trying to catch them? And so the model we're seeing, either on stage or on television, is totally different from anything that's in Scripture.[1]

I will use several illustrations which both reveal the polarities which we are addressing and the biases of my own heart.

## Contemporary Illustrations

Early in my ministry, I was preaching in a small town in the province of Saskatchewan, Canada. It was a traditional two-week campaign that went every night except Saturday. As the campaign moved toward its conclusion, there was born in my heart the belief that on the Lord's day there would be the descent of the Holy Spirit in such power that many in the congregation would be "cut down."

That expectation never was fulfilled. Instead, in the Friday evening service, immediately prior to the final Sunday, there was a pervasive response to the evangelistic and deeper life invitation. One young woman was particularly moved as she knelt at a chair in the inquiry room sobbing and groaning in prayer. Suddenly, she slipped off the chair (where she had been kneeling) and onto the floor. Immediately the pastor said, "That is not of the Holy Spirit."

In that moment, something died in my soul. I was inwardly grieved as I had never been to that point in my life. I believe still that the Holy Spirit, as I understand His working, was also grieved, and whatever He had in mind for the Lord's day was no longer on the horizon. Sunday was a powerful closing day to the evangelistic campaign, but there were none "cut down"—none at all. I had not sought such manifestations. I had not prayed or preached to trigger them. But the public grieving of the Holy Spirit quenched what had been, in my view, intended by Divine Providence. The incident still grieves me.

I was preaching in Burkina Faso, Africa, in a city whose name is long forgotten. At the end of the message, one man came forward and asked for prayer. Intuitively I knew that he had a sexual problem, but that did not become a public issue. We simply prayed that he would be released from demonic powers, and I commanded the evil spirit out in Spanish, a language unknown by those in the service. The man fell to the floor as if shot.

I was invited to preach in a church which I knew was in the habit of falling in its services. I went and preached in predictable fashion. After the service, the pastor asked if I would pray for him. I did so, placing my hands on his head. He began to go down. As he did, I held him up! My bias, stated earlier, is that I would rather avoid these kinds of situations.

## Biblical Illustrations

Most important to this text is the following question: What do the Scriptures illustrate? What do they teach? Having offered these several case studies, let's turn to the Bible.

Moses, Ezra and Daniel are among those who fell in the Old Testament (Deuteronomy 9:18; Ezra 9:5; Daniel 8:17-18). In Moses' case, he fell because of the sin of Israel. In the Ezra incident, self-abasement was the apparent motive. In the case of Daniel, he fell into a deep sleep, his face to the ground.[2] These Old Testament incidents do not exactly parallel the current religious phenomena, but there was falling for religious and spiritual reasons—that much is clear.

In the New Testament, people physically fell when they encountered Jesus Christ. The best-known example would be Saul on the Damascus road.

> As he [Saul] neared Damascus on his journey, suddenly a light from heaven flashed around him. He fell to the ground and heard a voice say to him, "Saul, Saul, why do you persecute me?"
>
> "Who are you, Lord?" Saul asked.
>
> "I am Jesus, whom you are persecuting," he replied. "Now get up and go into the city, and you will be told what you must do." (Acts 9:3-6)

It is clear also that the Apostle John fell on his face when the visions of revelation began to come (Revelation 1:17). Interestingly enough, no one has informed us moderns that Jesus Christ no longer does things like that!

## Mrs. Edwards

The wife of Jonathan Edwards of New England fame fell under the influence of "religious ecstasy." It happened amidst the fervor of revival:

> We remained in the meeting house about three hours after the public exercises were over. During most of the time, my bodily strength was overcome: and the joy and thankfulness which were excited in my mind, as I contemplated the great goodness of God, led me to converse with those who were near me, in a very earnest manner.
>
> . . . The intenseness of my feelings took away my bodily strength. . . . I felt such a sense of the deep ingratitude manifested by the children of God, in such coldness and deadness, that my strength was immediately taken away, and I sunk down on the spot . . . when they took me up and laid me on the bed, where I lay for a considerable time, faint with joy, while contemplating the glories of the heavenly world.[3]

## Happy Distemper

When others questioned the manifestations in Mrs. Edwards' life, her husband came to her defense. (It should be noted, however, that he did not defend all falling or all phenomena.)

> Now if such things are enthusiasm, and the offspring of a distempered brain; let my brain be possessed evermore of that happy distemper! If this be distraction; I pray God that the world of mankind may all be seized with this be-

nign, meek, beneficent, beatific, glorious distraction!
What notion have they of true religion who reject what
has been here described?[4]

It has been claimed by some that the Toronto Blessing exhibited
the same kind of phenomena as were present in Edwards' day. Of
course, no one can know for sure since it is impossible to time warp
back to the New England revival to see for ourselves.

A few years ago several of us went into an after-service of the Toronto Blessing. Most of the audience had gone home, but there were
perhaps twenty people still lying in the aisles. Various teams of
workers sought to minister to them with broad sweeping motions as
if they were sweeping the Holy Spirit in various directions with their
hands. In a search-for-discernment mode and not at all sure that it
was the Holy Spirit of Almighty God who was involved, I had no
willingness to be touched by any of them.

## Cane Ridge, 1801

At Cane Ridge in Bourbon County, Kentucky in 1801, at the most
famous of America's camp meetings, there were many manifestations.
In crowds estimated to be as large as 20,000, the people fell by the
hundreds. Set in a context of Presbyterianism, eventually the camp
meeting embraced the Baptists and Methodists as well. It was focused
on the communion service and the Presbyterian habit of "fencing the
table," i.e., erecting the proper scriptural barriers and restrictions associated with the Lord's Supper. In that intense atmosphere, revival—
with many conversions accompanying it—broke out:

> By the fall of 1801 evangelical visitors to the central coun-
> ties of Kentucky marveled at a near utopia. The Spirit of
> God had burned and cleansed the whole area. Practically
> everyone had been somehow affected by the revival.
> George Baxter, when he arrived from the Shenandoah Val-

ley, thought he breathed a special, cleansed air in Kentucky. He found "the most moral place I had ever been in."[5]

Some pastors, true to their calling as shepherds and overseers of God's flock, felt the need to judge the evidences of the revival.

> All the ministers accepted pastoral responsibility toward their people, even when they had no personal taste for their wild behavior. At times the exercises [manifestations] skirted the bounds of Presbyterian propriety—women fell in unladylike positions, legs and breasts might be scandalously exposed, people in comas might become incontinent, men and women occasionally fell off horses. . . . At least at a distance some of the more frenzied dances bore an uncommon similarity to those in taverns; some bodily convulsions hinted at sexual congress.[6]

## Crucified with Christ

In 1956, a revival, much less publicized than those we have just discussed, took place in Owen Sound, Ontario. The evangelist was Clarence Shrier who had been miraculously healed of terminal tuberculosis some years before. Never formally trained, Shrier preached and prayed for the sick with great power—sometimes accompanied by the phenomenon of falling. One leader, who was particularly arrogant, was inexplicably struck down as he walked across the platform. A common testimony from those who experienced the falling was that they seemed to be "being crucified with Christ." I must admit that this kind of report resonates within me. That falling can happen and that it can be a true manifestation of the authentic Holy Spirit is a conclusion we should not lightly put aside.

Although, as already admitted, I would prefer not to embrace phenomena such as these, I must be fair with Scripture and the history of the Christian Church: These phenomena do exist and apparently, as indicated in both Testaments, may be traced to various sources. E.M. Bounds records Wesley saying, "The power of God came mightily upon us, so that many cried out for exceeding joy, and many fell to the ground."[7] George Whitfield criticized Wesley for allowing the phenomenon until it began happening in his own meetings.[8] Bill McLeod, on the basis of a 1979 book by Arnold A. Dallimore, observes (March 2001) that both Wesley and Whitfield eventually resisted the exhibitionist falling experiences, considering them to be not from God and hindrances to revival.[9] Charles G. Finney, R.A. Torrey and Jonathan Goforth also relate incidents in their ministries where the phenomenon took place.[10]

Keith M. Bailey makes these observations:

> The expressions "falling under the power" and "slain in the Spirit" are non-biblical. They do not describe the experiences of falling found in Scripture. In both the Old and New Testaments incidents are found where godly people were overcome by the extraordinary presence of God. The biblical manifestations show little if any similarity to the modern falling experiences.
>
> Most fallings today happen in church services. I find no scriptural example that took place in the assembly of God's people. This is a striking difference. Individuals in a private encounter with God were those who experienced the Bible fallings. Most of the fallings were associated with a man of God receiving divine revelation which later became a part of Scripture.
>
> The biblical incidents were also different in that the individuals did not pass out but were fully aware of what was going on around them. Demons put people in a coma-like state. Those who have been involved in the deliverance ministry have encountered such states imposed

on the possessed. Many present-day fallings seem to follow the same pattern as the demonic.

The fallings in the Bible were special works of God usually associated with the inspiration of Scripture and were
never intended to be a continuing norm. John, Paul, Peter
and some of the prophets were overcome by extraordinary
circumstances but experienced divine strength and great
spiritual awareness. Since the devil can produce false
fallings, every precaution must be taken to discern his evil
work and rebuke it. The popular mass fallings in public
assemblies are certainly suspect since they resemble the
satanic model more than the biblical.[11]

## A Different Source

These phenomena do exist, and they may be traced to different
sources. The Scriptures are clear that people may physically fall when
demons are in control or when they are confronted and driven out.

> The next day, when they came down from the moun-
> tain, a large crowd met him. A man in the crowd called
> out, "Teacher, I beg you to look at my son, for he is my
> only child. A spirit seizes him and he suddenly screams; it
> throws him into convulsions so that he foams at the
> mouth. It scarcely ever leaves him and is destroying him. I
> begged your disciples to drive it out, but they could not."
>
> "O unbelieving and perverse generation," Jesus replied,
> "how long shall I stay with you and put up with you?
> Bring your son here."
>
> Even while the boy was coming, the demon threw him
> to the ground in a convulsion. But Jesus rebuked the evil
> spirit, healed the boy and gave him back to his father.
> (Luke 9:37-42)

If the falling that sometimes takes place in religious contexts is of the devil—a distinct possibility since Jesus encountered a demonized man in a synagogue (4:33)—then the falling phenomena may sometimes be occult phenomena and therefore responsive to authoritative Christian influences.

Bill McLeod, the pastor in whose church the Western Canadian Revival of 1971-1972 began, and an evangelist and revivalist in his own right, addresses this phenomena in the following manner:

> An internationally known preacher [and a student of occult phenomena] . . . told me of an experience he had had with a certain . . . healer. He said he saw what looked like genuine miracles. But when he saw people going down on the floor he told me it looked to him like an occult thing. He then prayed in the following fashion. He told the Lord that he was going to go forward with the next group that went to the altar, and he prayed that, if the power putting these people on the floor was NOT the power of God, that he would be the only one left standing. Of forty or so people, he was the only one that did not go down.[12]

McLeod continues.

> I was in Illinois and a young man told me of a similar experience he had. I had not told him of this other experience I have just outlined, but he told a story that was almost identical in every respect. He also had prayed [in a similar situation] that if the power was not of God that he would be the only one left standing. He said that at one point, his knees started to sag but he recovered strength and was the only one who did not go down.[13]

## *Angelology and Demonology*

A certain pastor was working through a teaching series on angelology and demonology. One night, as he was watching a satanic television program for research purposes, he prayed for the spiritual protection of his own person but inadvertently did not pray for his wife. When she entered the room, she went down flat, out cold in what he believed to be a satanic attack.[14]

People may fall when the Lord wishes to demonstrate His power. Jesus did that when He was in the Garden of Gethsemane just before His capture, surrounded by a crowd which included a detachment of soldiers, some officials and the betrayer, Judas.

> Jesus, knowing all that was going to happen to him, went out and asked them, "Who is it you want?"
>
> "Jesus of Nazareth," they replied.
>
> "I am he," Jesus said. (And Judas the traitor was standing there with them.) When Jesus said, "I am he," they drew back and fell to the ground. (John 18:4-6)

In the revival of 1859 in Ireland, prostrations, as they were called, seemed to be greatly blessed. "Another man, going home from the market where he had sold his produce, was walking along the road, counting his money. Suddenly he was struck by such conviction that he fell on the ground, like Saul of Tarsus, and his money was scattered on the road."[15]

Another account was similar. "A visitor began to describe revival scenes he had seen in another county. Suddenly a servant boy who was listening in felt convicted. Moments later a servant girl and then the brother of the visitor lay prostrate with conviction. None of these people had shown any religious interest before."[16]

Sometimes those who had fallen in the Irish revival exhibited supernatural recall.

. . . one pastor told of a girl who lay with fixed eyes turned to heaven for four hours. She quoted over a hundred Scriptures all related and applied to her own case. She repeated sermons and exhortations that the pastor had preached over previous months, quoting large sections of these verbatim. Afterward the pastor questioned her, but she could not remember the sermons or quote those Scripture passages accurately as she had done when gripped by the Holy Spirit.[17]

I have seen a young woman in the midst of her own deliverance from demonic power behave similarly. She called out Scripture references which she could not have known, but which when read aloud were instrumental in discharging the evil powers.

## Free Falling

The final observation is that people may fall of their own free will and volition. There were times in the Scripture when people fell down in such a manner. An incident in Luke chapter 5 can be chosen at random: "When Simon Peter saw this [the marvelous catch of fishes], he fell at Jesus' knees and said, 'Go away from me, Lord; I am a sinful man!' . . . When he [the man with leprosy] saw Jesus, he fell with his face to the ground and begged him, 'Lord, if you are willing, you can make me clean' " (5:8, 12).

Just as human beings can and do fall with purpose and intent, to say nothing of accident, there could be those times (particularly in meetings where falling is expected and even anticipated by the appointment of catchers along with ushers) that men and women may fall for reasons other than divine. By that I mean that simply having a passion to conform could lead those who fall to do no more than the men mentioned in the just-cited Scripture who fell because they wanted to.

There is no doubt that some of the "falling under the power" and being "slain in the Spirit" experienced today is no more than the carnal nature exhibiting itself. A pastor friend describes some manifestations of falling in a church where he ministered: "There were others that faked it. One young man went down almost every night with a smile on his face. But every once in a while he would open an eye to see how things were going. When he discovered that I was watching, he quickly closed it again."[18]

Another consideration in this matter must be passivity. Keith Bailey comments as follows:

> The New Testament examples [of falling] such as Peter in a trance and John on Patmos do not indicate a state of passivity. They were conscious and fully aware of the circumstances about them. The "slain" that I have observed were not conscious of their surroundings and had no recollection of anything during the time they remained unconscious.
>
> I have seen people fall, unable to move, who were fully conscious and prayed earnestly for forgiveness and salvation. They were unsaved people under deep conviction—people that had resisted God for a long time.[19]

It is commonly known that occult and paranormal events may be triggered through passivity. William James, the apostle of American pragmatism, recorded the experience of a Mr. LeBaron who willed himself into a state of passivity so that he could observe and experience the paranormal.[20] Bailey and other contemporary authors warn against passivity in Christian experience, particularly among those in pursuit of tongues-speaking.[21] There are other modern writers who play at the edge of passivity. John Dahms suggests that Richard Foster exhibited a worrisome tendency on this issue.[22] Schuster, citing ther authorities, says that the experiencing of the paranormal may virtually *require* the development of a passive, receptive mode.[23] *Surely any falling manifestation that involves passivity deserves to be suspect.*

In summary, both the Scriptures and various incidents make clear that falling—being slain, prostrations or whatever the phenomenon may be called—can and do accompany profound works of the Holy Spirit as well as demonic deceptions and fleshly events which are no more than expressions of the carnal nature given over to mimicry, ostentation and exhibitionism.

My point in this book is that, since there is always the need to be discerning and to distinguish between phenomena, I am encouraging readers to ask the question and thereby "prove all things; hold fast that which is good" (1 Thessalonians 5:21, KJV).

### Endnotes

1. John Wimber, "Spiritual Phenomena: Slain in the Spirit—Part 1," Vineyard Christian Fellowship, Anaheim, California, 1981, audiotape.

2. Robert J. Kuglin, *Handbook on the Holy Spirit* (Camp Hill, PA: Christian Publications, 1996), 121-122.

3. Sereno E. Dwight, *The Works of Jonathan Edwards* (Carlisle, PA: The Banner of Truth Trust, 1987), lxiv.

4. Ibid., lxix.

5. Paul K. Conkin, *Cane Ridge America's Pentecost* (Madison, WI: The University of Wisconsin Press, 1990), 115-116.

6. Ibid., 113.

7. E.M. Bounds, *The Complete Works of E.M. Bounds on Prayer* (Grand Rapids, MI: Baker Book House, 1990), 138.

8. John Wesley, *The Journal of John Wesley* (Chicago: Moody Press, 1980), 76.

9. Bill McLeod, personal conversation, March 2001. See Arnold A. Dallimore, *George Whitfield: The Life and Times of the Great Evangelist of the Eighteenth Century* (Westchester, IL: Cornerstone Books, 1979), vol. 1, 321-331, 490-491.

10. Paul L. King, "Holy Laughter and Other Phenomena in Evangelical and Holiness Revival Movements," *Alliance Academic Review,* 1998 (Camp Hill, PA: Christian Publications, 1998), 110.

11. Keith M. Bailey, personal correspondence, March 2001.

12. W.L. McLeod, *Charismatic or Christian?* (Saskatoon, SK: Western Tract Mission, 1978), 149-150.

13. Ibid.

14. Charles Martzall, personal conversation, June 14, 1998.

15. Wesley Duewel, *Revival Fire* (Grand Rapids, MI: Zondervan, 1995), 154-155.

16. Ibid., 155.

17. Ibid., 154.

18. Kuglin, 125.

19. Keith M. Bailey, personal correspondence, June 19, 1999.

20. Andrew I. Drummond, *Edward Irving and His Circle* (London: James Clarke and Co., 1934), 295.

21. Dorothy Brotherton, *Quiet Warrior* (Beaverlodge, AB: Spectrum Publications, 1991), 145.

22. John V. Dahms, "A Critique of Richard Foster's *Celebration of Discipline*," *His Dominion*, Volume 12, Fall, 1985, 33-35. (Foster later moved away from passivity as revised editions of his book indicate.)

23. Marguerite Schuster, "Power, Pathology and Paradox," Ph.D. thesis since published (Pasadena, CA: Fuller Theological Seminary, 1977), 227.

# 16

## Revival
## and Revival

# Judge Brillante

LET ME INTRODUCE YOU TO Judge Brillante and his gracious wife. At the time of this story, they lived in the Philippines and attended an evangelical church. Typical of some parents, they had favorites among their children. The judge particularly lavished his love on one child to the neglect of the other six. He was also a new believer and very anxious to walk carefully with God. So when revival exploded in their church, the judge was one of the first to respond.

> The Holy Spirit . . . pointed out that one of his daughters was his favorite while at the same time he lacked love for his little boy. There was no recourse but to go to the boy and beg forgiveness. With tears, [this] man of God did just that. "Bobo," he said, "please forgive me for not loving you."
>
> Mrs. Brillante had a similar issue to meet. She lacked love for her daughter who just happened to be her husband's favorite![1]

After the judge and his wife had gotten thoroughly right with God, they became members of a revival team that visited a church whose name I have long forgotten. All I remember is its beautiful location near the shore and surrounded by majestic palms. Internally, it was another matter. The church for many years had been riven with hatreds and bitternesses of long standing. Our revival team came for only one afternoon meeting. What a whirlwind it turned out to be.

Mr. and Mrs. Brillante, along with other members of the group, shared passionately from their hearts. I preached only ten minutes or so, but the response came from the deeps. Confessions and apologies were made on every side, for hours it seemed. Wrongs were righted after many years of disobedience. I have never witnessed a revival of such short duration or such awesome power. Truly God sent us a veritable whirlwind of His power. His works were marvelous in our eyes.

### *Endnote*

1. K. Neill Foster, *Revolution of Love* (Camp Hill, PA: Horizon Books, 1973), 52.

# Counterfeit Revival

*by E.M. Bounds*

THERE ARE COUNTERFEIT REVIVALS well executed, well calculated to deceive the most wary. These are deceptive and superficial, with many pleasant, entertaining, and delusive features. These are entirely lacking in the offensive features which distinguish the genuine ones. The pain of penitence, the shame of guilt, the sorrow and humiliation of sin, fear of hell—these marks of the genuine are lacking in the counterfeit. The test of a genuine revival is in its staying qualities. The counterfeit is but a winter spurt. . . . The genuine revival goes to the bottom of things.[1]

### *Endnote*

1. Lyle Wesley Dorsett, *E.M. Bounds: Man of Prayer* (Grand Rapids, MI: Zondervan, 1991), 177.

# Revival and Revival

I HAD ATTENDED A BILLY GRAHAM CRUSADE in Minnesota. I had seen Merv Rosell, a great evangelist of the 1950s, gather in the soul-winning net. I had attended another evangelist's tent crusade and witnessed the clarity of the preaching of the gospel along with the profound and numerous response to the altar call. Moreover, I had, as an itinerant evangelist for more than twenty years, been a witness to and participant in numerous situations in which many had come to Jesus Christ in response to my preaching. But I had never come close to calling any of that revival.

The first time I ever witnessed revival—and knew within my own soul that it was revival just as I knew I was a Christian—was in Kelowna, British Columbia in 1972. The Sutera Twins, Italian-American evangelists, had advised me to attend the morning service with them in a participating church. I decided to sit in the balcony. The most unforgettable thing I saw was a line of believers stretching along the side of the auditorium and up onto the platform. They were awaiting their turn to confess their sins publicly and to beg God's forgiveness and the forgiveness of their brethren. The confessions were wrenching admissions of wrong doing; I cannot remember even thinking that a single testimony might be out of order or offensive to the Holy Spirit.

As the revival unfolded, it became clear that what had begun in Saskatoon, Saskatchewan in October, 1971 in the Ebenezer Baptist Church was spreading around the world through many denominations. Revival fires had spread to eastern Canada and to some parts of the United States, but it was generally focused, at its inception at least, in Western Canada. A curious feature of the 1971-1973 revival was that it did not generally penetrate the Pentecostal churches or churches in which the pastor, whatever the denomination, was unwilling to welcome it or unwilling to personally come to a place of new obedience and repentance. Still, the sense of God's presence and power was abroad in the land.

"Revival" is a loaded word in the evangelical context, and it means many things to many people. By now you know that I am not referring to a series of meetings which a local church conducts along with public announcements and perhaps a banner advertising it as a "revival."

The famous Welsh revivalist, Duncan Campbell, expresses similar sentiments:

> "Oh, that thou wouldest rend the heavens, that thou wouldest come down, that the mountains might flow down at thy presence" (Isaiah 64:1-2 [KJV]). You will observe that in that prayer of the prophets two fundamental things are suggested. That unless God comes down, mountains will not flow and sinners will not tremble. But if God comes down, if God manifests His power, if God shows His hand, if God takes the field, mountains will flow . . . mountains of indifference, mountains of materialism, mountains of humanism, will flow before His presence, and nations, not just individuals, but nations, shall be made to tremble.
>
> We haven't seen nations trembling, but we have seen communities; we have seen districts; we have seen parishes in the grip of God in a matter of hours when God comes down. . . .

Howard Spring was right when he wrote, "The kingdom of God is not going to advance by our churches becoming filled with men, but by men in our churches becoming filled with God." And there's a difference! . . . Crowded churches, deep interest in church activity is possible on mere human levels leaving the community untouched.

The difference between successful evangelism (and I use the word "successful") and revival is this: In evangelism, the two, the three, the ten, the twenty and possibly the hundred make confessions of Jesus Christ, and at the end of the year you are thankful if half of them are standing. But the community remains untouched. The public houses are crowded, the dances, dancing ballrooms, packed. The theater and the picture houses are patronized by the hundreds. No change in the community!

But in revival, when God the Holy Ghost comes, when the wind of heaven blows, suddenly the community becomes God-conscious! A God-realization takes hold of young, middle-aged and old. So that, as in the case of the Hebrides Revival, 75% of those saved one night were saved before they came near the meeting![1]

Revival, defined, is a sovereign movement among God's people in which, through a new and determined obedience, a profound working of the Holy Spirit takes place by which the Church of Jesus Christ is cleansed and renewed—so profoundly as to create a holy contagion, so powerfully that unusual events take place, and so remarkably that both the church and the world are aware that God is visiting His people, renewing fruitfulness and exhibiting mighty power. The natural outworking of that revival is a cleansing of the culture and a renewed evangelistic harvest.

The first time (of perhaps eight or ten) I ever saw revival as defined above in my own ministry was in General Santos City on the is land of Mindanao in the Philippines in June 1973. The meetings were marked by strong confessions of sin, powerful testimonies and the formation of teams of lay-witnesses who went out to tell the story and who in turn saw the same kind of phenomena. A veteran missionary, after observing for a while, sent a telegram to the field office, announcing that revival had come. The dominant trait of the revival was the powerful expression of Christian love.

The question must be asked: Within the evangelical context, are there really revivals and revivals? My answer is an unequivocal "yes." I see the criteria as follows.

## Revival Is for Believers

True revivals take place among Christians as they become unusually conscious of their own sinfulness and begin to confess this condition to God and to one another. As James exhorted, "Confess your sins to one another, and pray one for another, so that you may be healed" (5:16, NASB). Even by definition, a revival—a revivification—infers that something was already alive. The present events simply purify and enhance life that is already there.

## Revival Comes from the Sovereign Hand of God

True revivals come from the sovereign hand of God. Were that not true, I do not think I could bear ever to preach again after emerging from the atmosphere of true revival. Returning home from Mali, Burkina Faso and Côte d'Ivoire in 1972, I had been in the midst of revival power for several weeks. Suddenly, in Kingston, Ontario I was preaching the same messages, but I was bereft of the holy flame. I was, I believed, the same person—but there was no revival. The pain was unspeakably intense. The sovereignty of God became my sanity. Conversely, any revival manipulated by the hand of man deserves only God's "Ichabod" upon it (1 Samuel 4:21).

## Revival Is Contagious

Revivals have a contagion all their own. The analogy of fire attached to them is fitting because, like a consuming fire, they spread, often in unpredictable ways. There often are connecting cords between one revival and another. The Western Canadian Revival, for example, was linked to the ministry of Duncan Campbell and the revival in the Hebrides.

Prior to 1972, Campbell visited Canada and told observers that he "saw" Canada enveloped in revival flames. And while he was in Winnipeg, Manitoba, he said that revival would begin in the Ebenezer Baptist Church in Saskatoon, Saskatchewan. My understanding is that he did not tell this to Ebenezer's pastor, but to the pastor's brother.

Later, indeed, revival exploded in that city and in that particular church, and it soon enveloped the whole evangelical community. From there, through the witness of revived men and women, it spread particularly powerfully throughout Western Canada, less powerfully to the east, to the United States and beyond to many countries of the world. As the new millennium dawns, the most prominent of the enduring effects of that revival continues through the ministry of Henry Blackaby, author of *Experiencing God,* who at the time of the revival was pastoring Faith Baptist Church in Saskatoon, Saskatchewan.[2]

## Revival Is Accompanied by Phenomena

Phenomena of various kinds accompany revival. Sometimes these evidences are more dramatic than at other times. The ministry of Duncan Campbell was no exception.

> Rev. Campbell, the minister, and about two hundred people started across the fields, taking a shortcut to the other church. Suddenly the sky was filled with the sound of an-

gelic voices singing. Everyone heard it, and they fell on their knees in the field. . . . After Duncan Campbell had spoken for an hour, six young men sitting side by side suddenly saw the glory of God come down upon Campbell. They fell on the floor weeping.[3]

## Revivals Are Circumscribed by Time

Revivals begin and end. When revival came to Western Canada, we were for the most part novices in that kind of spiritual power. But we soon learned that there was a prelude, a build-up to the revival. Then came the mighty power, and then, for one reason or another, the emergence of resistance and/or the grieving of the Holy Spirit. The fire was quenched, the cloud of God's manifest presence lifted. What once was spontaneous can become manipulated. What once was true can become false.

## Revival Has a Backwash

Beyond revivals there are after-events which are not always attractive nor God-owned. I recall preaching in a church which had participated in and experienced revival. It was clear that the revival had been through, followed by a backwash of reactions to some extravagances which had resulted. It was beginning to abate about the time I arrived. Such a series of events would not have been considered before revival came.

## Revival Has a Particular Message

There is an essential theological message to revival. It involves a profound consciousness of sin, a powerful awareness of the reality of forgiveness, a deep consciousness of the presence of the Holy Spirit and the urgent necessity of obeying Him utterly. Those ingredients, variously and uniquely framed in every true revival, make up its message. Any revival which does not focus on the "preaching of the cross" (1 Corinthians 1:18, KJV) and does not lift up the Savior as "Christ crucified" should be rejected out of hand.

Once when Evan Roberts, the human instrument of the Welsh Revival, was asked if he had a message for America, he offered his framing of the theology of the revival in Wales:

> The prophecy of Joel is being fulfilled. There the Lord says, "I will pour out my Spirit upon all flesh." If that is so, all flesh must be prepared to receive. (1) The past must be clear; every sin confessed to God, any wrong to man must be put right. (2) Everything doubtful must be removed once for all out of our lives. (3) Obedience prompt and implicit to the Spirit of God. (4) Public confession of Christ. Christ said, "I, if I be lifted up, will draw all men unto Me." There it is. Christ is all in all.[4]

In a similar manner, the practical theology of the revivals in the ministry of Jonathan Goforth had its own awesome power.

> At the close of his autobiographical account of revival in China, *By My Spirit*, Jonathan Goforth asserted, "We wish to state most emphatically as our conviction that God's revival may be had when we will and where we will. . . . Our reading of the Word of God makes it inconceivable to us that the Holy Spirit should be willing, even for a day, to delay His work. We may be sure that, where there is a lack of the fullness of God, it is ever due to man's lack of faith and obedience. If God the Holy Spirit is not glorifying Jesus Christ in the world today, as at Pentecost, it is we who are to blame."
>
> Goforth then asks, "Are we ready to pay the price of Holy Ghost revival?" He outlines what he considers to be the indispensable factors in preparing God's way in re-

vival: (1) prayer, (2) a "back-to-the-Bible" movement, and (3) exalting Jesus Christ as King of kings and Lord of lords.

The old Presbyterian missionary and prayer warrior, the man of unshakable faith in the Word of God, concluded his book with these words: "Brethren, the Spirit of God is with us still. Pentecost is yet within our grasp. If revival is being withheld from us it is because some idol remains enthroned; because we still insist in placing our reliance on human schemes; because we still refuse to face the unchangeable truth that 'it is not by might, but by my Spirit.' "[5]

## Revivals Come through Special Servants

There are usually key human instruments in revival. The great revivals have been and are associated with people, God's burning brands, His special servants. In Wales, Evan Roberts. In the Hebrides in this century, Duncan Campbell. In the Western Canadian Revival, Ralph and Lou Sutera and Bill McLeod. J. Edwin Orr's various catalogs of revival sound ever so much like a biblical genealogy, showing the personalities of the various revivals just as certainly as their interconnectedness. Women like Pandita Ramabai and others were as greatly used as some of the men.[6] Jonathan Goforth of China caught the fire from Wales. Duncan Campbell spread the flame to Canada, and so it goes.

It is probably true to say that in many cases the human instruments do not see themselves as specially chosen by God—though they are indeed that. Failure to see themselves as sovereign instruments sometimes leads them to suggest that revivals simply come when certain conditions are met. *Charles G. Finney was possibly one of these.* The incarnational presence of a revivalist who has been in the fire and is anointed by the Holy Spirit especially for the task is often not included as one of the conditions for revival, not included because the role of revivalists and the sovereignty of God have been inadequately connected.

Likewise and regrettably, revivals that do not come from the Holy Spirit and do not exalt the Lord Jesus Christ are also led by special people, who, like Aaron's sons, Nadab and Abihu, carry with them their own false and bloodless fire.

## Revivals May Be Counterfeited

Counterfeits to revival do exist, and when they emerge, God's people must be discerning; they must distinguish between the true and the false. John noted the necessity of such sorting: "Many false prophets have gone out into the world" (1 John 4:1).

## The Revival Wars

Hank Hanegraaff's book *Counterfeit Revival*[7] has triggered new arguments in the revival wars. Rebuttals have been circulated as well. The debate of the late 1990s was whether or not the Toronto Blessing or the Brownsville Outpouring were true revivals. Lost somewhere in the discussion has been the historical record. What the past could teach us is that the revivals of history are not much like these current movements and that, given enough time, the final fruit will be revealed. They will either enter into history as authentic movements, or they will be set aside as insignificant parentheses.

In Gamaliel's case (Acts 5:34-39), he urged the Sanhedrin to wait and see if the infant Church had anything of God in it. As events turned out, the Christian Church took root and has never disappeared. Whether these events of the twentieth and twenty-first centuries will leave enduring marks is still to be determined.

## *Endnotes*

1. Duncan Campbell, *The Nature of a God-Sent Revival* (Vinton, VA: Christ Life Publications, n.d.), 5-7.

2. Henry Blackaby, *Experiencing God* (Nashville, TN: Broadman and Holman, 1994).

3. Wesley Duewel, *Revival Fire* (Grand Rapids, MI: Zondervan, 1995), 312, 317.

4. S.B. Shaw, *The Great Revival in Wales* (Chicago: S.B. Shaw, 1905), 40-41.

5. Duewel, 276-277.

6. J. Edwin Orr, *Evangelical Awakenings in Southern Asia* (Minneapolis, MN: Bethany Fellowship, 1975), 142-146.

7. Hank Hanegraaff, *Counterfeit Revival* (Dallas, TX: Word Publishing, 1997).

# Afterword

# God's Glory

THIS IS A DELIBERATELY unfinished book. There is however, one salient point that must be made. And it must be made exactly here.

God is jealous for His glory. He will not share it with another. The Scriptures make this exceptionally clear. "I am the LORD: that is my name: and my glory will I not give to another. . . . I will not give my glory to another" (Isaiah 42:8; 48:11, KJV).

And in the case of the polarities, the true and the false, there is always the "Counterkingdom Competitor." I am speaking of the devil. The imitations and counterfeits are all attempts on his part to regain lost glory and to supplant the King of Glory. That he has failed, is failing and will fail to do that is self-evident in God's Word.

But here we say, solemnly, carefully and prayerfully, "Let God be glorified in all these pages. May those things that inadvertently do not glorify our Lord fall to the ground. And may those things that truly glorify Him endure for the ages."

K. Neill Foster
March 17, 2001

# The Wheat and the Tares

Jesus told them another parable: "The kingdom of heaven is like a man who sowed good seed in his field. But while everyone was sleeping, his enemy came and sowed weeds among the wheat, and went away. When the wheat sprouted and formed heads, then the weeds also appeared.

"The owner's servants came to him and said, 'Sir, didn't you sow good seed in your field? Where then did the weeds come from?'

" 'An enemy did this,' he replied.

"The servants asked him, 'Do you want us to go and pull them up?'

" 'No,' he answered, 'because while you are pulling the weeds, you may root up the wheat with them. Let both grow together until the harvest. At that time I will tell the harvesters: First collect the weeds and tie them in bundles to be burned; then gather the wheat and bring it into my barn.' " (Matthew 13:24-30)

# Appendix 1

# Where Do We Go from Here?

As stated in the preface of this book, the singular purpose of this writing was simply "to point out the biblical reality of true and false—the polarities within the realm of the supernatural—and thereby raise the level of discernment."

But what are the sources of discernment? The answer is singular—from the Scriptures. I offer the following list for your consideration.

## Channel 1—The Word of God

Every word of the Word of God is inspired, God-breathed and completely trustworthy. The Scriptures plainly claim for themselves complete inspiration and freedom from error (2 Samuel 23:2-3; Isaiah 59:21; Jeremiah 1:9). The Old Testament writers affirm it, as do the apostles (Acts 1:16; 4:24-25; 28:25; Hebrews 3:7). Jesus, too, affirmed the inspiration of the Old Testament (Mark 12:36; John 10:35), as well as the New Testament (John 16:12). Peter, in Second Peter 3:16, refers to Paul's letters as Scripture. And "[t]he early apostolic church received the New Testament Scriptures as the inspired Word of God as they were written, though formal recognition of the entire canon came more slowly. Because the Scriptures are inspired, they are authoritative and without error in their original words, and constitute the infallible revelation of God to man."[1]

Understanding the Scriptures is key, as well as the contextual setting. As one person has observed, "It is not the things in the Bible that I do not understand that bother me; it is the things I do understand." The Bible, rightly and clearly understood, will solve all kinds of discernment difficulties. It is unfailingly discerning, and no one who neglects or distorts the Word of God can be discerning.

## Channel 2—The Holy Spirit

The passages in John 14, 15, 16 make clear that the Holy Spirit has come into the world to be the divine Advocate and Guide for the Church. It is His clear goal to lead Christian believers into "all truth" (John 16:13). The Holy Spirit is in the business of giving wisdom and discernment to Christians. He needs to be recognized, appreciated, respected. He must not be grieved or quenched. He wants to exercise spiritual gifts through the believers. He wants to adore and exalt Jesus Christ. He is the Spirit who searches the hearts, who knows all things. Because He is a Spirit, He communicates with the human spirit. He will never deny the Word He has inspired. We have a marvelous Helper. The Comforter has come. And with His coming, penetrating Christian insight and discernment have become possible.

## Channel 3—The Body

The church is the Bride of Christ. It is also His body, assembled and joined together by the Holy Spirit. Ephesians 4 and First Corinthians 12 are the classic passages explaining this mystical relationship in the kingdom of God. We are members one of another. And as the eye needs the hand, and the mind needs the feet, so the members of our Lord's body are mutually interdependent. Since the gifts are given severally as God wills and since no one has all the gifts, an interdependence exists. The children of God need each other, and they obtain discernment from one another. The writer of the proverb put it this way, "In  multitude of counsellors there is safety" (Proverbs

24:6, KJV). We are foolish indeed if we feel we have no need of others.

Some discussion of authority in the church is in order. The Scriptures teach that Christians should obey those that have the rule over them (Hebrews 13:7, 17). (This has been abused, of course, and some believers have been spiritually imprisoned by zealous overseers.) Authority is a protective device. It allows the discernment of the body to have time and space to work. The spiritual gifts resident in the church contribute to discernment. Should one assume he has no need for the checks and balances the membership of the body brings into the life of a Christian, he is confused, if not deceived.

The discerning gifts, if allowed interplay in our lives, bring safety and protection to the body. When all is in order, the body provides discernment. We ignore it at our peril.

## Channel 4—The Discerning of Spirits

This gift of the Holy Spirit has often been called the gift of discernment, but it is not that. It is the gift, the charism that enables one to discern *spirits* (1 Corinthians 12:10). According to the Bible, there are at least four different kinds of spirits—the Holy Spirit, the human spirit, angelic spirits, and finally, fallen or evil spirits. The gift of discerning of spirits has to do with the intricate workings which take place in the spiritual world. A person with this gift will be more aware than others of the action and interaction of these spiritual forces.

## Channel 5—Experience

Discernment comes by experience. That is why an adage "Experience is the best teacher" has had such a long life. "But solid food is for the mature, who by constant use have trained themselves to distinguish good from evil" (Hebrews 5:14). Discernment comes with time, trial and error, age and experience. That is why Paul ord⁻⁻⁻

elders, not "youngers." Age in itself does not assure discernment, but discernment comes with the exercise of the senses, and that takes time.

## Channel 6—Patience

The passage of time itself clarifies issues. The Scriptures are full of exhortations in favor of patience.

> It is not good to have zeal without knowledge, nor to be *hasty* and miss the way. (Proverbs 19:2, emphasis added)

> But you, man of God, flee from all this, and pursue righteousness, godliness, faith, love, *endurance* and gentleness. (1 Timothy 6:11, emphasis added)

> You need to *persevere* so that when you have done the will of God, you will receive what he has promised. (Hebrews 10:36, emphasis added)

## Channel 7—Full Surrender

> Therefore, I urge you, brothers, in view of God's mercy, to offer your bodies as living sacrifices, holy and pleasing to God—which is your spiritual act of worship. Do not conform any longer to the pattern of this world, but be transformed by the renewing of your mind. Then you will be able to test and approve what God's will is—his good, pleasing and perfect will. (Romans 12:1-2)

There is a very real sense in which abandonment to God provides a large measure of discernment, so much so that, I venture to say, abandonment of oneself to God, to the will of God, to the Word of God will certainly produce discernment. The verb used in Romans

12:1 and 2 is an aorist which demands a once-and-for-all abandonment to God. I am persuaded that every Christian should abandon himself to God's will and that he should renew those vows from time to time. This is godly good sense. This surrender also reveals God's perfect will. It brings the penetrating insight in Christian discernment we need so much. When we abandon ourselves to God, we should be clearly giving ourselves to the God of the Bible who sent His only Son, Jesus Christ into the world and who manifests Himself in the person of the Holy Spirit today.

## Channel 8—Godly Discipline

At the very heart of Christianity is discipleship. Devotion to Jesus Christ is logically followed by appropriate disciplines. Not surprisingly, discipline sharpens spiritual discernment and insight. The classic example is that of the Savior Himself. As the divine Son of God possessing all the attributes of God, there was probably no deep need for Jesus to be fasting when He was being tempted by the devil in the wilderness (Matthew 4:1-11). But He did it anyway. Holy and godly discipline is assuredly a channel of true Christian discernment.

## Channel 9—Observing the Enemy

In some ways, I'm inclined to omit this section. Succinctly stated, I believe that sometimes we become truly discerning when we detect the activity of Satan, when we finally observe his direction and intent. To be anti-devil is fairly good Christianity, even if it is backdoor theology! My advice: Do not expect or seek discernment in this way. But it may happen.

## Channel 10—Christ, the Living Word

The word of God is living and active. Sharper than any double-edged sword, it penetrates even to dividing soul and spirit, joints and marrow; it judges the thoughts and attitudes of the heart. Nothing in all creation is hidden from God's sight. Everything is uncovered and laid bare before the eyes of him to whom we must give account. (Hebrews 4:12-13)[2]

Christ is the secret of all discernment. His indwelling presence is the key to understanding, wisdom, insight and discernment. Little wonder that great men of God like Dr. A.B. Simpson became so enamored of the concept. "Christ in you, the hope of glory" (Colossians 1:27). Christ is literally the total answer for every need in the Christian life. Allow the Lord Jesus to dwell in you and manifest Himself through you, and you will share His holiness, manifest His faith and demonstrate His discernment.

### Endnote

1. C.I. Scofield, ed., *The New Scofield Reference Bible* (New York: Oxford University Press, 1967), 1, 304.

2. The ten channels are taken from K. Neill Foster, *The Discerning Christian* (Camp Hill, PA: Christian Publications, 1981), pp. 60-75.

## Appendix 2

# True and False Prophets

Beware of false prophets" (Matthew 7:15, KJV). These well-known words of Jesus immediately imply two things: there are false prophets—and they are dangerous.

The existence of true and false and the danger of deception in the Christian life were not limited to the life and times of Jesus Christ. Moses, before Him, also warned the people of Israel against false prophets (Deuteronomy 13 and 18). And there are false prophets today as well. Just a few years ago a young friend of mine, along with his wife, became infatuated with a false prophet. At the time they were living in a western community isolated from other Christians and so began to attend meetings in which the "prophet" unveiled "new" truth and "deeper" truth that, according to him, traditional churches and pastors were too dull to accept.

Some of my colleagues alerted the young man and his wife to their danger, repeatedly warning them to get out and not to follow "that man." I held my peace. But finally the day came. The two of us were in his place of business alone. He knelt to pray—and prayed in tongues.

After the prayer time was over, he asked, "Neill, what do you think?" It was my signal to give him the exhortation that had been building up in me. I told him that the man he was following was wrong, unfaithful to the Scriptures—and false. Since there were many prophecies in the movement, I told him that he would get prophecy upon prophecy, and when one was not fulfilled there would be another to explain why the first had failed. My exhortation was lengthy and vigorous.

The reader must not assume that I am against prophecies. Remember that Paul instructed us not to despise prophecies (1 Thessalonians 5:20). I seek to obey that injunction. Neither should the reader assume that I am against tongues-speaking. While I never promote tongues-speaking, the New Testament tells us not to forbid speaking in tongues (1 Corinthians 14:39). In this case described above, however, both of these phenomena were threads in a web of deception. Had I understood then what I learned later about testing the validity of tongues and prophecy (1 John 4:1-3), I might have been able to help my friend escape his deception.

Although my words hammered him, and he seemed literally to reel before all that I was saying, he did not—seemingly could not—leave off following that false prophet. Still today, he and his wife continue to follow. The prophet was killed in a plane crash, but his tape recordings go on, and the evil powers that worked and still work through him hold their victims. As I write, I grieve for a brother so long deceived and for a friendship that could have been.

## Two Kinds of False Prophets

Though a great many who are familiar with the Old and New Testaments are aware that there are false prophets, not as many realize that there are two major kinds of false prophets.

- The first, the lying false prophet, announces events or says things that do not come true. He is obviously a false prophet (Deuteronomy 18:20-22). The penalty in Old Testament times was death for false prophets (18:20). This kind of false prophet is the most easily recognized and least dangerous of the two.

- The second kind of false prophet is more deceptive (Deuteronomy 13:1-3). He is impeccable in his words at first. All he says comes to pass. No fault can be found with his speech. Nevertheless, over time he draws the hearts of the people away from the Lord God Almighty. Finally, he leads them off to serve other gods. This kind of person is very dangerous, indeed the more dangerous of the two.

## Four Kinds of False Prophecy

Most of us are inclined to forget that there are false prophets. However, the frightening facts are these: there are at least two kinds of false prophets and four kinds of false prophecies. The details of these false prophecies are listed in Jeremiah 14:14.

- *False Visions.* These may come from the evil heart of the false prophet, or they may come from an evil spirit that controls him. The false visions are truly "seen" by the false prophet, but their source is devilish.

- *Divinations.* This is another form of false prophecy. Diviners may examine the entrails of animals or how rice floats in water. Or they may use a thousand other ways to divine. But their information is finally false even though some things may appear to be true, and entrapment of the simple is made easy. True prophets of God do not read palms or witch water.

- *Idolatries.* This breaking of the first of the Ten Commandments (Exodus 20:3) is the third form of false prophecy. Idols in themselves are nothing, nothing at all (Jeremiah 10:1-5). However, if they are seized by demons, then the idols reflect the power of the demons involved. The Ten Commandments explicitly forbid idols or graven images of any kind. When demons empower the idols, it is not long before prophecies emerge from the demons. We dare not have anything to do with such demons (1 Corinthians 10:21). Their prophecies are false.

- *Delusions.* These are the final kind of false prophecy—delusions of the mind. They are not necessarily from the devil; they may simply be fabricated by the persons themselves. They are still false, however, and very dangerous. And we recall again that false prophets were under severe judgment in the Old Testament. Jeremiah reminds us that even though false prophets prophesy and say all kinds of fascinating things, the Almighty is saying, "I did not send them" (Jeremiah 14:15).

One might even think that false prophets would have no power to attract at all. But the commentators, Keil and Delitzsch, observe in this Jeremiah passage that these willing listeners are under judgment just as severe as those who prophesy falsely: "They are not . . . excused because false prophets told them lies, for they have given credit to these lies."[1]

## Four Characteristics of False Prophets

False ministers exhibit a number of peculiar characteristics. Though not every false prophet necessarily displays all of the traits mentioned here, these are common.

- *The Love of Preeminence.* They like to be important and to have others believe and follow them. Diotrephes is a case in point. He loved to have the preeminence, but his heart was wholly evil (3 John 9). If someone has an inordinate desire to be a leader, if he thrusts himself forward to gain ascendancy, ask yourself a very important question: Is that person a false prophet?

  *Love of Money.* We know from Scripture that the love of ey is the root of all evil (1 Timothy 6:10). The early Christians wrote that if a man asked for money, he was surely a false prophet.[2] Those writings did not get into the New Testament, and certainly godly pastors and evangelists should encourage God's people to give their tithes and offerings. However, if someone is always pressing for money and seems likely to benefit personally from that gift or offering—beware!

- *The Love of Immorality.* Adultery and fornication are never too far removed from the doors of most false prophets (Jude 4; Revelation 2:20). Some may appear to be holy, even sanctimonious, but their apparent "purity" does not negate the rule (2 Corinthians 11:15). If you have doubts about someone, watch that person's interpersonal behavior.

- *The Love of Miracles and Spectacles.* The God of the Bible is certainly a God of miracles. No one can read the New Testament and come to any other conclusion. Faithful preaching of the Word of God even today will be followed by miracles and deliverances (Hebrews 13:8). At the same time, Jesus clearly warned that the presence of miracles and the casting out of demons are not necessarily authentications of true prophets. Rather, some who do those things, according to Scripture, may be the ones who will hear Christ's words: "I never knew you; DEPART FROM ME" (7:23). He will say this even to those who have been using His name in the doing (Matthew 7:15-23, NASB).

As the return of Jesus Christ nears, we may expect an abundance of false prophets and ultimately the appearance of the Antichrist. He will be a man of lying signs and wonders (2 Thessalonians 2:9). We are not to be deceived.

## The Fourfold Message of the False Prophet

False prophets never speak all lies. Rather, they speak mostly truth, but woven in and through the many true statements is a lie—

probably a major lie. Paul was amazed that the Corinthian church had been taken in by pseudo-apostles (2 Corinthians 11:1-15). The message of the false apostle may demonstrate and/or be characterized by a number of things.

- *He has his own gospel.* Are you surprised at that? Don't be. If the prophet is false, and inspired by the devil, he will have a special message. It will make sense. It will have its own reasons and rationale. It is also likely to be accompanied by its own miracles and providences. This was exactly the case among the Corinthians. But do not be deceived—it is a different gospel, a different message. Even though the Corinthians knew the Apostle Paul and had been taught by him, they loved the new gospel, and it went down smoothly (2 Corinthians 11:4; see also Galatians 1:6).

- *He has his own Jesus.* If a false prophet comes to a Christian, he will need a Jesus of some kind. He will never deceive any Christian unless he has a Jesus (2 Corinthians 11:4). There are many beings called Jesus in the world, just as there are many antichrists (1 John 2:18) and many false Christs (Matthew 24:24). I learned many years ago that when someone comes to me talking about Jesus, I must wait. I wait for the verbal use of His full title. I want to discover which Jesus is being talked about. Is he the Jesus of the New Testament, of Matthew, Mark, Luke and John? Is He the Jesus Christ described by the Apostle Paul? Did He come in the flesh (1 John 4:1-3), and is he Lord of all (1 Corinthians 12:3)? Is He the Jesus we confess in the Apostles' Creed?

- *He has his own spirit* (2 Corinthians 11:4). There is a reason why Christians must never invite false prophets into their homes (2 John 10). It has to do with doctrine, yes, but it has much more to do with spirits and contagion. Evil power is contagious. Mormons and Jehovah's Witnesses have another gospel, true. And they preach an alternate Jesus, true. But they are most dangerous because they have another spirit, an evil spirit which can do great damage in the life of a Christian. "So behind every prophet is a spirit, and behind each spirit either God or the devil."[3] The apostle did not bother to say, "Do not believe every prophet." Rather he went straight to the point: "Do not believe every spirit." Dr. Stott, in looking further at this passage says, "There is an urgent need for discernment among Christians. We are often too gullible, and exhibit a naive readiness to credit messages and teachings which purport to come from the spirit-world. There is such a thing, however, as a misguided charity and tolerance towards false doctrine. Unbelief (*believe not every spirit*) can be as much a mark of spiritual maturity as belief."[4]

If Christians are discerning, they will have learned the habit of disbelieving all spirits. That, in fact, is what the Apostle Paul had in mind when he said, "Despise not prophesyings. Prove all things; hold fast that which is good" (1 Thessalonians 5:20-21, KJV).

- *He has his own anointing.* False prophets are sometimes very exciting and colorful. They speak with power. They may be interesting and dramatic. There is a reason for that; being false does not mean being without an anointing. He just has another kind of anointing, an alternate anointing (1 John 2:18-27). Antichrists in the New Testament are those who have substitute enduements. It is not just that they are against Jesus Christ—they are sometimes powerfully, dramatically and excitingly so. They have an alternate anointing that gives them power. The true prophet is supposed to have an anointing from the Holy Spirit of Almighty God. The false prophet has another kind of unction.

## Four Favorite Doctrines of False Prophets

I may be exaggerating when I say that the following are the four favorite doctrines of false prophets. You be the judge.

- *The Denial of the Deity of Jesus Christ.* For false prophets, Jesus Christ may be "a" god but not the Creator, God incarnate, God Almighty. They may even allow that Jesus Christ is the Son of God, but not God Almighty (John 1:1). Without exception, they find ways to diminish the integrity and deity of Jesus Christ. If these false prophets are inspired and empowered by Satan, as they are, we should not be surprised that they ultimately attack the Lord Jesus Christ. They do it because Satan is their father, and he has been a murderer and a liar from the beginning (8:44).

- *The Denial of the Incarnation of Jesus Christ.* John makes this very clear. Every spirit that does not continually confess that Jesus Christ is come "in the flesh" is not of God (1 John 4:1-3). Why is the incarnation so essential? Because Jesus Christ was not truly man if He was not clothed with flesh. If Jesus Christ did not come in the flesh, who died on the cross? And what was torn if not His flesh? And what was shed if not His blood? The Apostle Paul preached Jesus Christ crucified. He preached the cross. Why was he so emphatic? Because it is on the cross that the enfleshment and incarnation of Jesus Christ are most clearly seen. Beware when there is no mention of the blood of Jesus Christ. Beware when there is no preaching about the cross of Jesus Christ. "For the preaching of the cross is to them that perish foolishness; but unto us which are saved it is the power of God" (1 Corinthians 1:18, KJV). False prophets do not love the cross of Christ. They prefer rather not to mention it.

- *The Denial of the Lostness of Man.* The Scripture makes very clear that all men and women who have not believed in Jesus

Christ are eternally lost (John 3:16, 36). To question that there is a place called hell, and to suggest that eternity is not forever is a favorite device of false prophets. Jesus Christ was the most emphatic teacher of eternal punishment and the lostness of man in all of the Bible (Matthew 25:46; John 3:16, etc.). False prophets, moved and controlled by evil spirits, do not want to confess their own future since the lake of fire has been prepared for the devil and his angels (Matthew 25:41).

- *The Denial of the Inspiration and Integrity of Scripture.* The Bible teaches that God's Word has been inspired as holy men were moved by the Holy Spirit to write (2 Timothy 3:16). All that they have written are God's words (Romans 3:2). Every single word of the original texts has been given by God. Not even a tiny jot or tittle will pass away (Matthew 5:18). It is the practice of Satan to say, "Did God really say . . . ?" (Genesis 3:1). False prophets say the same thing because they are energized by the same spirit.

  False prophets also like to have their own revelations and attack the adequacy and inerrancy of the Holy Scriptures in order to introduce their own scriptures. If the prophet is adding new revelation to the Bible accepted by the Church for most of these 2,000 years, you can be sure that prophet is false.

## Four Favorite Tactics of False Prophets

False prophets are involved in spiritual warfare—against the Church and against the Lord Jesus Christ. In their wars on behalf of the counterkingdom ruled by Satan, they follow a number of common strategies.

- *Invasion from the Outside.* When Paul was bidding farewell to the Ephesian elders, he warned them that certain men would descend upon their church and cause havoc (Acts 20:29). This is one of the favorite tactics of the false prophet. Coming in from outside, he is unknown and, therefore, more easily able to deceive. The Church of the first century struggled mightily to distinguish between prophets false and true. Several of the criteria they emphasized in the Didache and other early writings have to do with distinguishing between those who come into the local assembly from the outside.

- *Emergence from the Inside.* Just as Paul warned the Ephesian elders about those coming from elsewhere, he proceeded to shock them further by insisting that even from among themselves false brethren would arise (Acts 20:30). We are not to be surprised by those who rise up and become false prophets. They come, still today, from among the faithful.

- *Resistance to Authority.* False prophets challenge the authority of the pastor and elders. If they are to be successful, they must challenge the existing leadership. The Scriptures teach that believers are to obey those who have the rule over them, those who oversee watch for their souls (Hebrews 13:17). If a true undershepherd, a true and godly pastor (1 Peter 5:1-4), is guarding his flock, his authority has to be overturned before the false prophet can rend and tear the sheep. It also must be admitted, unfortunately, that sometimes godly leaders become corrupt and end up as false prophets themselves, remaining in the places of authority all the while.

- *Isolation of Victims.* False prophets are rightly likened to wolves (Acts 20:29). All predators do one thing to their victims—they separate the one about to be destroyed from the protection of the flock or herd. Once the victim is separated from the rest, he becomes easy prey. The word "demon" means distributor and divider.[5] If false prophets are controlled by demons, we should not be surprised when they divide the flock, isolating their victims before destroying them. And if the young, the infirm and the aged are beguiled, we should not be surprised. Young people are inexperienced and unfortunately curious. The weak and aged sometimes do not have the strength or clarity to escape.

## The Four Main Weapons against False Prophets

Fortunately, there are a number of powerful spiritual weapons that can and must be used in the Christian's struggle against the deception of false prophets (2 Corinthians 10:4-6).

- *God's Word.* The more one reads and studies the Bible, the more likely he is to recognize false prophets. Conversely, the less one knows about the Word of God, the more easily he will be deceived and led astray. Like Timothy of old, we should give attendance to reading (1 Timothy 4:13), and we should study to show ourselves approved unto God, not ashamed, but able to rightly divide the word of truth (2 Timothy 2:15).

    Familiarity with the Bible also needs some basic laws of interpretation to go along with it. One of the most helpful is this: If the literal sense makes common sense, seek no other sense. Another helpful rule of interpretation to remember is that the Bible is by far the best interpreter of itself.

- *A Multitude of Counselors.* In a multitude of spiritual counselors there is safety (Proverbs 11:14). God's servants are part of a body—the body of Christ (Ephesians 4:15-16). Christians can be very helpful to one another. If pastors or elders or older brothers and sisters in the church warn you, listen! They are probably correct. Their wisdom is exceptionally valuable. Having seen various false prophets over the years, they have learned not to be taken in by them.

- *Tough Truth* (2 Timothy 4:2-3). False prophets tickle the ears of the people (4:3). They often pronounce that they have deeper truths to share (Revelation 2:24). Paul observed that those who wish to turn away from the Lord Jesus Christ will not "endure sound doctrine" (2 Timothy 4:3). The message that is very smooth and attractive probably has something wrong with it. Real truth has an edge; it has bite to it. It makes demands. It sometimes hurts when we hear it. One of the best understandings with which to protect oneself from following false teachers is this: Sound doctrine must be endured.

• *Pursuit of Love* (1 Corinthians 14:1). There are always those who wish to pursue miracles and spectacles. There are always those who wish to have their ears tickled. But love is preeminent. Miracles and martyrdom cannot compare with it (13:3). It is greater than faith and hope (13:13). Jesus Christ commanded His disciples to love one another (John 13:34-35). The great commandment is to love the Lord our God with all our heart and soul and mind and strength (Mark 12:29-30). "By this all men will know that you are my disciples," Jesus said (John 13:35).

Paul's prayer for the Philippian church was that their love would abound more and more in order that they could discern (Philippians 1:9-10). The most discerning apostle was John. True, he wrote his Gospel, his epistles and the Revelation as he was inspired by the Holy Spirit, but he was the obvious choice among the apostles to write the Revelation—because he was the apostle of love, because he loved the Master so deeply (John 13:23). He saw more because he loved more.

In conclusion, I must recount the story of a false prophetess who lived in a Latin American city. The beginning of a movement that was called a revival was underway in that city. It featured a lot of falling under the power, being "slain in the Spirit." Eventually, the woman, along with her brother who was the pastor, withdrew from her home church with perhaps 200 others. Because the church leadership was wrong, and because they were not following the Holy Spirit, she said, it would soon become clear that she was to be a prophetess and would lead a great movement for God. To validate her calling and future status, she also announced that on a certain day her invalid husband would die. His death would demonstrate the rightness of her prophecies and launch her out into a wide prophetic ministry.

The predicted day arrived. The sick husband, a believer, dressed himself in his best finery. Many people gathered to witness the passing of this saint of God into the presence of the Lord. They waited the whole day and even partly into the next, but nothing happened. The husband did not die on the day appointed. The woman obviously was a false prophetess. To his credit, her brother who was pastor of the new group publicly rebuked her. The original church that had lost hundreds of people returned to evangelism and soulwinning. The congregation grew until once more the sanctuary was filled. But, in the meantime, the false prophetess had caused a great deal of trauma and pain.

## A Final Word

One might assume after reading this appendix that discerning false prophets is a simple matter. If that impression has been conveyed, it is most assuredly wrong. I have been deceived more than once. The struggle to be discerning faces duplicity so great, Matthew says, that even the elect are barely able to discern (Matthew 24:24).

If you have a great concern about false prophets, my advice is ultimately twofold: 1) immerse yourself in the Scriptures (2 Timothy 2:15), and 2) pursue love, so that it may abound on every side and bring you discernment in the end (Philippians 1:9).

Beware of false prophets.

# Endnotes

1. C.F. Keil and F. Delitzsch, *Commentary on the Old Testament in Ten Volumes* (Grand Rapids, MI: Eerdmans, 1980), volume 8, 250.

2. Alexander Roberts and James Donaldson, *Anti-Nicene Christian Library* (Edinburgh: T & T Clark, 1916), volume 5, 114.

3. John R.W. Stott, *The Epistles of John* (Grand Rapids, MI: Eerdmans, 1960), 153.

4. Ibid.

5. W.E. Vine, *The Expanded Vine's Expository Dictionary of New Testament Words,* edited by John R. Kohlenberger, III (Minneapolis, MN: Bethany House, 1984), 283.

# Appendix 3

# The Specific Jesus

*Excerpted from "Discernment, the Powers,
and Spirit-Speaking" by K. Neill Foster*

Having discussed the matter of Jesus and Jesus in chapter 12, and having no other Jesus than the Lord Jesus Christ firmly established in our minds, we wish to consider an alternate reading of First John 4:3: " . . . every spirit that does not confess that Jesus Christ is come in the flesh is not of God" (NKJV).

The controversy is summarized as follows: Most manuscripts read *may homologei,* "does not confess," but the Vulgate, many Old Latin manuscripts and a number of Latin Fathers have readings that assume *luei,* "looses, destroys, annuls," as original. The Latin texts have *solvit* ("severs"), and the Fathers have *destruit* ("destroys"). Some modern scholars have accepted the Latin reading. . . .[1]

The alternate reading, [*luei*], becomes strikingly significant in view of the tendency of . . . [some movements] to focus on Jesus . . . [to truncate His name] and to "Jesusize" the Christian faith. Though we are not at this point suggesting that the Jesusizing of Christianity is necessarily a reflection of latent Gnosticism or doctrinal error, the loosing and disassociating of Jesus from Christ obviously can be an indication of deception as indicated in our earlier discussion about "this Jesus," and the prevalence of Jesus spirits [as observed by those who engage in the deliverance ministry. Frankly, manifestations of pseudo-jesus spirits happen frequently.] . . .

The alternate reading is precise, *pan pneuma ho luei ton Jesus,* "every spirit that loosens this Jesus . . . [is not from God]." But the arguments for it are exceptionally interesting. *Lueo* is a primary verb meaning to loosen, . . . break up, destroy, dissolve or . . . unloose. It also carries meanings of "to melt and to put off."[2] If the apostle speaks of disassociating Jesus from Christ, or if he means loosening Jesus from Christ as Cerinthus certainly wished to do, then the verb is aptly chosen.

The [alternate] reading is often associated with [the heretic] Cerinthus who was a contemporary of the Apostle John.[3] Irenaeus tells the story that when John found himself in the same bathhouse as Cerinthus, he fled fearing disaster.[4] Frederick W. Farrar, though he casts doubt on the bathhouse story . . . , explains that Cerinthus

> was one of those who believed in two principles, making a distinction between God and . . . the Creator. Further than this, he was one of the founders of docetism, in that form of it which spoke of "Jesus" as being a mere man, on whom "Christ," the Son of the Most High God, had descended at His baptism. . . .[5]

As Farrar makes clear, the Cerinthian tendency to sever Jesus from Christ is . . . [rebutted by] the alternate reading.

Findlay presents a good summary of the case for *luei.*

> hough *ho may homologei* [the accepted rendering] stands
> all the extant Greek codices, earlier and later, *ho luei ton*
> us is vouched for by Irenaeus and Origen (in Latin

translations), by Tertullian, Lucifer, and Augustine. The patristic Socrates, in his *Hist. Ecclesiae, vii. 32,* approves the reading *luei*, stating that "it had been so written in the old copies," and argues from it against the Nestorians; he even asserts, on the testimony of the "old interpreters," that the disappearance of *luei* from the current text was due to its depravation by heretics! This is strong evidence for the . . . [genuineness] of the Greek reading *luei.*[6]

. . . Farrar ventures [in verse three] a translation thus: "Every spirit *which severs Jesus . . . [is not from God]."*[7] *He bases it in part on Socrates who tells us that Nestorius "was ignorant that in the ancient manuscripts* of the Catholic Epistle of John *it had been written* that, 'Every spirit *which severs Jesus* is not from God.' "*[8]

And rather impatiently, Farrar says, "How Dusterdieck [another commentator] and others can here maintain that Socrates does not mean to assert that the reading 'severs Jesus' *was actually found* in these old manuscripts is more than I can understand."[9]

Still, an authority [of Farrar's era] like Westcott considers *luei* carefully, but prefers not to embrace it, believing that Polycarp in an indirect reference to the writings of John affirms the accepted reading.[10] Plummer [a more modern authority] discusses the variant reading but concludes, "it can scarcely be genuine, for it is *not found in a single Greek MS.,* nor in any version except the Vulgate."[11] [Charles Gore (1920)[12] and Ronald A. Ward (1965),[13] both from the interim period argue for the "severs" language.] . . .

Marshall's [1978] summary of the reasons why *luei* should be accepted as the original reading are as follows:

In favor of this reading it is argued: (1) The attestation [for severs] is very old, going back to the mid-second century. (2) The grammatical irregularity of using *may* with the indicative *homologei* suggests that this reading [confess] is not original. (3) *Luei* is a pregnant expression while *may homologei* is a colorless substitution. (4) The sharp continuation in verse 3b demands the stronger word. (5) It is easier to explain the scribal word [as *may homologei*] to bring the saying into conformity with verse 2.[14]

On the probability scale of our day (2001), I place "severs" as an eight or a nine. The original text probably contained *luei*. But it is not a ten and may not ever be unless older and better manuscripts of the New Testament are discovered. Still, and this is an extremely important caveat, orthodox Christians must regard with a jaundiced eye every tendency and every current which seems intent on severing Jesus in any way from His Lordship, His Deity and His Messiahship.

### Endnotes

1. Donald W. Burdick, *The Letters of John the Apostle* (Chicago: Moody Press, 1985), 297.

2. James Strong, *The Exhaustive Concordance of the Bible* (New York: Abingdon, 1890), 3089.

3. John Fletcher Hurst, *Short History of the Christian Church* (New York: Harper and Brothers, 1893), 27.

4. David J. Wright, "The Gnostics," *Eerdman's Handbook to the History of Christianity* (Grand Rapids, MI: Eerdmans, 1977), 100.

5. Frederick W. Farrar, *The Early Days of Christianity* (New York: Cassell, Petter Galpin & Co., 1882), volume 2:162-163.

6. George C. Findlay, *Fellowship in the Life Eternal* (London: Hodder and Stoughton, 1909), 316.

7. Farrar, 2:447.

8. Ibid., 448-449.

9. Ibid., 449.

10. Brook Foss Westcott, *The Epistle of St. John* (New York: MacMillan, 1886), 142.

11. Alfred Plummer, *The Epistles of St. John* (Grand Rapids, MI: Baker Book House, 1980), 96.

12. Charles Gore, *The Epistle of St. John* (London: John Murray Publishing, 1920), cited on page 193, "Discernment, the Powers and Spirit-Speaking," by K. Neill Foster.

13. Ronald A. Ward, *The Epistles of John and Jude* (Grand Rapids, MI: Baker Book House, 1965), cited on page 173, "Discernment, the Powers and Spirit-Speaking," by K. Neill Foster.

14. I. Howard Marshall, *The New International Commentary on the New Testament, The Epistles of John* (Grand Rapids, MI: Eerdmans, 1978), 207.

# Appendix 4

# Jonathan Edwards' Evaluative Criteria

This appendix also consists of material assembled in the endnotes of my dissertation.[1] It is dependent on and is an interpretation of another significant work.[2] The following pages are as cited in the dissertation. D.W. Waanders' section, called "[Jonathan] Edwards' Evaluative Criteria," is exceptionally interesting. He observes that "within Edwards' historical context, the problem of evaluating religious experience was a serious one because the Great Awakening brought a great interest in religious experience to New England and much disagreement about the evaluation and interpretation of religious experience."[3]

Edwards' twelve signs of the working of the Holy Spirit are better known than another set of twelve signs about which he also wrote. In *Religious Affections* he [Edwards] gives a cumbersome section entitled "Shewing What Are No Certain Signs that Religious Affections Are Truly Gracious, or that They Are Not." In the context of discernment in which this is written, the first twelve signs summarized here are fully as interesting as the later twelve, perhaps more so.

1. Great religious experiences in themselves are no sign of their validity or that necessarily they are from God.

2. Religious experiences which have great effect upon the body are not necessarily valid.

3. Fluent, fervid and abundant spiritual speaking in no way demonstrates that the religious experience is necessarily divine.

4. If a person does not create his own religious experience, or by his own strength does not initiate the experience, the experience is still not necessarily valid or divine.

5. If a religious experience comes with texts and Scripture remarkably brought to mind, it is not necessarily valid or divine.

6. The appearance of love in a religious experience is no proof that it is a valid or saving experience.

7. Multiplied religious experiences, accompanying one another are no evidence that the experience is necessarily saving or divine.

8. Religious experiences in which comforts and joys seem to follow conviction in a certain order are not necessarily saving or divine.

9. Spiritual experiences which stimulate the spending of much time in religious activity and zealous participations in the externals of worship are not necessarily saving experiences.

10. Religious experiences which cause men and women to praise and glorify God with their mouths are not necessarily saving and divine.

11. Religious experiences which produce confidence of being in a good estate in the people that have them are not necessarily saving or divine.

12. Religious experiences which are outwardly pleasing and very acceptable to the truly godly are not necessarily saving or divine.[4]

With each of these initial twelve signs, Edwards is careful to buttress his statements with Scripture. That he had been witness to many unusual events in the Great Awakening is reported in *A Faithful Narrative of the Surprising Work of God,* published in 1737. That he was a discerning witness in the two sets of signs both the former and the latter attest. It is significant in that Edwards was an ardent biblicist who believed this. Therein lies its significance and value.

The first twelve signs, already summarized above, were set negatively. The second twelve signs, positively framed, are also essential to his thought.

1. In the first sign of the second twelve, Edwards draws a sharp distinction between affections which are natural and commonplace on the one hand and affections which are "spiritual, supernatural" and "divine" on the other hand.[5] True believers exhibit divine affections, whereas false professors show natural and carnal affections.

2. The second sign has to do with what Edwards calls the objective or foundation of gracious affections, or what Waanders calls "the love of divine things."[6]

3. The third sign, built upon the second, was an appreciation for "the loveliness of the moral excellency of divine things."[7] Genuine Christians develop an appreciation for the beauty that is revealed in moral excellency.

4. His fourth sign emphasized rationality, calling it the "sense of the heart."

5. Edwards' fifth sign was a spiritual conviction "of the reality and certainty of divine things."[8]

6. Sixth, Edwards saw that humility needed to be spiritual and thoroughgoing and godly.

7. Seventh, he insisted that "spiritual discoveries make an alteration in the very nature of the soul."[9]

8. The eighth sign of spiritual authenticity was a spirit of gentleness, leading to a spirit of love, meekness, quietness, forgiveness and mercy.

9. Edwards insisted as a ninth sign that gracious affections that soften the heart are attended and followed with a Christian tenderness of spirit.[10]

10. Tenth, Edwards called for symmetry and proportion. The modern parallel of this sign would be a plea for balance from spiritual leaders.

11. In the case of the eleventh sign, Edwards believed that there would be striving for spiritual attainment in true believers whereas the false ones would rest assured in themselves and their spiritual achievements.

12. Finally, Edwards insisted that conduct and behavior must demonstrate by outward evidence the inward changes that have taken place.

These views of Jonathan Edwards reveal a discerning and insightful leader. These lists, just enumerated, are together one of the most important legacies of discernment ever given to the Church. Interestingly enough, it was extensive experience in the midst of revival that produced Edwards' summations.

## *Endnotes*

1. K. Neill Foster, "Discernment, the Powers and Spirit-Speaking," unpublished dissertation (Pasadena, CA: Fuller Theological Seminary, 1988).

2. D.W. Waanders, *Illumination and Insight* (Ann Arbor, MI: University Microfilms International, 1982).

3. Ibid, 271.

4. Jonathan Edwards, *Religious Affections,* edited by James M. Houston (Minneapolis, MN: Bethany House, 1959), 127-181.

5. Waanders, 279.

6. Ibid., 282.

7. Ibid., 284.

8. Ibid., 289.

9. Ibid., 294.

10. Ibid., 357.

# Appendix 5

# False and True Fire

*by A.B. Simpson*

"Aaron's sons Nadab and Abihu took their censers, put fire in them and added incense; and they offered unauthorized [strange] fire before the LORD." (Leviticus 10:1)

What a difference there is between fire and fire! What a difference between the fire that warms the hearth and cheers the home and the devouring flame that consumes the dwelling and leaves the homeless household shivering in the darkness and the cold!

What a difference between the lightning stroke that shatters the tree, or strikes down some fugitive from the tempest that has taken refuge beneath its branches, and the same lightning when it has been caught in the electric battery or conveyed along the conducting wires as the motive power that runs our factories, carries our trolleys or conveys our messages.

Just as great is the difference between the true fire of the Holy Ghost and the flames of wild fanaticism and strange fire which the devil is kindling as his counterfeit wherever God is working.

1. The true fire is kindled at the Altar of Sacrifice. The false fire ignores the blood. There is much religious fire today which is merely the so-called "enthusiasm of humanity," or the emotion stirred by eloquence, art or zeal for some human cause and selfish interest. It is not enough to believe in the Spirit, for spiritism and spiritualism all do this; *but the true Spirit always comes in association with the blood* [emphasis added].

2. The true fire is always found in the golden censer which represents the priesthood of the Lord Jesus Christ. While the altar represents His earthly sacrifice, the censer represents His heavenly intercession. Only through His name and mediation can sinful man find access to the presence of a holy God.

3. The true fire is kindled by the Holy Ghost and comes down from above. The false is earth born and comes from mere human emotion, intellectual culture, heart stirring eloquence or selfish zeal. It may even come from a spirit of fear and a guilty conscience.

4. The true fire is fed by the fuel of God's Word. The strange fire depends upon human reasoning or interior revelations which come only from the *ignus fatuus* light of our own imagination.

   The world is full of this kind of light and flame. We have the revelations of spiritualism, the dreams of theosophy and the *fatuus* foolers of Christian Science. The desire of many people for a religion of feeling and a life guided by impulse rather than conviction and truth is the beginning of the same process and sure to lead eventually to the most dangerous delusions. There is no surer test of any religious experience than the simple Word of God.

5. The true fire not only descends from heaven, but goes back to heaven in a supreme purpose to glorify God, whereas the strange fire always seeks to exalt and promote the glory of some man or woman.

The more truly we are filled with the Holy Spirit, the more we will forget ourselves and seek the glory of Him that sent us. Whenever you see a religious movement or a religious leader trying to promote his fame, to demand his rights or to pose upon the stage of sensationalism and spectacular popularity, you may well say, "strange fire."

6. True fire purifies, while strange fire manifests itself in unhallowed forms of sinful self-indulgence and excess. The fire of the Holy Ghost instinctively seeks out every sinful thing and all that is of the flesh and the world and consumes it by a divine necessity.

7. The true fire warms and blesses, melts the heart into tenderness and inspires the soul with love. The false fire leads to criticism, division, censoriousness, harshness and judgment. James and John are the types of the latter seeking to call fire down from heaven to consume the people who refuse to honor and agree with them.

The fire of God is gentle, tender, loving, patient, free from self-assertion, strife and harshness, ready to make concessions, easy to get along with and as sweet as it is strong.

8. The true fire works along the ordinary channels of duty while the false fire is apt to be eccentric, abnormal and extravagant. The true fire does not take people out of their place, but fits them better to fill it. It makes the mother a better mother, the pupil a better scholar, the employee a more faithful servant, the artisan a more skillful workman, the businessman more efficient in his calling, the worshiper more regular in his pew and systematic in his contributions and the Christian, whatever his place in the secular and spiritual world, more simple, practical and efficient in every sphere of duty and place of service. When people are struck with the false fire they become eccentric.

9.   The true fire energizes and makes things go. The false fire is satisfied to watch its own blaze and hear its own report.

The Holy Ghost always puts the "go" in us and turns our blessing into the multiplied blessing of our fellowmen.[1]

## *Endnote*

1. A.B. Simpson, *When the Comforter Came* (Camp Hill, PA: Christian Publications, 1991), 118-121.

# Bibliography

Airhart, Arnold E. *Beacon Bible Commentary* 9. Kansas City, MO: Beacon Hill Press, 1965.

*The Analytical Greek Lexicon.* London: Samuel Bagster and Sons, n.d.

Anderson, Christopher. *Bill and Hillary: The Marriage.* New York: William Morrow and Company, 1999.

Anderson, Neil T. *Helping Others Find Freedom in Christ.* Ventura, CA: Regal Books, 1995.

_____. *Setting Your Church Free.* Ventura, CA: Regal Books, 1994.

_____. *Victory Over the Darkness.* Glendale, CA: Regal Books, 1990.

_____. *Winning Spiritual Warfare.* Eugene, OR: Harvest House, 1990.

Anderson, Neil T. and Dave Park. *The Bondage Breaker*, Youth Edition. Eugene, OR: Harvest House, 1993.

Arnold, Clinton E. *3 Crucial Questions about Spiritual Warfare.* Grand Rapids, MI: Baker Book House, 1997.

Aune, David E. *Prophecy in Early Christianity.* Grand Rapids, MI: Eerdmans, 1983.

Bailey, Keith M. Personal correspondence, June 1999.

_____. Personal correspondence, March 2001.

Bauer, Walter, William Arndt and F. Wilbur Gingrich. *A Greek English Lexicon of the New Testament and Other Early Christian Literature.* Grand Rapids, MI: Zondervan, 1968.

Beverley, James A. "Vineyard: Leading Church Leaves Association," *Christianity Today* 40, no. II (October 7, 1996).

Birch, George. *The Deliverance Ministry.* Camp Hill, PA: Horizon Books, 1988.

Blackaby, Henry. *Experiencing God.* Nashville, TN: Broadman and Holman, 1994.

Bornkamm, G., VII. *"Seismos." Theological Dictionary of the New Testament.* Grand Rapids, MI: Eerdmans, 1985.

Boschman, La Mar. *The Rebirth of Music.* Springdale, PA: Revival Press, 1980.

Botha, E. "Exploring gesture and nonverbal communication in the Bible and the ancient world: some initial observations." *Neotestamentica* 30, no. 1 (1996), 1-19.

Bounds, E.M. *The Complete Works of E.M. Bounds on Prayer.* Grand Rapids, MI: Baker Book House, 1990.

_____. *Power Through Prayer.* London: Marshall, Morgan and Scott, n.d.

Bowman, Robert M. *Orthodoxy and Heresy.* Grand Rapids, MI: Baker Book House, 1992.

Bradley, Bert E. *Fundamentals of Speech Communication: The Credibility of Ideas.* Dubuque, IA: Wm. C. Brown, 1991.

Brevere, John. *Thus Saith the Lord?* Lake Mary, FL: Creation House, 1999.

Brotherton, Dorothy. *Quiet Warrior.* Beaverlodge, AB: Spectrum Publications, 1991.

Brown, Harold O.J. *Heresies*. Garden City, NY: Doubleday and Company, 1984.

Bubeck, Mark. *Overcoming the Adversary*. Chicago: Moody, 1984.

Budgen, Victor. *The Charismatics and the Word of God*. Phillipsburg, NJ: Presbyterian and Reformed, 1987.

Burdick, Donald W. *The Letters of John the Apostle*. Chicago: Moody, 1985.

Campbell, Duncan. *The Nature of a God-Sent Revival*. Vinton, VA: Christ Life Publications, n.d.

Carson, D.A. *Showing the Spirit: A Theological Exposition of 1 Corinthians 12-14*. Grand Rapids, MI: Baker Book House, 1987.

Chadwick, Henry. *Augustine*. Oxford, England: Oxford University Press, 1986.

Chafer, Lewis Sperry. *The Epistle to the Ephesians*. Grand Rapids, MI: Kregel Publications, 1991.

Choy, Leona. "Conversations with Andrew Murray," *Classic-Christianity*, the e-zine, April 1, 1999.

_____. *Powerlines*. Camp Hill, PA: Christian Publications, 1990.

Clark, Gordon H. *First John*. Phillipsburg, NJ: Presbyterian and Reformed Publishing, 1981.

Clarke, Michael D. *Canada Portraits of Faith*. Chilliwack, BC: Reel to Real, 1998.

Conkin, Paul K. *Cane Ridge: America's Pentecost*. Madison, WI: The University of Wisconsin Press, 1990.

Cook, Arnold L. *Historical Drift: Must My Church Die?* Camp Hill, PA: Christian Publications, 2000.

Cooper, Ken. *Nonverbal Communication for Business Success.* New York: AMACOM, a division of American Management Association, 1979.

Cuccaro, Elio. Personal correspondence, April 6, 1999.

_____. Cited by K. Neill Foster, "Apologetics and the Deliverance Ministry," Evangelical Theological Society, 1995.

Cymbala, Jim. *Fresh Faith.* Grand Rapids, MI: Zondervan, 1999.

_____. *Fresh Wind, Fresh Fire.* Grand Rapids, MI: Zondervan, 1997.

Dahms, John V. "A Critique of Richard Foster's *Celebration of Discipline.*" *His Dominion* 12, (Fall 1985).

Dallimore, Arnold A. *George Whitfield: The Life and Times of the Great Evangelist of the Eighteenth Century.* Westchester, IL: Cornerstone Books, 1979.

Dana, H.E. and Julius R. Mantey. *A Manual Grammar of the Greek New Testament.* New York: MacMillan, 1927.

David, W. Cloud. *Fundamentalist Baptist News Service.* Oak Harbor, WA: Way of Life Literature, February 17, 1996.

De Soyres, John. *Montanism and the Primitive Church.* Cambridge, MA: Deighton, Bell and Sons, 1878.

Deere, Jack. *Surprised by the Voice of God.* Grand Rapids, MI: Zondervan, 1996.

Delph, Edward William. *The Silent Community.* Beverly Hills, CA: Sage Publications, 1978.

DeVito, Joseph A. and Michael L. Hecht. *The Nonverbal Communication Reader.* Prospect Heights, IL: Waveland Press, 1990.

Dorsett, Lyle Wesley. *E.M. Bounds: Man of Prayer.* Grand Rapids, MI: Zondervan, 1991.

Druckman, Daniel, Richard M. Rozelle and James C. Baxter. *Nonverbal Communication: Survey Theory, Research*. Beverly Hills, CA: Sage Publications, 1982.

Drummond, Andrew I. *Edward Irving and His Circle*. London: James Clarke and Co., 1934.

Duewel, Wesley. *Revival Fire*. Grand Rapids, MI: Zondervan, 1995.

Dunn, Richard. *Will God Heal Me?* Lottbridge Drove, England: Kingsway Publications, 1997.

Dwight, Sereno E. *The Works of Jonathan Edwards*. Carlisle, PA: The Banner of Truth Trust, 1987.

Edwards, Jonathan. *Religious Affections*. Minneapolis, MN: Bethany House, 1959.

Ellicott, Charles John. *Ephesians*. Vol. 8. Grand Rapids, MI: Zondervan, n.d.

Elwell, Walter A. *Evangelical Dictionary of Biblical Theology*. Grand Rapids, MI: Baker Book House, 1996.

Ensign, Grayson H. and Edward Howe. *Bothered? Bewildered? Bewitched?* Amarillo, TX: Recovery Publications, 1984.

Fant, David J. *Modern Miracles of Healing*. Harrisburg, PA: Christian Publications, 1943.

Farnell, F. David. "The Current Debate about New Testament Prophecy." *Bibliotheca Sacra* (July-September 1992): 149, 277-303.

_____."Does the New Testament Teach Two Prophetic Gifts?" *Bibliotheca Sacra* (January-March 1993): 150, 62-88.

_____. "Fallible New Testament Prophecy/Prophets? A Critique of Wayne Grudem's Hypothesis," *The Master's Seminary Journal* (Fall 1991): 157-80.

_____. "The Gift of Prophecy in the Old and New Testaments." *Bibliotheca Sacra* (October-December 1992): 149, 387-410.

_____. "When Will the Gift of Prophecy Cease?" *Bibliotheca Sacra* (April-June 1993): 150, 171-202.

Farrar, Frederick W. *The Early Days of Christianity.* New York: Cassell, Petter, Galpin & Co., 1882.

Findlay, George C. *Fellowship in the Life Eternal.* London: Hodder and Stoughton, 1909.

Foster, K. Neill. "Apologetics and the Deliverance Ministry," paper delivered at the Evangelical Theological Society, 1995.

_____. *The Believer's Authority.* Camp Hill, PA: Christian Publications, 1995.

_____. *Dambreak in Georgia.* Camp Hill, PA: Horizon Books, 1978.

_____. *The Discerning Christian.* Camp Hill, PA: Christian Publications, 1981.

_____. "Discernment, the Powers and Spirit-Speaking." Unpublished dissertation. Pasadena, CA: Fuller Theological Seminary, 1988.

_____. *Fasting: The Delightful Discipline.* Camp Hill, PA: Christian Publications, 1995.

_____. *Lessons Learned When a Teenager Was Liberated from LSD.* Beaverlodge, AB: Evangelistic Enterprises Society of Alberta, 1964.

_____. *Revolution of Love.* Camp Hill, PA: Horizon Books, 1973.

_____. *The Third View of Tongues.* Camp Hill, PA: Horizon Books, 1994.

_____. *Warfare Weapons.* Camp Hill, PA: Christian Publications, 1994.

Gaffin, Richard B., Jr. *Perspectives on Pentecost.* Phillipsburg, NJ: Presbyterian and Reformed, 1979.

Geisler, Norman. "Beware of Philosophy: A Caution to Biblical Exegetes." Tape recording. Orlando, FL: Evangelical Theological Society, 1998.

Gentry, Kenneth L., Jr. *The Charismatic Gift of Prophecy*, 2nd ed. Memphis, TN: Footstool, 1989.

Goff, J.R., Jr. "Charles Fox Parham." *Dictionary of Pentecostal and Charismatic Movements.* Grand Rapids, MI: Zondervan, 1988.

Gore, Charles. *The Epistle of St. John.* London: John Murray Publishing, 1920.

Grady, Lee. "Wimber Plots New Course for Vineyard." *Charisma*, February 1993.

Gross, Edward N. *1 Peter.* Grand Rapids, MI: Eerdmans, 1998.

————. *Miracles, Demons & Spiritual Warfare.* Grand Rapids, MI: Baker Book House, 1990.

Grudem, Wayne, gen. ed. *Are Miraculous Gifts for Today?* Grand Rapids, MI: Zondervan, 1996.

Grudem, Wayne. *The Gift of Prophecy in 1 Corinthians.* Washington, DC: University Press of America, 1982.

————. *Systematic Theology.* Grand Rapids, MI: Zondervan, 1994.

Grudem, Wayne and John Piper. *Recovering Biblical Manhood and Womanhood.* Wheaton, IL: Crossway Books, 1991.

Grundmann, W. *Theological Dictionary of the New Testament.* Grand Rapids, MI: Eerdmans, 1985.

Hanegraaff, Hank. *Counterfeit Revival.* Dallas, TX: Word Publishing, 1997.

————. "Pensacola Outpouring." *Christian Research Journal* (November-December 1997): 11-20.

Harris, Gregory H. "Satan's Deceptive Miracles in the Tribulation." *Bibliotheca Sacra* 156 (July-September 1999): 308-324.

Harris, R. Laird, Gleason L. Archer and Bruce K. Waltke. *Theological Wordbook of the Old Testament*, 2 vols. Chicago: Moody, 1980.

Harvey, John. "Music of the Spirit." *Alliance Life* (January 2001).

Harvey, Richard H. *70 Years of Miracles*. Camp Hill, PA: Horizon Books, 1992.

Hecker, Sid and David W. Stewart. *Nonverbal Communication and Advertising*. Lexington, MA: Lexington Books, 1988.

Heine, Ronald E. *The Montanist Oracles and Testimonia*. Macon, GA: Mercer University Press, 1989.

Hendrickson, William. *Exposition of Ephesians*. Grand Rapids, MI: Baker Book House, 1955.

Henley, Nancy M. *Body Politics, Power, Sex and Nonverbal Communication*. New York: Simon and Schuster, 1977.

Henry, Matthew. *Matthew Henry's Commentary*. New York: Fleming H. Revell, 1721.

Hiebert, Paul G. "Discerning the Work of God," Unpublished paper. Pasadena, CA: Fuller Theological Seminary, n.d.

Hill, Charles. Interview with George McPeek, November 22, 2000.

Hill, Clifford and Peter Fenwick, David Forbes and David Noakes. *Blessing the Church?* Guildford, Surrey, UK: Inter Publishing Service, 1995.

Hobbs, Herschel H. *The Epistles of John*. Nashville, TN: Thomas Nelson, 1983.

House, Wayne. "With an Apology to Arius: When and How Should We Deal with Heretics and Heresy?" *Journal of Christian Apologetics*. Plymouth, MI: Michigan Theological Seminary, 1997.

Houston, James M., editor. *Religious Affections, Jonathan Edwards*. Minneapolis, MN: Bethany House Publishers, 1996.

Howe, Edward and Barbara Davenport. *Who Are These People?* Enumclaw, WA: Winepress Publishing, 1999.

Hurst, John Fletcher. *Short History of the Christian Church.* New York: Harper and Brothers, 1893.

*Hymns of the Christian Life.* "The Apostles' Creed." Camp Hill, PA: Christian Publications, 1978.

Jamieson, Robert with A.R. Fausset and David Brown. *Commentary, Critical and Explanatory, on the Whole Bible.* Grand Rapids, MI: Zondervan, n.d.

Kaiser, Walter C., Jr. *Back Toward the Future.* Grand Rapids, MI: Baker Book House, 1989.

_____. "False Prophet," "Prophet, Prophetess, Prophecy." *Evangelical Dictionary of Biblical Theology.* ed. Walter A. Elwell. Grand Rapids, MI: Baker Book House, 1996.

Katz, Albert M. and Virginia T. Katz. *Foundations of Nonverbal Communication.* Carbondale, IL: Southern Illinois University Press, 1983.

Keil, C.F. and F. Delitzsch. *Commentary on the Old Testament.* 10 vols. Grand Rapids, MI: Eerdmans, 1980.

Key, Dana with Steve Rabey. "Tool of Satan or Tool of God?" *Contemporary Christian Music,* 1989.

Kilpatrick, John. *In Times Like These.* Videotape. Pensacola, FL: Brownsville Assembly of God, May 30, 1996.

King, Francis X. and Stephen Skinner. *Nostradamus: Prophecies Fulfilled for the Millennium and Beyond.* New York: St. Martin's Press, 1994.

King, Paul L. *A Believer with Authority: The Life and Message of John A. MacMillan.* Camp Hill, PA: Christian Publications, 2001.

_____. "Holy Laughter and Other Phenomena in Evangelical and Holiness Revival Movements." *Alliance Academic Review,* 1998. Camp Hill, PA: Christian Publications, 1998.

_____. Personal correspondence, 1999.

King, Roberta. *Pathways in Christian Music Communication: The Case of the Senufo of Côte d'Ivoire*. Pasadena, CA: Fuller Theological Seminary, 1989.

Kittel, Gerhard and Gerhard Friedrich, editors. *Theological Dictionary of the New Testament*. Grand Rapids, MI: Eerdmans, 1985.

Koch, Kurt. *Christian Counseling and Occultism*. Grand Rapids, MI: Kregel Publications, 1965.

_____. *Demonology, Past and Present*. Grand Rapids, MI: Kregel Publications, 1973.

Kruger, Paul A. " 'Nonverbal Communication' in the Hebrew Bible: A Few Comments." *Journal of Northwest Semitic Languages* 24, no. 1 (1998).

Kuglin, Robert J. *Handbook on the Holy Spirit*. Camp Hill, PA: Christian Publications, 1996.

Leahy, Frederick S. *Satan Cast Out*. Edinburg, PA: Banner of Truth Trust, 1975.

Leno, Garth. *Hebrews*. Camp Hill, PA: Christian Publications, 1996.

Lloyd-Jones, D. Martyn. "Biblical Intolerance," *Banner of Truth*. August/September 1994.

MacArthur, John, Jr. *Charismatic Chaos*. Grand Rapids, MI: Zondervan, 1992.

_____. *Our Sufficiency Is in Christ*. Dallas, TX: Word Publishing, 1991.

MacMillan, J.A. *The Authority of the Believer*. Camp Hill, PA: Christian Publications, 1997.

_____. *Encounter with Darkness*. Camp Hill, PA: Christian Publications, 1980.

MacMullen, Ramsay. *Christianizing the Roman Empire A.D. 100-400*. New Haven, CT: Yale University Press, 1984.

Malandro, Loretta A, Larry L. Barker and Debrah G. Barker. *Nonverbal Communication*. New York: Random House, 1983.

Marchand, Philip. "Marshall McLuhan," *Canada Portraits of Faith*. Chilliwack, BC: Reel to Real, 1998.

Mare, W. Harold. *Expositor's Bible Commentary*. *1 Corinthians*. Grand Rapids: Zondervan, 1976.

Marshall, I. Howard. "The Epistles of John," *The New International Commentary on the New Testament*. Grand Rapids, MI: Eerdmans, 1978.

Martzall, Charles. Personal conversation, June 14, 1998.

Maudlin, Michael G. "Seers in the Heartland," *Christianity Today* 36, no. 1 (January 14, 1991).

McLuhan, Marshall. *Understanding Media: The Extension of Man*. New York: McGraw Hill, 1964.

McElheran, Clifton. *Let the Oppressed Go Free*. Calgary, AB: Self-published, n.d.

McGraw, Gerald. Personal conversation, 1999.

_____. "Tongues—True or False?" and "Tongues Should Be Tested." *The Alliance Witness*, 1974 (May 22 and June 5).

McLeod, W.L. *Charismatic or Christian?* Saskatoon, SK: Western Tract Mission, 1978.

Mickelsen, A. Berkeley. *Interpreting the Bible*. Grand Rapids, MI: Eerdmans, 1963.

Mish, Frederick C., ed. *Merriam-Webster's Collegiate Dictionary*, 10th ed. Springfield, MA: Merriam-Webster, Inc., 1996.

Mitchell, L. David. *Liberty in Jesus*. Edinburgh: The Pentland Press, 1999.

Morris, Leon. *Tyndale New Testament Commentary. 1 Corinthians,* vol. 7; *1 and 2 Thessalonians,* Volume 13. Grand Rapids, MI: Eerdmans, 1983.

Murray, Andrew. *Key to the Missionary Problem*. Contemporized by Leona Choy. Fort Washington, PA: Christian Literature Crusade, 1979.

Murrell, Conrad. *Practical Demonology*. Pineville, LA: Saber Publications, n.d.

Myers, Bill and David Wimbish. *The Dark Side of the Supernatural*. Minneapolis, MN: Bethany House, 1999.

Neff, David and George K. Brushaber. "The Remaking of British Evangelicalism," *Christianity Today* 34, no. 2 (February 5, 1990).

Nevius, John L. *Demon Possession and Allied Themes*. Grand Rapids, MI: Kregel Publishing, 1894.

Niederwimmer, Kurt. *The Didache*. Minneapolis, MN: Fortress Press, 1998.

Oden, Thomas C. *Requiem*. Nashville, TN: Abingdon Press, 1995.

Oesterreich, T.K. *Possession, Demoniacal and Other*. New Hyde Park, NY: University Books, 1966.

Orr, J. Edwin. *Evangelical Awakenings in Southern Asia*. Minneapolis, MN: Bethany Fellowship, 1975.

Overholt, Thomas W. *Prophecy in Cross-Cultural Perspective*. Atlanta, GA: Scholars Press, 1986.

Owen, Timothy. *Cancer—A Healing Encounter with God*. Camp Hill, PA: Christian Publications, 2001.

Parham, Charles F. *The Everlasting Gospel*. Baxter Springs, KS: Apostolic Faith Bible College, 1911.

Paull, Janet. Diagram used in Sunday school class, 2000.

BIBLIOGRAPHY

Penn-Lewis, Jessie. "How to Pray for Missionaries," *The Alliance Weekly*, June 12, 1937.

————. *War on the Saints*. New York: Thomas Lowe, 1912.

————. *The Warfare with Satan*. Fort Washington, PA: Christian Literature Crusade, 1963.

Phillips, McCandlish. *The Bible, the Supernatural and the Jews*. Camp Hill, PA: Christian Publications, 1970, 1995.

Piper, John. *God's Passion for His Glory: Living the Vision of Jonathan Edwards*. Wheaton, IL: Crossway Books, 1998.

Plummer, Alfred. *The Epistles of St. John*. Grand Rapids, MI: Baker Book House, 1980.

Polano, H. *The Talmud*. Philadelphia, PA: Leary's Book Store, 1876.

Poyatos, F. *Cross-Cultural Perspectives in Nonverbal Communication*. Toronto, ON: C.J. Hofgre, 1987.

Redfield, James. *The Celestine Prophecy*. New York: Warner Books, 1993.

Reston, James, Jr. *The Last Apocalypse*. New York: Doubleday, 1998.

Rich, Frank. "Betty Currie's P.C. Pass." *New York Times*. January 30, 1999.

Roberts, Alexander and James Donaldson. *Ante-Nicene Christian Library*. Edinburgh: T & T Clark, 1916.

Rockstad, Ernest B. *Demon Activity and the Christian*. Andover, KS: Faith and Life, 1972.

Rosenthal, Robert. *Skill in Nonverbal Communication*. Cambridge, MA: Oelgeschlager, Grum and Hein, 1979.

Ruesch, J. and W. Kees. *Nonverbal Communication: Notes on the Visual Perception of Human Relationships*. Berkeley, CA: University of California Press, 1956.

Runge, Albert. Personal correspondence, 1998.

_____. "Response to Wayne Grudem's View of Prophecy." Unpublished manuscript, 1998.

Saucy, Robert L. "Open But Cautious." *Are Miraculous Gifts for Today?* Ed. Wayne Grudem. Grand Rapids, MI: Zondervan, 1996.

Schroeder, David E. *Matthew*. Camp Hill, PA: Christian Publications, 1995.

Schuster, Marguerite. "Power, Pathology and Paradox." Ph.D. thesis, since published. Pasadena, CA: Fuller Theological Seminary, 1977.

Scofield, C.I., ed. *The New Scofield Reference Bible*. New York: Oxford University Press, 1967.

Shaw, S.B. *The Great Revival in Wales*. Chicago: S.B. Shaw, 1905.

Sillivant, Terri. "Paul Cain's Ministry: Recent Manifestations of the Spirit." *Grace City Report: Special Edition.*, n.d.

Simpson, A.B. "Matthew." *Christ in the Bible Commentary*. Camp Hill, PA: Christian Publications, 1994.

_____. *The Holy Spirit*. Harrisburg, PA: Christian Publications, n.d.

_____. *When the Comforter Came*. Camp Hill, PA: Christian Publications, 1991.

Snyder, James L. *In Pursuit of God*. Camp Hill, PA: Christian Publications, 1991.

Sproul, R.C. *The Invisible Hand*. Dallas, TX: Word Publishing, 1997.

Stevens, George Barker. *The Christian Doctrine of Salvation*. New York: Charles Scribners Sons, 1917.

_____. *The Teaching of Jesus*. New York: MacMillan, 1901.

Storms, C. Samuel. "A Third Wave View." *Are Miraculous Gifts for Today?* Ed. Wayne A. Grudem. Grand Rapids, MI: Zondervan, 1996.

Stott, John R.W. *The Epistles of John.* Grand Rapids, MI: Eerdmans, 1964.

Strong, James. *The Comprehensive Concordance of the Bible.* Iowa Falls, IA: World Bible Publishers, n.d.

_____. *The Exhaustive Concordance of the Bible.* New York: Abingdon, 1890.

Thickle, Phyllis. "Verbatim." *Current Thoughts & Trends.* Colorado Springs, CO: The Navigators, 1999.

Thomas, Robert L. "Prophecy Rediscovered? A Review of the Gift of Prophecy in the New Testament and Today." *Bibliotheca Sacra* (January-March 1992).

_____. *The Expositor's Bible Commentary. 1, 2 Thessalonians.* Grand Rapids, MI: Zondervan, 1976.

Thompson, David. *Beyond the Mist.* Camp Hill, PA: Christian Publications, 1998.

Tozer, A.W. *The Best of A.W. Tozer.* Camp Hill, PA: Christian Publications, 1978.

_____. *Born after Midnight.* Camp Hill, PA: Christian Publications, 1989.

_____. *Man: The Dwelling Place of God.* Camp Hill, PA: Christian Publications, 1989.

_____. *The Pursuit of Man.* Camp Hill, PA: Christian Publications, 1997.

_____. *Total Commitment to Christ: What Is It?* Camp Hill, PA: Christian Publications, 1995.

_____. *Worship: The Missing Jewel.* Camp Hill, PA: Christian Publications, 1999.

Trevett, Christine. *Montanism, Gender, Authority and the New Prophecy*. Cambridge, MA: Cambridge University Press, 1996.

Unger, Merrill F. *Biblical Demonology*. Wheaton, IL: Scripture Press, n.d.

Vine, W.E. *The Expanded Vine's Expository Dictionary of New Testament Words*. Ed. John R. Kohlenberger III. Minneapolis, MN: Bethany House, 1984.

Waanders, D.W. *Illumination and Insight*. Ann Arbor, MI: University Microfilms International, 1982.

Wagner, C. Peter. *Confronting the Powers*. Ventura, CA: Regal Books, 1996.

Wallis, Arthur. *In the Day of Thy Power*. Fort Washington, PA: Christian Literature Crusade, 1956.

Ward, Ronald A. *The Epistles of John and Jude*. Grand Rapids, MI: Baker Book House, 1965.

Warner, Timothy. "The Power of Truth to Dispel Deception." Unpublished lecture notes. Gettysburg, PA: Susek Evangelistic Association, 1997.

Wesley, John. *The Journal of John Wesley*. Chicago: Moody Press, 1980.

Westcott, Brook Foss. *The Epistle of St. John*. New York: MacMillan, 1886.

Wigton, James. "History of the Charismatic Movement." Tape recording. Bay City, MI: Midland Street Peoples Church, 1980.

_____. "Why I Left the Charismatic Movement." Tape recording. Bay City, MI: Midland Street Peoples Church, 1980.

Williams, Don. *Signs, Wonders and the Kingdom of God*. Ann Arbor, MI: Servant Publications, 1989.

Williamson, G.A. *History of the Church from Christ to Constantine*. Minneapolis, MN: Augsburg Publishing House, 1975.

Willoughby, W. Robert. *First Corinthians*. Camp Hill, PA: Christian Publications, 1996.

_____. Private correspondence, 1998.

_____. "Responses to Wayne Grudem's View of Prophecy." Unpublished manuscript, 1998.

Wilson, Bright, Jr. *An Introduction to Scientific Research*. New York: Dover Publications, 1990.

Wimber, John. "Spiritual Phenomena: Slain in the Spirit—Part 1." Audiotape. Anaheim, CA: Vineyard Christian Fellowship, 1981.

Wimber John and Kevin Springer. *Riding the Third Wave*. Basingstoke, Hants, UK: Marshall Pickering, 1987.

Wood, J.A. *Perfect Love*. Abridged by John Paul. Kansas City, MO: Beacon Hill Press, 1944.

Woodcock, Eldon. Personal correspondence, 1998.

Wright, David J. "The Gnostics." *Eerdman's Handbook to the History of Christianity*. Grand Rapids, MI: Eerdmans, 1977.

# Scripture Index

# Subject Index

## A

# E

# F

# G

# H

# M

## S

# T

# Publications by K. Neill Foster

## Books

*Sorting Out the Supernatural*
*Binding and Loosing* (with Paul King)
*Dam Break in Georgia* (with Eric Mills)
*The Discerning Christian*
*Revolution of Love*
*The Third View of Tongues*
*Warfare Weapons*

## Booklets

*The Believer's Authority*
*Fasting: The Delightful Discipline*
*Six Conditions for the Filling of the Holy Spirit*

## Books Edited

*Healing Voices* (with Stephen Adams)
*Holiness Voices* (with H. Robert Cowles)
*Missionary Voices* (with H. Robert Cowles and David Jones)
*Prayer Voices* (with H. Robert Cowles)
*Voices on the Glory* (with Stephen Adams and George McPeek)

Available from Christian Publications at
1-800-233-4443 or www.christianpublications.com